Oscar Fay Adams

A Brief Hand Book of American Authors

Sixth Edition

Oscar Fay Adams

A Brief Hand Book of American Authors
Sixth Edition

ISBN/EAN: 9783337280765

Printed in Europe, USA, Canada, Australia, Japan

Cover: Foto ©Thomas Meinert / pixelio.de

More available books at **www.hansebooks.com**

A

BRIEF HANDBOOK

OF

AMERICAN AUTHORS

BY

OSCAR FAY ADAMS

AUTHOR OF " A BRIEF HANDBOOK OF ENGLISH AUTHORS"

SIXTH EDITION.

REVISED AND ENLARGED

BOSTON

HOUGHTON, MIFFLIN AND COMPANY

New York: 11 East Seventeenth Street

The Riverside Press, Cambridge

1889

The Riverside Press, Cambridge, Mass., U. S. A.
Electrotyped and Printed by H. O. Houghton & Company.

THE WRITER

GRATEFULLY DEDICATES TO

WILLIAM J. ROLFE

The Little Book

MADE POSSIBLE BY HIS KINDLY

ENCOURAGEMENT.

NOTE TO SECOND EDITION.

In the preparation of this edition the writer has received material assistance from several of the persons named in the former preface, as also from Mr. C. W. Ernst, and Mrs. Grace A. Oliver, of Boston, Mass.; Mr. William Leete Stone, of New York city; and Mr. Appleton Morgan, of Flushing, L. I.; and for the aid so kindly extended he desires in this place to render his grateful acknowledgments.

PREFACE.

In preparing this brief handbook the writer has especially considered the needs of that large class of readers who have neither means nor disposition to provide themselves with costly biographical works of reference. Necessarily subject to limitations, the book nevertheless includes in its scope more or less extended notice of most of the persons known to American literature. In no other work, so restricted as to size, can be found as many names, or mention of so many authors who have recently achieved distinction. A few names which might reasonably be looked for in this volume are omitted by the wish of their owners, and the absence of data after some others may be similarly explained. The names of two or three persons are included which also have place in the "Handbook of English Authors," their literary work having been done in both countries.

To the many authors in England and America who have cordially coöperated with the writer in his work he desires to express his sincere thanks, as well as to the following persons who have rendered valuable assistance: Mr. Horace E. Scudder, Colonel T. W. Higginson, and Miss C. F. Bates, of Cambridge, Mass.; Mr. E. C. Stedman, Mr. Rossiter Johnson,

Mr. G. P. Lathrop, and Mr. Wm. Winter, of New York City; Mr. James Berry Bensel, of Lynn, Mass.; Mr. David Hutcheson, of Washington, D. C.; Miss Frances Bigelow, of Worcester, Mass.; Mr. Wm. M. Rossetti, Mr. Austin Dobson, Mr. M. D. Conway, and Mrs. Howitt-Watts, of London, England.

That the work as it stands leaves much to be desired no one is more fully conscious than the writer; but if, imperfect as it may be considered, it shall yet be found of substantial service to those for whom it was written, it will have attained the end which he had in view.

OSCAR FAY ADAMS.

PLAINFIELD, NEW JERSEY, *April* 23, 1884.

PUBLISHERS REFERRED TO IN THIS VOLUME

Dra.	Draper, Warren F..	Andover, Mass.
Dut.	Dutton, E. P., & Co.. . . .	New York City.
El.	Ellis, George H.	Boston, Mass.
Eld.	Eldredge & Bro. . . . , .	Philadelphia, Pa.
Est.	Estes & Lauriat	Boston, Mass.
Fo.	Fords, Howard & Hulbert .	New York City.
For.	Fortescue, W. S., & Co. . .	Philadelphia, Pa.
Fow.	Fowler & Wells	New York City.
Fu.	Funk, I. K., & Co.	" " "
Gi.	Ginn & Co.	Boston, Mass.
Go.	Goodrich, E. J.	Oberlin, O.
Gri.	Griggs, S. C., & Co. . . .	Chicago, Ill.
Ha.	Hale, E. J., & Son . . .	New York City.
Hal.	Hall & Whiting.	Boston, Mass.
Har.	Harper & Bros.	New York City.
Ho.	Holt, Henry, & Co. . . .	" " "
Hol.	Holbrook, M. L.	" " "
Hou.	Houghton, Mifflin & Co. .	Boston, Mass.
Iv.	Ivison, Blakeman, Taylor & Co.	New York City.
Jan.	Jansen, McClurg & Co. . .	Chicago, Ill.
J. H. U.	Johns Hopkins University .	Baltimore, Md.
Jo.	Johnson, T. & J. W. . . .	Philadelphia, Pa.
Jon.	Jones, G. I.	St. Louis, Mo.
La.	Lea's, Henry, Son & Co. .	Philadelphia, Pa.
Le.	Lee & Shepard	Boston, Mass.
Lip.	Lippincott, J. B., & Co.. .	Philadelphia, Pa.
Lit.	Little, Brown & Co. . . .	Boston, Mass.
Lo.	Lothrop, D., & Co.	" "
Loc.	Lockwood, Brooks & Co. . .	" "
L. P. S.	Lutheran Publication Society	Philadelphia, Pa.
Mac.	Macmillan & Co.	New York and London.
Me.	Merriam, G., & Co.	Springfield, Mass.
Mil.	Miller, James	New York City.
Mur.	Murphy, John, & Co.. . .	Baltimore, Md.
Og.	Ogilvie, J. S., & Co. . . .	New York City.
Os.	Osgood, James R., & Co. .	Boston, Mass.
P. B.	Presbyterian Bd. of Publication	Philadelphia, Pa.
Pe.	Peck, H. H.	New Haven, Ct.
Pet.	Peterson, T. B., & Bros. .	Philadelphia, Pa.
Phi.	Phillips & Hunt	New York City.
Pi.	Piet, John B.	Baltimore, Md.
Pl.	Plon & Co.	Paris, France.
Por.	Porter & Coates	Philadelphia, Pa.
Pot.	Potter, Ainsworth & Co.. .	New York City.
Pott.	Potter, John E.	Philadelphia, Pa.
Put.	Putnam's, G. P., Sons . .	New York City.

Ran.	Randolph, A. D. F., & Co.	New York City.
Re.	Reid, J. A. & R. A.	Providence, R. I.
Rev.	Revell, Fleming H.	Chicago, Ill.
Rob.	Roberts Brothers	Boston, Mass.
Sad.	Sadlier, D. & J., & Co.	New York City.
Sau.	Saunders, Otley, & Co.	London, England.
Scr.	Scribner's, Charles, Sons	New York City.
Sev.	Sever, C. W.	Cambridge, Mass.
Sh.	Sheldon & Co.	New York City.
So.	Sower, Potts & Co.	Philadelphia, Pa.
Ste.	Steiger, E., & Co.	New York City.
Sto.	Stoddart, J. M., & Co.	Philadelphia, Pa.
Su.	Sumner, Henry A., & Co.	Chicago, Ill.
Th.	Thomas, F. H.	St. Louis, Mo.
Un.	University Publishing Co.	New York City.
Va.	Van Antwerp, Bragg & Co.	Cincinnati, O.
W.	White, Stokes & Allen	New York City.
Wa.	Ware, W., & Co.	Boston, Mass.
Wd.	Ward & Drummond	New York City.
We.	West, Johnson & Co.	Richmond, Va.
Wh.	Whittaker, Thomas	New York City.
Wi.	Wilson, John	Cambridge, Mass.
Wid.	Widdleton, W. J.	New York City.
Wil.	Wiley, John, & Sons	" " "
Wils.	Wilstach, Baldwin & Co.	Cincinnati, O.
Wu.	Wilson, John	London, England.
Wo.	Wood, W. & Co.	New York City.
Wor.	Worthington, R.	" " "
Yo.	Young, E. & J. B.	" " "
Yt.	Yost, Samuel M., & Son	Staunton, Va.
Ze.	Zell, T. Ellwood	Philadelphia, Pa.

The place of birth of the larger number of the authors mentioned in this volume is indicated by an abbreviation placed after the date of birth, which the following list of abbreviations will serve to explain. It has not, however, been thought best to mention locality more exactly than by reference to State or foreign country.

Al.	Alabama.	Ms.	Massachusetts.
A. M.	Asia Minor.	N.	Norway.
B.	Brazil.	N. B.	New Brunswick.
Ba.	Bermuda.	N. C.	North Carolina.
B. G.	British Guiana.	N. H.	New Hampshire.
Bh.	Burmah.	N. J.	New Jersey.
Bm.	Belgium.	N. S.	Nova Scotia.
Cal.	California.	N. Y.	New York.
Ct.	Connecticut.	O.	Ohio.
Del.	Delaware.	P.	Prussia.
D. C.	District of Columbia.	Pa.	Pennsylvania.
E.	England.	Per.	Persia.
F.	France.	Q.	Quebec.
Fl.	Florida.	Ra.	Russia.
G.	Germany.	R. I.	Rhode Island.
Ga.	Georgia.	S.	Scotland
Gr.	Greece.	S. C.	South Carolina.
I.	Ireland.	Sd.	Switzerland.
Ia.	Iowa.	Sh.	Sandwich Islands.
Il.	Illinois.	Sl.	Senegal.
Ind.	Indiana.	Sn.	Sweden.
Iy.	Italy.	Sxy.	Saxony.
J.	Jamaica.	Sy.	Sicily.
Ky.	Kentucky.	Tn.	Tennessee.
La.	Louisiana.	Ts.	Texas.
L. I.	Long Island.	Va.	Virginia.
Mch.	Michigan.	Vt.	Vermont.
Md.	Maryland.	W.	Wales.
Me.	Maine.	Wis.	Wisconsin.
Mg.	Mecklenburg.	W. I.	West Indies.
Mi.	Mississippi.	W. Va.	West Virginia.
Mo.	Missouri.		

Abbey, Henry. 1842 *N. Y.* ——. Poet. Author Ballads of Good Deeds and Other Poems, Poems, and The City of Success and Other Poems. *Pub. Apl.*

Abbot, Ezra. 1819 *Me.*–1884. Unitarian biblical scholar of note. Author Literature of the Doctrine of a Future Life, Authenticity of the Fourth Gospel, etc. *Pub. El. Wid.*

Abbot, Gorham Dummer. 1807 *Me.*–1874. Bro. to J. Abbott and J. S. C. Abbott. Educational writer. Author Prayer-Book for the Young, Pleasure and Profit, etc.

Abbott, Austin. 1831 *Ms.* ——. Son to J. A. Legal writer. Co-author with B. V. A. of several works.

Abbott, Benjamin Vaughan. 1830 *Ms.* ——. Son to J. A. Legal writer. Author Law Dict., Year-Book of Jurisprudence for 1880, Judge and Jury, etc. *Pub. Har. Lit.*

Abbott, Charles Conrad. 1843 *N. J.* ——. Archæologist and physician. Author The Stone Age in New Jersey, Primitive Industry, etc. *Pub. Ba. Cass. Apl.*

Abbott, Edward. 1841 *Me.* ——. Son to J. A. Editor Literary World. Author Paragraph Hist. U. S., Paragraph Hist. Am. Revolution, Revolutionary Times, etc. *Pub. Ran. Rob.*

Abbott, Jacob. 1803 *Me.*–1879. Writer for the young. Author of the famous and deservedly popular Rollo Books, Histories of Celebrated Sovereigns, Young Christian series, etc. *Pub. Clk. Cr. Do. Har.*

Abbott, John Stephens Cabot. 1805 *Me.*–1877. Bro. to J. A. Historian. Author Hist. of Napoleon, Napoleon at St. Helena, Hist. French Revolution, etc. The merit of his works is greatly impaired by their partisan spirit. *Pub. Do. Har. Lo.*

Abbott, Lyman. 1835 *Ms.* ——. Son to J. A. Religious writer. Editor Christian Union. Author Jesus of Nazareth, Old Testament Shadows of New Testament Truths, Illustrated Commentary on the New Testament, A Layman's Story, etc. *See Lit. World, Jan. 27, 1883. Pub. Do. Fo. Fu. Har.*

Adams, Mrs. Abigail [Smith]. 1744 *Ms.*–1818. Wife to J. A. Known to literature by her entertaining Letters, edited by Chas. Francis Adams. *Pub. Hou.*

Adams, Charles Baker. 1814 *Ms.*–1853. Naturalist. Author Contributions to Conchology, Monographs of Several Species of Shells, etc.

Adams, Charles Francis. 1807 *Ms.*–1886. Son to J. Q. A. Statesman. Editor Life and Works of John Adams, Letters of Mrs. Abigail Adams, Life and Works of John Q. Adams, etc. *See Lippincott's Mag. April, 1871, and Carroll's Twelve Americans. Pub. Apl. Hou. Lip. Lit. Scr.*

Adams, Charles Francis, Jr. 1835 *Ms.* ——. Son to preceding. An authority upon railway science. Author Chapters of Erie, Railroads, A College Fetich, etc. *Pub. Put.*

Adams, Charles Kendall. 1835 *Vt.* ——. Historical writer. Author Manual of Historical Lit., Democracy and Monarchy in France, etc. *Pub. Ho.*

Adams, George Burton. 1851 *Vt.* ——. Historical writer. Author Mediæval Civilization in Appleton's History Primers. *Pub. Apl.*

Adams, Hannah. 1755 *Ms.*–1831. Historian. Author of A View of Religious Opinions, Hist. New England, Hist. of the Jews, Evidences of Christianity, etc. A writer of much merit, and the first woman in America who made literature a profession.

Adams, Herbert Baxter. 1850 *Ms.* ——. Historical writer. Author The Germanic Origin of New England Towns, Saxon Tithingmen in America, Norman Constables in America, Village Communities of Cape Ann and Salem, etc. *Pub. J. H. U.*

Adams, John. 1735 *Ms.*–1826. Pres. U. S. Author Essay on Canon and Feudal Law, Defence of the Am. Constitution, Hist. of the Dispute with America, etc. *See Complete Works. See Bancroft's Hist. U. S., McMaster's Hist. of the People of the U. S., N. A. Rev. Oct. 1850, Quarterly Rev. Dec. 1841, and Sparks's Diplomatic Correspondence of the Revolution. Pub. Lit.*

Adams, John Quincy. 1767 *Ms.*–1848. Son to preceding. Pres. U. S. Author Lect. on Rhetoric and Oratory, The Bible and its Teachings, Poems of Religion and Society, Letters on Freemasonry, and many State Papers. *See Life by Seward, Memoir by Josiah Quincy, and John Q. Adams by John T. Morse in Am. Statesmen. Pub. Lip.*

Adams, Nehemiah. 1806 *Ms.*–1878. Congregationalist religious writer. Author Remarks on Unitarian Belief, Life of John Eliot, Agnes and the Little Key, etc. His most noted work, A South Side View of Slavery, provoked much criticism. *Pub. Lo.*

Adams, Samuel. 1722 *Ms.*–1803. Cousin to J. A. Political writer. *See Life and Public Services of, by W. V. Wells, and Harper's Mag. July, 1876.*

Adams, Wm. 1807 *Ct.*–1880. Presbyterian religious writer. Author The Three Gardens: Eden Gethsemane Paradise, etc. *Pub. Scr.*

Adams, Wm. Taylor, "Oliver Optic." 1822 *Ms.* ——. Author of many popular juvenile works. *Pub. Le.*

Adler [äd′ler], **Georg.** 1821 *G.*-1868. Philologist. Author of a valuable German and English Dict., and other educational works. *Pub. Apl.*

Agassiz [ag′a-see or ä-gäs-se′], **Louis Jean Rudolph.** 1807 *Sd.*-1873. Naturalist. Author of Nat. Hist. of Fresh-Water Fishes of Central Europe, Études sur les Glaciers, Système Glacière, Methods of Study in Nat. Hist., Geological Sketches, Structure of Animal Life, Journey in Brazil, etc. *See Whipple's Character and Characteristic Men, Atlantic Monthly, Jan. 1858 and Feb. 1874, and Life, by his wife. Pub. Hou.*

Ainslie, Hew. 1792 *S.*-1878. Poet. Author Pilgrimage to the Land of Burns, and Scottish Songs, Ballads, and Poems.

Albee, John. 1833 *Ms.* ——. Author of Literary Art, St. Aspenquid, a poem, etc. *See Lit. World, Sept. 10, 1881. Pub. Put.*

Alcott [awl′kot], **Amos Bronson.** 1799 *Ct.*-1888. Philosopher. Author Conversations, Essays, Tablets, Concord Days, Sonnets and Canzonets, etc. *Pub. Rob.*

Alcott, Louisa May. 1832 *Pa.*-1888. Dau. to A. B. A. Author of Moods, Little Women, Little Men, An Old-Fashioned Girl, Eight Cousins, Under the Lilacs, etc. *Pub. Car. Rob.*

Alcott, Wm. Alexander. 1798 *Ct.*-1859. Cousin to A. B. A. Diet reformer. Author The House I Live in, Vegetable Diet, Library of Health, etc. An energetic, earnest writer. *Pub. Pott.*

Alden [awl'den], **Henry Mills.** 1836 *Vt.* ——. Editor of Harper's Magazine. Author Lect. on the Structure of Paganism, the poem The Ancient Lady of Sorrow, and co-editor with A. H. Guernsey of Harper's Pictorial Hist. of the Great Rebellion, etc. *Pub. Har.*

Alden, Mrs. Isabella [Macdonald], "Pansy." 1841 *N. Y.* ——. Writer of religious tales for young people. Author Four Girls at Chautauqua, Chautauqua Girls at Home, etc. *Pub. Lo.*

Alden, Joseph. 1807 *N. Y.*–1885. Educational writer of note. Author Example of Washington, Citizen's Manual, Christian Ethics, The Science of Government, etc. *Pub. Apl. Bar. Bard. Iv. Le. Phi. Put. Sh.*

Alden, Wm. L. 1837 *Ms.* ——. Son to J. A. Author Domestic Explosions, Shooting Stars, Moral Pirates, Cruise of the Canoe Club, Life of Christopher Columbus, etc. *Pub. Har. Ho. Put.*

Aldrich [awl'dritch], **Thomas Bailey.** 1837 *N. H.* ——. Poet and novelist. Author of the novels Prudence Palfrey, The Queen of Sheba, and The Stillwater Tragedy, The Story of a Bad Boy, a volume of sketches containing the famous Marjorie Daw, etc. Among his finest poems are Spring in New England, Baby Bell, and the XII. Sonnets. *See Atlantic Monthly, Dec. 1874. See Complete Poems, one vol., 1882. Pub. Hou.*

Alexander, Archibald. 1772 *Va.*–1851. Presbyterian theologian. Evidences of Christianity, The Canon of Scripture, Moral Science, and Bible Dict. are some of his numerous works. Style idiomatic and forcible. *See Life, by J. W. Alexander, and Sprague's Annals of the Am. Pulpit, vol. 3. Pub. P. B. Scr.*

Alexander, James Waddell. 1804 *Va.*–1859. Son
to A. A. Presbyterian religious writer. Author
Thoughts on Preaching, Life of Archibald Alexander, Consolation, etc. *Pub. P. B. Ran. Scr.*

Alexander, Joseph Addison. 1809 *Pa.*–1860. Son
to A. A. Presbyterian theologian and reviewer.
Author Commentaries on the Psalms, Isaiah, Acts,
Matthew, and Mark, and of ninety-two articles in
the Princeton Rev. A strong writer, possessing
an attractive and forcible but often extremely sarcastic style. *See Life, by H. C. Alexander, and
Hart's Am. Lit. Pub. P. B. Scr.*

Alexander, Samuel Davies. 1819 *N. J.* ——. Son
to A. A. Presbyterian religious writer. Author
Princeton College in the 18th Cent., etc.

Alexander, Stephen. 1806 *N. Y.*–1883. Astronomer. Author Physical Phenomena of Solar Eclipses,
etc.

Alger [ăl'jĕr or awl'jĕr], **Horatio, Jr.** 1832 *Ms.* ——.
Author of a long series of popular juvenile tales.
Pub. Le. Og. Por.

Alger, Wm. Rounseville. 1823 *Ms.* ——. Unitarian religious writer. Author Symbolic Hist. of
the Cross, The School of Life, Hist. of the Doctrine of a Future Life, The Solitudes of Nature
and Man, The Friendships of Women, Poetry of
the Orient, etc. Style meditative and suggestive.
Pub. A. U. A. Lip. Rob.

Allen, Mrs. Elizabeth Ann [Chase] [Akers], "Florence Percy." 1832 *Me.* ——. Poet. "Rock me
to sleep, mother," is her most noted poem.

Allen, Joseph Henry. 1820 *Ms.* ——. Unitarian
theologian. Author Ten Discourses on Orthodoxy,
Hebrew Men and Times, Christian Hist. in Three
Great Periods, and several classical text-books.
Pub. El. Gi. Rob.

Allen's Wife, Josiah. See Holley.

Allen, Wm. 1784 *Ms.*-1868. Author of a valuable Biographical and Historical Dict., the first edition of which appeared in 1809 and the last in 1857, and works of lesser note.

Allibone, Samuel Austin. 1816 *Pa.* ——. Literary lexicographer. Best known by his Critical Dict. of English Literature and British and American Authors. *Pub. Lip.*

Allston [awl'ston], **Washington.** 1779 *S. C.*-1843. Artist and poet. Author Sylphs of the Seasons and Other Poems, The Romance of Monaldi, Lect. on Art, etc. *See Tuckerman's Book of the Artists, and Sunday Afternoon, May, 1878.*

Alsop [awl'sop], **Richard.** 1761 *Ct.*-1815. Poet. Author of A Monody on the Death of Washington, and many witty and satirical political poems. *Pub. Apl.*

Ames, Fisher. 1758 *Ms.*-1808. Statesman. Author of Speeches, Orations, and Essays. His style is one of much beauty and vigor. *See Works, with Memoir, 1854.*

Ames, Mrs. Mary Clemmer. See Hudson, Mrs.

Ames, Nathaniel. 1708 *Ms.*-1764. Author of a widely popular Almanac of the eighteenth century. *See Tyler's Am. Lit. vol. 2.*

Anderson, John Jacob. 1821 *N. Y.* ——. School historian of note. *Pub. Clk.*

Anderson, Rasmus B. 1846 *Wis.* ——. Norse scholar. Author America not Discovered by Columbus, Norse Mythology, Viking Tales of the North, The Younger Edda, The Elder Edda, etc. *See Lit. World, Aug. 28, 1880. Pub. Gri.*

Anderson, Rufus. 1796 *Me.*-1880. Author Foreign Missions, Hist. of Am. Board's Missions in Sand-

wich Islands, Turkey and India, Peloponnesus and
Greek Islands, etc. *Pub. C. P. S.*

Andrews, Ethan Allen. 1787 *Ct.*-1858. Classical
scholar. Author of a Latin-English Dict. and a
valuable series of classical text-books. *Pub. Hou.*

Andrews, Israel Ward. 1815 *Ct.*-1888. Pres. Marietta College. Author Manual of the Constitution of the U. S., etc. *Pub. Va.*

Andrews, Samuel J. 1817 *Ct.* ——. Bro. to I. W.
A. Author The Life of Our Lord. *Pub. Scr.*

Andrews, Stephen Pearl. 1812 *Ms.*-1886. Author
of several works on Phonography, The Science of
Society, Love, Marriage and Divorce, etc.

Anthon, Charles. 1797 *N. Y.*-1867. Classical
scholar. Author of a Classical Dict. and many
valuable classical text books. *See Galaxy Mag.
Sept. 1867. Pub. Har.*

Anthon, John. 1784 *Mch.*-1863. Bro. to C. A.
Jurist. Author Essay on the Study of Law, Analysis of Blackstone, etc.

Appleton, Thomas Gold. 1812 *Ms.*-1884. Essayist.
Author of A Sheaf of Papers, A Nile Journal,
Windfalls, Syrian Sunshine, and Chequer-Work.
Pub. Rob.

Armstrong, John. 1758 *Pa.*-1843. Author War of
1812 and the famous Newburg Address, 1782.

Arnold, George. 1834 *N. Y.*-1865. Poet. Jubilate,
Recrimination, Beer, and Cui Bono are some of
his best poems. His style lacks finish and his
verse is wanting in strength. *See edition with
Memoir by Wm. Winter, and Scribner's Mag.
July, 1881. Pub. Os.*

Arr, E. H. See Rollins, Mrs. Ellen.

Arthur, Timothy Shay. 1809 *N. Y.*-1885. A prolific writer of moral tales, among which Ten Nights

in a Bar-Room is the most famous. His works are all popular and well intentioned, but their literary merit is not high. *Pub. Col. Lip. Lo. Og. Pet. Por. Pott.*

Atwater, Lyman. 1813 *Ct.*–1883. A noted contributor to the Princeton Rev. and author of a Manual of Logic. *Pub. Lip.*

Audubon, John James. 1780 *La.*–1851. Ornithologist of eminence. Author Birds of America, Quadrupeds of N. A., etc. *See London Quarterly Rev. July, 1832; Audubon, the Naturalist, by Mrs. St. John; and Journal of Life and Labors of Audubon.*

Austin, Benjamin. 1752 *Ms.*–1820. Political writer. Author Constitutional Republicanism.

Austin, James Trecothic. 1784 *Ms.*–1870. Author Life of Elbridge Gerry, etc.

Austin, Mrs. Jane [Goodwin]. 1831 *Ms.* ——. Novelist. Author Cipher, Shadow of Moloch Mountain, Mrs. Beauchamp Brown, The Desmond Hundred, A Nameless Nobleman, two vols. of fairy tales, Nantucket Scraps, etc. Style animated and natural. *Pub. Os. Put. Rob. Sh.*

Austin, Wm. 1778 *Ms.*–1841. Best known as the author of the famous sketch Peter Rugg: the Missing Man.

Ayres, Alfred. See Osmun, Thomas E.

Azarias, Brother. See Mullany, Patrick F.

Bache [bātch], Alexander Dallas. 1806 *Pa.*–1867. Philosopher. Author of numerous valuable scientific papers and coast survey reports.

Bache, Franklin. 1792 *Pa.*–1864. Cousin to A. D. B. Physician and chemist. Author of A System of Chemistry for Students in Medicine, and co-author

with Wood of a noted Dispensatory of the U. S.
See Memoir of, by Geo. B. Wood.

Bachman [bäk'man], **John.** 1790 *N. Y.*-1874. Naturalist and theologian. B. was the assistant of Audubon, writing the larger part of The Quadrupeds
of N. A., and also author of many scientific and
theological works.

Backus, Isaac. 1724 *Ct.*-1806. Baptist historian.
Author of A Hist. of New England with Particular
Reference to the Baptists.

Bacon, Della. 1811 *O.*-1859. Author Philosophy of
the Plays of Shakespeare Unfolded, an attempt to
prove Lord Bacon to be the author of Shakespeare's plays. *See Hawthorne's Recollections of a
Gifted Woman.*

Bacon, Leonard. 1802 *Mch.*-1881. Bro. to D. B.
Congregationalist theologian. Author Historical
Discourses, Essays on Slavery, Genesis of ·the
New England Churches, etc. *See Century Mag.
March, 1883. Pub. Clk. Har.*

Bacon, Leonard Woolsey. 1830 *Ct.* ——. Son to
L. B. Congregationalist religious writer. Author
A Life Worth Living, etc. *Pub. Ran.*

Bagby, George Wm. 1828 *Va.*-1883. Humorist. Author Letters to Mozis Addums, etc.

Baird, Charles Washington. 1828 *N. J.* ——.
Son to R. B. Presb. religious writer. Author Eu-
taxia, or the Presbyterian Liturgies, Book of Public Prayer, and Hist. of Rye. *Pub. Do.*

Baird, Henry Martyn. 1832 *Pa.* ——. Son to R.
B. Author Modern Greece, Life of Robert Baird,
and Hist. of the Rise of the Huguenots of France.
Pub. Har. Ran. Scr.

Baird, Robert. 1798 *Pa.*-1863. Presbyterian religious writer. Author Hist. of the Temperance So-

cieties, View of Religion in America, Hist. of the
Waldenses, Albigenses, and Vaudois, etc. *See
Life, by H. M. Baird. Pub. Har.*

Baird, Samuel John. 1817 *O.* ——. Presbyterian
theologian. Author of numerous works on the
polity and history of the Presbyterian church.

Baird, Spencer Fullerton. 1823 *Pa.*–1887. Naturalist. Secretary of the Smithsonian Institution.
Translator and editor of the Iconographic Ency.,
and co-author with J. Cassin of Birds of N. A. and
Mammals of N. A. Editor Annual Record of Science and Industry. *Pub. Cass. Har. Lip. Lit.*

Baker, George M. 1832 *Me.* ——. Author Amateur
Dramas, The Social Stage, and works of a similar
character. *Pub. Le.*

Baker, Mrs. Harriette Newell [Woods], "Madeline Leslie." 1815 *Ms.* ——. Author The Courte-
sies of Wedded Life, and nearly two hundred moral
and religious tales. *Pub. Le. Su.*

Baker, Wm. Mumford. 1825 *D. C.*–1883. Novelist.
Author The Virginians in Texas, Inside, The
New Timothy, Mose Evans, His Majesty Myself,
Blessed St. Certainty, Thirlmore, and The Ten The-
ophanies, a religious work. Style vigorous and
original. *Pub. Har. Le. Ran. Rob.*

Baldwin, John Denison. 1809 *Ct.*–1883. Archæologist. Editor of the Worcester Spy. Author Pre-
Historic Nations, Ancient America, etc. His works
show great research and are of much value. *Pub.
Har.*

Ballou, Hosea. 1771 *N. H.*–1852. Universalist theologian and controversialist. The founder of Universalism in the U. S. An Examination of the
Doctrine of Future Retribution is his chief work.
See Biography, by M. M. Ballou.

Ballou, Hosea. 1796 *Vt.*-1861. Neph. to preceding. Author Ancient Hist. of Universalism, etc.

Ballou, Maturin Murray. 1822 *Ms.* ——. Son to H. B. 1st. Littérateur. Author History of Cuba, Biog. of Hosea Ballou, Due West, a vol. of travels, and compiler of Pearls of Thought, and similar works. *Pub. Hou.*

Ballou, Moses. 1811 *Ms.* ——. Neph. to H. B. 1st. Universalist theologian.

Bancroft, Aaron. 1755 *Ms.*-1840. Unitarian religious writer, and author of A Life of Washington. *Pub. Por.*

Bancroft, George. 1800 *Ms.* ——. Son to A. B. Historian. The first vol. of his great work, The Hist. of the U. S., appeared in 1834, and the twelfth and concluding one in 1880. A thoroughly revised edition has since been published in six volumes. *Pub. Apl.*

Bancroft, Hubert Howe. 1832 *O.* ——. Historian. Author The Native Races of the Pacific States, History of the Pacific States, and The Early Am. Chroniclers. These works are exceedingly comprehensive in their scope, and are prepared with the assistance of a number of collaborateurs. *Pub. Apl. Ban.*

Bangs, Nathan. 1778 *Ct.*-1862. Methodist theologian. A prolific writer, whose Hist. of the M. E. Church is his most valuable work. *See Life and Times of, by Abel Stevens. Pub. Phi.*

Banneker, Benjamin. 1731 *Md.*-1806. Astronomical writer. *See Atlantic Monthly, Jan. 1863.*

Banvard, Joseph. 1810 *N. Y.*-1887. Miscellaneous writer. Author Romance of Am. Hist., Plymouth and the Pilgrims, Novelties of the New World, etc. *Pub. Loc.*

Barber, John Warner. 1798 *Ct.*–1885. Historical compiler. Author Historical Collections of Mass., Historical Collections of Conn., and similar annals of several other States.

Barclay, James Turner. 1807 *Va.*–1874. Campbellite religious writer. Best known as the author of The City of the Great King, a valuable work relating to Jerusalem.

Barlow, Joel. 1755 *Ct.*–1812. Poet. Author The Columbiad, a pretentious, stilted production, and Hasty Pudding, a genuinely humorous poem. *See Edinburgh Rev. Oct. 1809, and Life by Todd.*

Barnard, Charles. 1838 *Ms.* ——. Littérateur. Author The Tone Masters, The Soprano, The Strawberry Garden, etc. Style bright and spirited. *See Hart's Am. Lit. Pub. Le. Put. Scr.*

Barnard, Frederick Augustus Porter. 1809 *Ms.*–1889. Educational writer. Pres. Columbia Coll. Author Letters on College Government, etc.

Barnard, Henry. 1811 *Ct.* ——. Educational writer of eminence. Author National Education in Europe, School Architecture, Hints and Methods for Teachers, Pestalozzi and Pestalozzianism, etc. Editor of several journals of education. *Pub. Ste.*

Barnard, John. 1681 *Ms.*–1770. Congregationalist theologian. The style of his sermons is robust and logical. *See Tyler's Am. Lit. vol. 2.*

Barnes, Albert. 1798 *N. Y.*–1870. Presbyterian commentator. His Notes on the New Testament is his best known work. His scriptural expositions are clearly and distinctly stated. *Pub. Har. P. B.*

Bartlett, John. 1820 *Ms.* ——. Editor Familiar Quotations, The Shakespeare Phrase-Book, etc. *Pub. Lit.*

Bartlett, John Russell. 1805 *R. I.*–1886. Miscellaneous writer. Author Dict. of Americanisms, Progress of Ethnology, etc., and editor of the Letters of Roger Williams.

Bartlett, Joseph. 1763 *Ms.*-1827. Satirical poet. Author The New Vicar of Bray.

Bartlett, Wm. Henry Chambers. 1804 *Pa.* ——. Scientist. Author treatises on Optics, Mechanics, Spherical Astronomy, etc.

Bartol, Cyrus Augustus. 1813 *Me.* ——. Unitarian theologian. Author Pictures of Europe, Christian Spirit and Life, Radical Problems, The Rising Faith, Principles and Portraits, etc. *Pub. A. U. A. Rob.*

Bartram, John. 1701 *Pa.*-1777. "The Father of American Botany." A shrewd, careful observer. *See Memorials of, by Wm. Darlington, and Tyler's Am. Lit. vol. 2.*

Bartram, Wm. 1739 *Pa.*-1823. Son to J. B. Botanist and traveler. Best known by his Travels in the South Atlantic States. An enthusiastic writer on all botanical topics.

Bascom, John. 1832 *N. Y.* ——. Philosopher. Pres. Wisconsin Univ. Author of Psychology, Æsthetics, Political Economy, Science, Philosophy and Religion, Natural Theology, The Science of Mind, The Words of Christ, etc. A keen, influential thinker. *Pub. Dra. Pot. Put.*

Bates, Arlo. 1850 *Me.* ——. Journalist and novelist. Author Mr. Jacobs and The Pagans. *Pub. Ho.*

Bates, Charlotte Fiske. 1838 *N. Y.* ——. Poet. Author of a volume of careful verse entitled Risk and Other Poems, and editor of The Longfellow Birthday-Book, The Cambridge Book, etc. *Pub. Cr. Hou.*

Baxter, Wm. 1820 *E.* ——. Poet and religious writer. Some of his War Lyrics were once widely popular.

Bayley, James Roosevelt. 1814 *N. Y.*–1877. R. C. Abp. Baltimore. Religious writer. *Pub. Cath.*

Beardsley, E. Edwards. 1808 *Ct.* ——. Ecclesiastical historian and biographer. Author Hist. P. E. Church in Connecticut, and Lives of Samuel Johnson, Wm. Samuel Johnson, and Bp. Seabury. Style dignified and careful. *Pub. Hou.*

Beasley, Frederick. 1777 *N. C.*–1845. Episcopal theologian. Author An Examination of the Oxford Divinity, Search of Truth in the Science of the Human Mind, and Reply to Dr. Channing.

Beck, Theodore Romeyn. 1791 *N. Y.*–1855. Medical writer of note. Co-author with his brother, J. B. Beck, of a much-valued Medical Jurisprudence.

Bedell [bē-dĕll′], Gregory Townsend. 1793 *N. Y.*–1834. Episcopal religious writer. Author Renunciation, Ezekiel's Vision, Sermons, etc. A preacher of much eminence in his day.

Beecher, Catherine Esther. 1800 *L. I.*–1878. Dau. to L. B. Best known by her works on physical training. Author Domestic Economy, Physiology and Calisthenics, Letters to the People, Religious Training of Children, etc. *See Mrs. Hale's Woman's Record. Pub. Fo. Har.*

Beecher, Charles. 1815 *Ct.* ——. Son to L. B. Congregationalist religious writer. Author Pen Pictures of the Bible, The Eden Tableau, Redeemer and Redeemed, etc. *Pub. Le.*

Beecher, Edward. 1804 *L. I.* ——. Son to L. B. Congregationalist theologian. Author The Conflict of the Ages, Papal Conspiracy Exposed, Baptism, etc. *Pub. Apl.*

Beecher, Henry Ward. 1813 *Ct.*–1887. Son to L. B. Congregationalist religious and miscellaneous writer. Life Thoughts, Star Papers, Yale Lect. on Preaching, Lect. to Young Men, and the novel Norwood are his best known works. A pulpit orator of great eminence. *See Parton's Famous Americans, and Abbott's Henry Ward Beecher. Pub. Arm. Fo. Har.*

Beecher, Lyman. 1775 *Ct.*–1863. Congregationalist theologian of note. Author Sermons on Temperance, Views in Theology, Scepticism, etc. A thinker of great boldness and energy. *See Life and Correspondence, edited by Chas. Beecher, 1864. Pub. Har.*

Beecher, Thomas Kennicutt. 1824 *Ct.* ——. Son to L. B. Religious and miscellaneous writer.

Belknap [bĕl'năp], **Jeremy.** 1744 *Ms.*–1798. Historian. Author Hist. of New Hampshire, Am. Biography, The Foresters, etc.

Bell, John. 1796 *I.*–1872. Medical lecturer and journalist of note. Author Health and Beauty, Regimen and Longevity, etc.

Bellamy, Joseph. 1719 *Ct.*–1790. Congregationalist theologian. Style able and learned.

Bellows, Henry Whitney. 1814 *N. H.*–1882. Unitarian theologian. Restatements of Christian Doctrine, Sermons, Relation of Public Amusements to Public Morality, and The Old World in its New Face are his principal works. *Pub. A. U. A. Har.*

Benedict, Frank Lee. 18— ——. Novelist. Author Miss Van Kortland, My Daughter Elinor, The Price She Paid, etc. *Pub. Har.*

Benezet, Anthony. 1713 *F.*–1784. Philanthropist. His works on slavery first aroused the attention of Clarkson and Wilberforce to the subject.

Benjamin, Park. 1809 *B. G.*–1864. Poet and journalist. Of his verse, mainly lyrical in character, The Old Sexton is the best remembered example.

Benjamin, Samuel Green Wheeler. 1840 *Gr.* ——. Artist and littérateur. Author Art in America, The Atlantic Islands, Contemporary Art in Europe, etc. *Pub. Har. Loc. Lo. Ran. Scr.*

Bennet, Emerson. 1822 *Ms.* ——. Sensational novelist. *Pub. Clx.*

Bennett, James Gordon. 1800 *S.*–1872. Journalist. *See Parton's Famous Americans.*

Bensel, James Berry. 1856 *N. Y.*–1886. Poet and novelist. Author In the King's Garden, the novel King Cophetua's Wife, etc. *Pub. Lo.*

Benson, Eugene. 1840 *N. Y.* ——. Artist and writer upon art. Author Gaspara Stampa, and Art and Nature in Italy. *Pub. Rob.*

Benton, Joel. 1832 *N. Y.* ——. Essayist and poet. Author Under the Apple Boughs, Emerson as a Poet, etc. Style thoughtful, graceful, and finished. *Pub. Hol.*

Benton, Thomas Hart. 1782 *N. C.*–1858. Statesman. Author Speeches, Thirty Years' View, and Abridgment of the Debates of Congress 1789–1856. Politically his works are of much value, and as literary productions are marked by taste and simplicity. *Pub. Apl.*

Berard, Augusta Blanche. 1824 *N. Y.* ——. Author of several excellent school histories. *Pub. Bar. Cop.*

Berg, Joseph Frederick. 1812 *W. I.*–1871. Dutch Reformed controversial writer.

Berrian, Wm. 1786–1862. Episcopal devotional writer. Author Family and Private Prayers, Historical Sketch of Trinity Church, etc.

Bethune [beh-thoon'], **George Washington.** 1805
N. Y.–1862. Dutch Reformed theologian and poet.
Author Hist. of a Penitent, Lays of Love and Faith,
etc. Style genial and scholarly. *See Memoir, by
A. R. Van Nest.*

Beverly, Robert. 16— *Va.*–1716. Colonial historian. Author Hist. of the Present State of Virginia, 1705. *See Tyler's Am. Lit. vol. 2.*

Biddle, Charles John. 1819 *Pa.*–1875. Son to N.
B. Journalist. Best known by his careful monograph on the execution of Major André.

Biddle, Nicholas. 1786 *Pa.*–1844. Financier. Author of A Commercial Digest and numerous brilliant and polished addresses.

Bigelow, Jacob. 1787 *Ms.*–1879. Medical and scientific writer of note. *See Memoir, by Ellis. Pub.
Har. Wo.*

Bigelow, John. 1817 *N. Y.* ——. Journalist. Author Life Benj. Franklin, Bryant in Am. Men of
Letters, etc. *Pub. Hou. Lip.*

Bigelow, Melville Madison. 1846 *Mch.* ——. Jurist. Author English Procedure in the Norman
Period, The Law of Fraud, Elements of Equity,
and other legal works of value, and editor 8th edition of Story's Conflict of Laws. *Pub. Hou. Lit.*

Billings, Josh. See Shaw, Henry.

Binney, Horace. 1780 *Pa.*–1875. Jurist. Author
Reports of Cases in the Supreme Court of Pennsylvania 1799–1814, Leaders of the Old Bar of Phil.,
etc.

Bird, Frederick Mayer. 1838 *Pa.* ——. Son to R.
M. B. Hymnologist. Compiler of several collections of hymns, and a high authority in his department. His hymn library is the largest in America.

Bird, Robert Montgomery. 1805 *Del.*–1854. Romantic novelist. Author Nick of the Woods, Peter Pilgrim, Sheppard Lee, etc., and The Gladiator and two other tragedies. *Pub. Arm.*

Bishop, Joel Prentiss. 1814 *N.Y.* ——. Jurist. Author Commentaries on Criminal Law, on Marriage and Divorce, on The Law of Married Women, on Criminal Law, on Criminal Procedure, etc. *Pub. Lit. Th.*

Bishop, Nathaniel Holmes. 1837 *Ms.* ——. Traveler. Author A Thousand Miles' Walk Across South America, The Voyage of the Paper Canoe, and Four Months in a Sneak Box. *Pub. Dou. Le. Pl.*

Bishop, Wm. Henry. 1847 *Ct.* ——. Novelist. Author Detmold, The House of A Merchant Prince, and a volume of travels entitled Old Mexico and her Lost Provinces. *Pub. Har. Hou.*

Blackburn, Wm. Maxwell. 1828 *Ind.* ——. Presbyterian religious and historical writer. Author Hist. of the Christian Church, Geneva's Shield, etc. *Pub. Do. Phi. P. B.*

Blake, John Lauris. 1788 *N. H.*-1857. Author of a valuable Family Encyclopædia, Gen. Biographical Dict., etc.

Bledsoe, Albert Taylor. 1808 *Ky.* ——. Metaphysical and mathematical writer. Author of Essay on Liberty and Slavery, Examination of Edwards on the Will, Philosophy of Mathematics, etc. *Pub. Lip.*

Blunt, Edmond March. 1770 *N. H.*-1862. Nautical writer. Author The Am. Coast Pilot.

Boardman, George Dana. 1828 *Bh.* ——. Baptist religious writer. Author Studies in the Creative Week, Epiphanies of the Risen Lord, Titles of a Pastor's Wednesday Evening Lectures, etc. *Pub. Apl. A. S. U.*

Boardman, Henry Augustus. 1808 *N. Y.*–1880. Presbyterian theologian. Author The Bible in the Family, The Bible in the Counting-House, The Christian Ministry not a Priesthood, etc. *Pub. Lip. P. B.*

Boker, George Henry. 1824 *Pa.* ——. Dramatic poet. Author of the tragedies Calaynos, Anne Boleyn, Lenor de Guzman, and Francesca da Rimini ; Poems of the War, The Book of the Dead, etc. With the exception of Francesca da Rimini his dramas are better suited for closet reading than for acting. *Pub. Lip.*

Bolton, Mrs. Sarah T. [Barritt]. 1820 *Ky.* —— Poet. Paddle Your Own Canoe is her most noted poem. ·

Bonner, Sherwood. See MacDowell, Mrs.

Bosman, John Leeds. 1757 *Md.*–1823. Legal and historical writer. Author Hist. Maryland, etc.

Botta, Mrs. Anne Charlotte [Lynch]. 1820 *Vt.* ——. Wife to V. B. Littérateur. Author Handbook of Universal Lit., Leaves from the Diary of a Recluse, etc. *Pub. Hou.*

Botta, Vincenzo. 1818 *Iy.* ——. Historical writer. Author Life of Cavour, Historical Account of Modern Philosophy in Italy, Dante as Philosopher, Patriot, and Poet, etc. *Pub. Scr.*

Boudinot [boo'de-not], Elias. 1740 *Pa.*–1821. Religious writer. Author The Age of Revelation and other works, much read at one time, but now nearly forgotten.

Bouvier [boo-veer'], Hannah M. 1811 *Pa.*–18——. Dau. to J. B. Author Familiar Astronomy. *Pub. So.*

Bouvier, John. 1787 *F.*–1851. Jurist. Author Law Dict., Institutes of Am. Law, etc. *Pub. Lip. Lit.*

Bowditch, Nathaniel. 1773 *Ms.*–1838. Mathematician. His translation of La Place is his greatest work. *See Memoir, by N. I. Bowditch.*

Bowen, Francis. 1811 *Ms.* ——. Philosopher. Author Critical Essays on Speculative Philosophy, Modern Philosophy, Treatise on Logic, Am. Political Economy, etc. *See Harvard Register, May, 1881. Pub. Al. Scr. Wa.*

Bowen, Mrs. Sue [Petigru] [King]. 1824 *S. C.*–1875. Novelist. Author Busy Moments of an Idle Woman, Sylvia's World, Gerald Gray's Wife, etc.

Bowles, Samuel. 1826 *Ms.*–1877. Journalist. Editor The Springfield Republican. Author Across the Continent, Our New West, etc.

Boyd, James R. 1804 *N. Y.* ——. Educational and religious writer. Author Elements of Rhetoric and Literary Criticism, Moral Philosophy, etc. *Pub. Har.*

Boyesen, Hjalmar Hjorth. 1848 *N.* ——. Novelist and poet. Author Gunnar, A Norseman's Pilgrimage, Tales from Two Hemispheres, Falconberg, A Daughter of the Philistines, etc. *See Scribner's Mag. Oct. 1877. Pub. Scr.*

Brace, Charles Loring. 1826 *Ct.* ——. Author Norsefolk, Home Life in Germany, The Races of the Old World, Gesta Christi, etc. *Pub. Arm. Scr.*

Brackenridge, Hugh Henry. 1748 *S.*–1816. Humorist. Author Modern Chivalry. Style keenly satirical. *See edition 1848, and Hart's Am. Lit.*

Bradstreet, Mrs. Anne [Dudley]. 1612 *E.*–1672. Poet. The first American woman of letters. Called by her contemporaries "The Tenth Muse." *See Tyler's Am. Lit. vol. 1, and Helen Campbell's Anne Bradstreet in Famous Women.*

Brainard, John Gardiner Calkins. 1796 *Ct.*–1828.

Poet. His chief claim to remembrance is the fine poem beginning, " I saw two clouds at morning." *See Griswold's Poets and Poetry of America.*

Breckinridge, Robert Jefferson. 1800 *Ky.*–1871. Presbyterian theologian of note. Author The Knowledge of God, etc. Style clear and forcible. *See Memorials and Biographical Sketches, by Jas. Freeman Clarke. Pub. Ca.*

Briggs, Charles Frederick. 1804 *Ms.*–1877. Journalist. Best known as the author of the novel Harry Franco. Style genial and pleasing. *See Lowell's Fable for Critics.*

Brinton, Daniel Garrison. 1837 *Pa.* ——. Physician and archæologist. Author The Myths of the New World, The Religious Sentiment, American Hero-Myths, Aboriginal Am. Authors, etc., and editor The Maya Chronicles, The Comedy-Ballet of Güeguence, etc. *Pub. Br. Ho.*

Bristed, Charles Astor. 1820 *N. Y.*–1874. Littérateur. Author Five Years in an English University, The Upper Ten Thousand, etc.

Brodhead, John Romeyn. 1814 *Pa.*–1873. Historian. Author Hist. of the State of New York, a valuable and standard work. *See Scribner's Mag. Feb. 1877. Pub. Har.*

Brooks, Charles Timothy. 1813 *Ms.*–1883. German scholar of eminence. His versions of Schiller, Richter, Goethe, and Scheffel take high rank among translations. Author Songs of Field and Flood, The Simplicity of Christ, etc. *Pub. Rob.*

Brooks, Edward. 1831 *N. Y.* ——. Educational writer of note. *Pub. So.*

Brooks, Mrs. Maria [Gowen]. 1795 *Ms.*–1845. Poet. Called by Southey "Maria del Occidente." Author of Zophiel, a powerful but morbid and fitfully vehement poem. *See Griswold's Female Poets of America, and Harper's Mag. Jan. and May, 1879. Pub. Le.*

Brooks, Nathan Covington. 1809 *Md.* ——. Author of an excellent series of classical text-books and A Complete Hist. of the Mexican War. *Pub. Bar. Clx.*

Brooks, Noah. 1830 *Me.* ——. Writer of tales for young people. Author The Boy Emigrants, The Fairport Nine, etc. *Pub. Scr.*

Brooks, Phillips. 1835 *Ms.* ——. Broad Church theologian. Author The Influence of Jesus, Lect. on Preaching, Sermons, Sermons in English Churches, etc. A leader of modern religious thought. *Pub. Dut.*

Brougham [broo'am or broo'm], **John.** 1814 *I.*–1880. Dramatist. Author of over a hundred comedies and farces, many of which have been very successful. *See Life, by Wm. Winter.*

Brown, Charles Brockden. 1771 *Pa.*–1810. Novelist. Author Wieland, Ormond, Arthur Mervyn, Edgar Huntly, Clara Howard, Jane Talbot, and Sky-Walk. Style vivid, often morbid, and highly inventive.

Brown, David Paul. 1795 *Pa.*–1872. Author of several tragedies, and The Forum, or Forty Years' Practice at the Bar.

Brown, Goold. 1791 *Ms.*–1857. Grammarian of note. Author Grammar of English Grammars, Institutes of English Grammar, etc. *Pub. Wo.*

Brown, Henry Armitt. 1846 *Pa.*–1878. Orator. *See Memoir, by Hoppin, and Atlantic Monthly, Aug. 1880.*

Brown, John W. 1814 *N. Y.*–1849. Poet. Author Christmas Bells, etc.

Browne, Charles Farrar, " Artemus Ward." 1834 *Me.*–1867. Humorist. Author Artemus Ward : his Book, Artemus Ward Among the Mormons, Artemus Ward in London, etc. *See Scribner's Mag. Oct. 1877, and May, 1881, and Haweis's Am. Humorists.*

Browne, John Ross. 1817 *I.*–1875. Humorist. Author American Family in Germany, Yusef, Land of Thor, and other vols. of travels. *Pub. Apl. Har.*

Brownell, Henry Howard. 1820 *R. I.*–1872. Neph. to T. C. B. Poet. Author Songs of a Soldier, etc. His war lyrics rank among the finest of their kind. *See edition 1866.*

Brownell, Thomas Church. 1779 *Ms.*–1865. Bp. Ct. Religious writer. Author Family Prayer-Book, Commentary on the Prayer-Book, Youthful Christian's Guide, etc. *Pub. Clx.*

Brownson, Orestes Augustus. 1803 *Vt.*–1876. Roman Catholic theologian. Author Charles Elwood, an autobiographic novel, Leaves from my Experience, etc. A clear, bold, and earnest thinker. As editor of Brownson's Review he ably defended the Roman Catholic faith. *Pub. Sad.*

Bruce, Wallace. 1844 *N. Y.* ——. Poet and lecturer. Author The Hudson, The Land of Burns, etc. *Pub. Hou.*

Bryant, John Howard. 1807 *Ms.* ——. Bro. to W. C. B. Poet. *See Griswold's Poets and Poetry of America.*

Bryant, Wm. Cullen. 1794 *Ms.*–1878. Poet and journalist. Editor The N. Y. Evening Post. Author The Flood of Years, The Little People of the Snow, Song of the Sower, Thanatopsis, etc. His greatest work is his translation of the Iliad and Odyssey. Among the best of his lighter poems is

The Planting of the Apple-Tree. *See Commemorative Address by G. W. Curtis, Scribner's Mag. Aug. 1878, Lippincott's Mag. July, 1882, Bryant in Am. Men of Letters, Life by Parke Godwin, and Biography by A. J. Symington. Pub. Apl. Hou.*

Buckingham, Joseph Tinker. 1779 *Ct.*–1861. Journalist. Author Specimens of Newspaper Literature, Personal Memoir, etc.

Bulfinch, Stephen Greenleaf. 1809 *Ms.*–1870. Unitarian religious writer. Author Poems, Lays of the Gospel, Communion Thoughts, etc. *Pub. A. U. A. Le.*

Bullions, Peter. 1791 *S.*–1864. Classical scholar. Author of a valuable series of classical text-books. *Pub. Sh.*

Bunner, Henry Cuyler. 18——. Ed. of Puck. Author of Airs from Arcady and Elsewhere, and the novel The Woman of Honor. *Pub. Os. Scr.*

Burdett, Charles. 1815 *N. Y.*–18—. Journalist and novelist. Author Life of Kit Carson, etc. *Pub. Por. Pott.*

Burdette, Robert Jones. 1844 *Pa.* ——. Humorist. Editor Burlington Hawkeye. Author Life of Wm. Penn, Hawkeyes, etc. *Pub. Ho.*

Burgess, George. 1809 *R. I.*–1866. Bp. Me. Author Ecclesiastical Hist. of New England, The Christian Life, The Book of Psalms in English verse, etc. *See Memoir, by A. Burgess. Pub. Bro. Ran.*

Burleigh, Wm. Henry. 1812 *Ct.*–1871. Poet. *See Memoir, by Celia Burleigh. Pub. Hou.*

Burnap, George Washington. 1802 *N. H.*–1859. Unitarian controversialist. Author Popular Objections to Unitarian Christianity Considered, etc.

Burnett, Mrs. Frances [Hodgson]. 1849 *E.* ——.

Novelist. Author Haworth, That Lass o' Lowrie's,
Through One Administration, Louisiana, Esme-
ralda, A Fair Barbarian, etc. *Pub. Os. Pet. Scr.*

Burnham, Mrs. Clara Louise [Root]. 1854 *Ms.*
——. Novelist. Author No Gentlemen, A Sane
Lunatic, etc. Style animated and pleasing. *Pub. Su.*

Burr, Enoch Fitch. 1818 *Ct.* ——. Congregationalist religious writer. Author Pater Mundi, Ad
Fidem, Doctrine of Evolution, Ecce Cœlum, Sunday Afternoons, Toward the Strait Gate, Ecce
Terra, etc. *Pub. A. T. S. Loc.*

Burritt, Elihu. 1811 *Ct.*–1880. Linguist. Called
" The Learned Blacksmith." Author Sparks from
the Anvil, a Voice from the Forge, Peace Papers
for the People, etc. *See Memorial, by C. Northend.*
Pub. Ran. Sh.

Burroughs, John. 1837 *N. Y.* ——. Essayist. Author Wake-Robin, Winter Sunshine, Locusts and
Wild Honey, Birds and Poets, Pepacton, etc. A
minute, keen observer of nature, possessing an
original, vivacious style. *See Scribner's Mag. Jan.*
1877. Pub. Hou.

Burton, Wm. Evans. 1804 *E.*–1860. Comedian and
miscellaneous writer. Best known by his Cyclopædia of Wit and Humor. *Pub. Apl.*

Bush, George. 1796 *Vt.*–1860. Swedenborgian biblical commentator of note. Author Commentaries
on Genesis, Exodus, Leviticus, Numbers, Joshua,
Judges, the Psalms, Life of Mohammed, etc. *Pub.*
Har.

Bushnell, Horace. 1802 *Ct.*–1876. Congregationalist theologian. Author Christian Nurture, God in
Christ, Christian Theology, The Vicarious Sacri-
fice, Politics the Law of God, Nature and the
Supernatural, Moral Uses of Dark Things, etc.

See Life and Letters, and Atlantic Monthly, Jan. 1881. Pub. Scr.

Butler, Wm. Allen. 1825 *N. Y.* ——. Satirical poet. Author Nothing to Wear, Two Millions, General Average, etc.

Byles, Mather. 1706 *Ms.*–1788. Poet. Of great renown in his day as a humorist. *See Sprague's Annals Am. Pulpit, vol. 1, and Tyler's Am. Lit. vol. 2.*

Byrd, Wm. 1674 *Va.*–1744. His Journals, first published in 1841, are known as The Westover Manuscripts. Style pleasing and quaintly humorous. *See Hart's Am. Lit.; also Tyler's Am. Lit. vol. 2.*

Cable, George Washington. 1844 *La.* ——. Novelist. Author Old Creole Days, The Grandissimes, Madame Delphine, Dr. Sevier, Simms in Am. Men of Letters, etc. *Pub. Scr.*

Caldwell, Charles. 1772 *N. C.*–1853. Physician. Author Life and Campaigns of Gen. Greene, and translator of Blumenbach's Elements of Physiology, etc. *See Autobiography, 1855, and Life, by Carruthers.*

Calef, Robert. 1652 *Ms.*–c. 1723. Author More Wonders of the Invisible World, a satirical work in opposition to witchcraft persecutions, which was publicly burnt by Increase Mather. *See Tyler's Am. Lit. vol. 2.*

Calhoun [kăl-hoon'], **John Caldwell.** 1782 *S. C.*–1850. Statesman. Author Treatise on the Nature of Governments, and six vols. of speeches. Style strong, concise, and severely logical. *See Life by Jenkins, Parton's Famous Americans, and Von Holst's Calhoun in Am. Statesmen. Pub. Apl.*

Calvert, George Henry. 1803 *Md.* ——. Poet and

essayist. Author Goethe : his Life and Works,
Dante and his Latest Translators, a translation of
Schiller's Don Carlos, Count Julian, a tragedy, and
many volumes of verse. His prose is scholarly and
refined, but his poetry has met with much adverse
criticism. *See Lit. World, June 16, 1883. Pub. Le.*

Campbell, Alexander. 1788 *I.*-1865. Theologian
and founder of the sect of Campbellites. His writings are mainly controversial, and are very numerous. *See Hart's Am. Lit. and Memoir by Richardson.*

Campbell, Bartley. 1843 *Pa.*-1888. Dramatist. Author My Partner, The Galley Slave, Matrimony,
Siberia, and other popular plays.

Campbell, Charles. 1807 *Va.* ——. Historian. Au-
.thor Hist. of the Colony of Virginia, Genealogy of
the Spotswood Family, etc. *Pub. Lip.*

Campbell, Mrs. Helen [Stuart]. 1839 ——. Nov-
elist and littérateur. Author Under Green Apple
Boughs, Unto the Third and Fourth Generation,
The Ainslee Stories, Anne Bradstreet in Famous
Women, Patty Pearson's Boy, etc. *Pub. Fo. Rob.*

Carey, Henry Charles. 1793 *Pa.*-1879. Son to
M. C. Political economist of eminence. Author
Principles of Political Economy, The Credit System, The Principles of Social Science, Lectures on
the Currency, etc. A strong, original writer, and a
leading authority in his department. *See Allibone's
Dict. and Memoir by Wm. Elder. Pub. Bai. Lip.*

Carey, Mathew. 1760 *I.*-1839. Political economist. Author Essays on Political Economy.

Carleton, Wm. 1845 *Mch.* ——. Poet. Author
Farm Ballads, Farm Festivals, Farm Legends, etc.
His verse does not take a high rank, but it has
been widely read, and displays a keen sympathy

for the commoner, harder phases of life. *See Harper's Mag. March, 1884, and Lit. World, Jan. 26, 1884. Pub. Har.*

Carruthers, Wm. A. 1800 *Va.*–1850. Author The Cavaliers of Virginia, Knights of the Horse-Shoe, etc.

Carter, Robert. 1819 *N. Y.*–1879. Littérateur. Author A Summer Cruise on the Coast of New England. Was one of the editors of Appleton's Am. Cyclopædia, to the earlier and later editions of which he contributed many articles, the most important being on Jefferson Davis and The Confederate States. *See Lit. World, Feb. 15, 1879.*

Cary, Alice. 1820 *O.*–1871. Poet. Author of Lyra and Other Poems, A Lover's Diary, etc., and Clovernook, Pictures of Country Life, and other prose works. *See Memorials of Alice and Phœbe Cary, by Mrs. [Clemmer] Hudson. Pub. Arm. Hou. Lip. Wid.*

Cary, Phœbe. 1824 *O.*–1871. Sister to A. C. Poet. Author Poems and Parodies, and Poems of Faith, Hope, and Resignation. Field Preaching and Nearer Home are among her best poems. Of the sisters, Phœbe possessed the most original and brilliant mind. *Pub. Hou. Lip.*

Casey, Silas. 1807 *R. I.*–1882. Military writer. Author several standard works on infantry tactics.

Cassin, John. 1813 *Pa.*–1869. Naturalist. Author Am. Ornithology, A General Synopsis of N. A. Ornithology, etc.

Catherwood, Mrs. Mary [Hartwell]. 1848 *O.* ——— Novelist. Author Craque o' Doom, Old Caravan Days, etc. *Pub. Lip.*

Catlin, George. 1796 *Pa.*–1872. Artist and traveler. Author Notes of Travel, and Illustrations of the

Manners, Customs, and Condition of the N. A. Indians, a work of lasting interest. *See Edinburgh Rev. Jan. 1842, and Tuckerman's Book of the Artists.*

Chadbourne, Paul A. 1823 *Me.*–1883. Pres. Williams Coll. Naturalist. Author Relations of Natural Hist. to Intellect, Taste, Wealth, and Religion, Natural Theology, Instinct in Animals and Men, etc. *Pub. Bar. Put.*

Chadwick, John White. 1840 *Ms.* ——. Poet and Unitarian religious writer. Author Poems, In Nazareth Town, The Man Jesus, The Faith of Reason, etc. A thinker of extremely radical views. *Pub. Put. Rob.*

Chalkley, Thomas. 1675 *E.*–1749. Quaker missionary. His writings, consisting of religious tracts and a Journal of his experiences, are noted for their simplicity and beauty.

Champlin, James Tifft. 1811 *Ct.*–1882. Educational writer. Author First Principles of Ethics, Lessons on Political Economy, Text-Book on Intellectual Philosophy, etc. *Pub. Al. Apl. Pot. Sev.*

Champlin, John Denison, Jr. 1834 *Ct.* ——. Educational writer. Author Young Folks' Cyclopædia of Common Things, Young Folks' Cyclopædia of Persons and Places, Young Folks' Hist. of the War for the Union, Young Folks' Catechism of Common Things, etc. *Pub. Ho.*

Champney, Mrs. Lizzie [Williams]. 1850 *O.* ——. Writer of tales and sketches. Author In the Sky-Garden, All Around a Palette, Bourbon Lilies, the novel Sebia's Tangled Web, etc. *Pub. Loc. Lo.*

Channing, Edward Tyrrel. 1790 *R. I.*–1856. Bro. to W. E. C. 1". Critical and biographical writer.

Channing, Walter. 1786 *R. I.*–1876. Bro. to W. E

C. 1ᵗ. Physician. Author of several valuable medical works.

Channing, Wm. Ellery. 1780 *R. I.*-1842. Unitarian theologian of eminence. Author Evidences of Christianity, Self-Culture, Sermons, etc. *See Westminster Rev. Jan. 1849, N. A. Rev. Oct. 1835, Sprague's Annals Am. Pulpit, vol. 1, Memoirs by W. H. Channing, Channing by C. T. Brooks, Reminiscences by Miss Peabody, and Correspondence of Channing and Lucy Aikin. Pub. A. U. A.*

Channing, Wm. Ellery. 1818 *Ms.* ——. Son to W. C. Poet. Author The Wanderer, Near Home, Thoreau, the Poet Naturalist, etc. Style meditative and refined. His verse is of a character more keenly appreciated by poets than by readers in general. *Pub. Hou. Rob.*

Channing, Wm. Francis. 1820 *Ms.* ——. Son to W. E. C. 1ᵗ. Medical writer.

Channing, Wm. Henry. 1810 *Ms.*-1884. Unitarian religious writer. Author Memoirs of Wm. E. Channing, The Christian Church and Social Reform, etc.

Chapin, Edwin Hubbell. 1814 *N. Y.*-1881. Universalist preacher of eminence. Author The Crown of Thorns, Humanity in the City, Christianity the Perfection of True Manliness, Moral Aspects of City Life, Discourses on the Lord's Prayer, etc. *See Life, by Sumner Ellis. Pub. Mil.*

Chaplin, Jeremiah. 1813 *Ms.*-1886. Baptist religious writer. Author Riches of Bunyan, Chips from the White House, etc. His best work is the Life of Henry Dunster, First President of Harvard College. *Pub. Lo. Wd. Wid.*

Chase, Ira. 1793 *Vt.*-1864. Baptist theologian. Author Life of Bunyan, Design of Baptism, etc.

Chase, Thomas. 1827 *Ms.* ——. Classical scholar.

Author of Hellas, her Monuments and Scenery, etc., and co-editor with Geo. Stuart of a series of classical text-books. *Pub. Eld.*

Chauncey [chän'sĭ or chaun'sĭ], **Charles.** 1589 *E.*–1672. Puritan theologian. Author of Justification, etc. *See Tyler's Am. Lit. vol. 1.*

Chauncey, Charles. 1705 *Ms.*–1787. Great-grandson to preceding. Congregationalist theologian. Author Seasonable Thoughts on the State of Religion in New England, etc. A writer of great research and intellectual vigor. *See Tyler's Am. Lit. vol. 2.*

Cheever, George Barrell. 1807 *Me.* ——. Religious and miscellaneous writer. Author Deacon Giles's Distillery, Studies in Poetry, Wanderings of a Pilgrim in the Shadow of Mont Blanc, etc. *Pub. Ca. Ran. Wil.*

Cheever, Henry Theodore. 1814 *Me.* ——. Bro. to G. B. C. The Island World of the Pacific is one of his most popular works. *Pub. Har. Lo.*

Chesebro [cheez'brō], **Caroline.** 1825 *N. Y.*–1873. Novelist. Author Peter Carradine, The Children, etc. The Foe in the Household, her finest work, is one of the best of American novels. *Pub. Do.*

Child, Francis James. 1825 *Ms.* ——. Critic and scholar. Editor Am. edition of The British Poets, of English and Scottish Popular Ballads, etc. A high authority upon all matters connected with English literature and philology. *Pub. Hou.*

Child, Mrs. Lydia Maria [Francis]. 1802 *Ms.*–1880. Hobomok, a novel, Philothea, Looking Toward Sunset, Romance of the Republic, and An Appeal for that Class of Americans Called Africans are her most noted works. A writer of lively sympathies and noble aims. *See Letters of, and Lowell's Fable for Critics. Pub. Hou. Lo. Rob.*

Choate, Rufus. 1799 *Ms.*-1858. Orator. Known to literature by his Lectures, Addresses, and Speeches. Style brilliant and persuasive. *See Works with Memoir, Life by E. G. Parker, Memoir by S. G. Brown, N. A. Rev. Jan. 1863, Harper's Mag. Nov. 1878, and Some Recollections of by E. P. Whipple. Pub. Lit.*

Choules [chōlz], **John Overton.** 1801 *E.*-1856. Miscellaneous writer. Author Hist. of Missions, Christian Offering, Young Americans Abroad, etc.

Church, Benjamin. 1734 *R. I.*-1776. Political satirist and poet.

Church, Pharcellus. 1801 *N. Y.*-1886. Baptist religious writer. Seed-Truths is his most important work. *Pub. Sh.*

Claiborne [klā'burn], **John F. H.** 1807 *Mi.*-1884. Historian. Author Hist. of the War of Secession, and Lives of Gen. Dale and Gen. Quitman. *Pub. Har.*

Clark, Davis Wasgatt. 1812 *Me.*-1871. Methodist religious writer. Author Mental Discipline, Death-Bed Scenes, etc. *Pub. Phi.*

Clark, Lewis Gaylord. 1810 *N. Y.*-1873. Humorous writer. Author Knick-Knacks, etc.

Clark, Thomas March. 1812 *Ms.* ——. Bp. R. I. Religious writer of the Broad Church school. Author Primary Truths, Lect. to Young Men and Women, Early Discipline and Culture, etc. *Pub. Apl. Le.*

Clark, Willis Gaylord. 1810 *N. Y.*-1841. Twin bro. to L. G. C. Poet. *See Griswold's Poets and Poetry of America.*

Clarke, Edward Hammond. 1820 *Ms.*-1877. Physician. Author Sex in Education, The Building of a Brain, Visions : a Study of False Sight, etc. *Pub. Hou.*

Clarke, James Freeman. 1810 *N. H.*–1888. Unitarian theologian. Ten Great Religions, Christian Doctrine of Prayer, Thomas Didymus, Common Sense in Religion, Steps of Belief, Events and Epochs in Religious Hist., and Self-Culture are some of his most important works. He is also the author of religious verse of much merit. *Pub. A. U. A. Hou. Le. Loc. Os.*

Clarke, MacDonald. 1798 *Ct.*–1842. Poet. Author of Elixir of Moonshine — a Collection of Prose and Poetry by the Mad Poet, etc. An erratic and fantastic writer. *See Baldwin's Monthly, Aug. 1880.*

Clarke, Rebecca Sophia, "Sophie May." 18— *Me.*
——. Writer of stories for young people. Author of Quinnebasset Girls, The Doctor's Daughter, etc. *Pub. Le.*

Clarke, Richard H. 1827 *D. C.* ——. Biographer. Lives of Deceased R. C. Bishops of the U. S. is his chief work.

Clay, Henry. 1777 *Va.*–1852. Statesman. Known to literature by his published speeches. *See N. A. Rev. Jan. 1866, Parton's Famous Americans, Lives by Mallory and Colton, and Henry Clay by Carl Schurz in Am. Statesmen.*

Clemens, Samuel Langhorne, "Mark Twain." 1835 *Mo.* ——. Humorist. Author Innocents Abroad, Roughing It, Tom Sawyer, The Gilded Age (with C. D. Warner), etc. *See Haweis's American Humorists, and Century Mag. Sept. 1882.*

Clement, Mrs. Clara Erskine. See Waters, Mrs.

Clemmer, Mrs. Mary. See Hudson, Mrs.

Cleveland, Charles Dexter. 1802 *Ms.*–1869. Educational writer. Author of Compendiums of English, American, and Classical Literature, Eng. Literature of the 19th Cent., etc. *Pub. Bar. Clx. Lip.*

Cobb, Sylvanus. 1823 *Me.*-1887. Writer of sensational tales of little merit.

Coffin, Charles Carleton. 1821 *N. H.* ——. Journalist and lecturer. Author My Days and Nights on the Battlefield, Building the Nation, Old Times in the Colonies, and other books for young people. *See Hart's Am. Lit. Pub. Est. Har. Le.*

Coffin, Robert Barry, "Barry Gray." 1826 *N. Y.*-1886. Author Matrimonial Infelicities, Who is the Heir ? etc.

Coffin, Robert S. 1797 *Me.*-1827. Poet. Called "The Boston Bard." *See Poems, pub. 1826.*

Cogswell, Joseph Green. 1786 *Ms.*-1871. Scholar. Superintendent Astor Library.

Coit, Thomas Winthrop. 1803 *Ct.*-1885. Episcopal theologian. Author Theological Commonplace Book, Puritanism, Lect. on the Early Hist. of Christianity in England, etc.

Colburn, Warren. 1793 *Ms.*-1833. Mathematician of note. *Pub. Hal. Hou. Loc.*

Colden, Cadwallader. 1688 *S.*-1776. A Hist. of the Five Nations is his chief work. An industrious, versatile writer. *See Tyler's Am. Lit. vol. 2.*

Collier, Joseph Avery. 1828 *Ms.*-1864. Religious writer for the young. Author Little Crowns, Dawn of Heaven, etc. *Pub. Ca.*

Collier, Robert Laird. 1837 *Md.* ——. Unitarian religious writer and littérateur. Author Every-Day Subjects in Sunday Sermons, Meditations on the Essence of Christianity, Henry Irving : a Sketch and a Criticism, etc. *Pub. A. U. A. Rob.*

Collyer, Robert. 1823 *E.* ——. Unitarian religious

writer. Author The Life That Now Is, Nature and Life, A Man in Earnest, etc. *Pub. Le. Put.*

Colman, Lyman. 1796 *Ms.*-1882. Religious writer. Author Ancient Christianity Exemplified, Manual of Prelacy and Ritualism, etc. *Pub. Lip.*

Colton, Calvin. 1789 *Ms.*-1857. Episcopal religious and miscellaneous writer. Author Life of Henry Clay, Junius Tracts, etc.

Colton, George Hooker. 1818 *N. Y.*-1847. Poet. Author Tecumseh. His verse is mediocre and flavorless. *See Griswold s Poets and Poetry of America.*

Colton, Walter. 1797 *Vt.*-1851. Bro. to C. C. Writer of travels. Author Ship and Shore, Deck and Port, The Sea and the Sailor, etc.

Colwell, Stephen. 1800 *Va.*-1871. Political economist, and author of several works on that subject. *Pub. Lip.*

Comstock [kŭm'stŏck], **John Lee.** 1788 *Ct.*-1858. Educational writer. Of his numerous scientific text-books, the most noted is The Elements of Chemistry. *Pub. Sh.*

Conant, Mrs. Hannah O'Brien [Chaplin]. 1812 *Ms.*-1865. Wife to T. J. C. Oriental scholar. Author Hist. of the English Bible, New England Theocracy, etc.

Conant, Mrs. Helen S. 1839 *Ms.* ——. Littérateur. Author The Butterfly Hunters, Primers of German and Spanish Literature, etc. *Pub. Har.*

Conant, Thomas Jefferson. 1802 *Vt.* ——. Baptist biblical scholar of note. *Pub. Fu. Sh.*

Conrad, Robert T. 1805 *Pa.*-1858. Poet. Author of the tragedies Aylmere and Conrad of Naples, and minor poems.

Conway, Moncure Daniel. 1832 *Va.* ——. Littéra

teur. Author of Idols and Ideals, Demonology and Devil Lore, The Wandering Jew, Sketch of Carlyle, etc. *Pub. Har. Ho.*

Conyngham, David Power. 1840 *I.*-1883. Editor N. Y. Tablet. Author of Sherman's March Through the South, Lives of the Irish Saints and Martyrs, several novels, and other works. *Pub. Sad.*

Cook, Clarence. 1828 *Ms.* ——. Art critic. Editor Lübke's Hist. of Art, and author The House Beautiful, etc. The possessor of a pleasing but occasionally captious style. *Pub. Do. Scr.*

Cook, Joseph. 1838 *N. Y.* ——. Lecturer. Author Boston Monday Lect., Biology, Transcendentalism, Orthodoxy, Heredity, Socialism, Labor, etc. An earnest, forcible thinker, whose somewhat ambitious style has received much hostile criticism. *Pub. Hou.*

Cooke, George Willis. 1848 *Mch.* ——. Critic. Author George Eliot: a Critical Study, and Ralph Waldo Emerson: his Life, Writings, and Philosophy. A critic of fine appreciation and judgment. *Pub. Os.*

Cooke, John Esten. 1830 *Va.*-1886. Novelist and littérateur. The Virginia Comedians and Henry St. John are his best novels. Among other works are able Lives of Gen. Lee and Gen. Stonewall Jackson, and Virginia in Am. Commonwealths. *See Lit. World, Jan. 13, 1883. Pub. Apl. Car. Clx. Har. Hou. Lip.*

Cooke, Josiah Parsons. 1827 *Ms.* ——. Chemist. Author Religion and Chemistry, Scientific Culture, Elements of Chemical Physics, etc. *Pub. Al. Apl. Bu. Scr.*

Cooke, Philip Pendleton. 1816 *Va.*-1850. Bro. to J. E. C. Poet. Author The Froissart Ballads, etc. Florence Vane is his most quoted poem. *See Griswold's Poets and Poetry of America.*

Cooke, Mrs. Rose [Terry]. 1827 *Ct.* ——. Poet and writer of short stories. Author Somebody's Neighbors, etc. The Two Villages is her best known poem. Her stories, mainly of New England life, for faithful description, excellence of character drawing, and constructive ability, take high rank. *Pub. Os.*

Cooley, Leroy C. 1833 *N. Y.* ——. Author of numerous scientific text-books. *Pub. Scr.*

Cooley, Thomas McIntyre. 1824 *N. Y.* ——. Jurist. Author of annotated editions of Blackstone's and Story's Commentaries, a Treatise on Constitutional Limitations, Constitutional Law, etc. *Pub. Lit.*

Coolidge, Susan. See Woolsey, Sarah.

Cooper, James Fenimore. 1789 *N. J.*-1851. Novelist and naval historian. His thirty novels are mainly sea stories and pioneer tales. Of the former, The Pilot and The Red Rover are the best. Of his other stories, The Spy, The Last of the Mohicans, The Prairie, The Pathfinder, The Deerslayer, and The Pioneer are the finest. The animation and vigor of his narratives atone for many faults in construction and character drawing. *See Lowell's Fable for Critics, and Lounsbury's Cooper in Am. Men of Letters. Pub. Apl. Arm. Hou.*

Cooper, Susan Fenimore. 1825 *N. Y.* ——. Dau. to J. F. C. Author Rural Hours, Country Rambles, Rhyme and Reason, Country Life, etc. Style even and picturesque, showing close observant powers. *Pub. Put.*

Cooper, Thomas. 1759 *E.*-1840. Political and legal writer of much local influence.

Coppée, Henry. 1821 *Ga.* ——. Historian and ed·

ucational writer.   Author Elements of Logic, Hist.
of the Conquest of Spain by the Arab Moors, etc.
Pub. Bu. Clx. Lit.

Copway, George, or **Kah-ge-ga-gah-bowh.**   1820
Mch. ——.   An Indian of the Ojibway tribe.   Au-
thor Recollections of a Forest Life, Copway's
American Indian, The Traditional Hist. of the
Ojibway Nation, etc.

Corbin, Mrs. Caroline Elizabeth [Fairfield].   1835
Ct. ——.   Writer of religious tales, of which Rebecca is the best example.   *See Lit. World, April,
1878.   Pub. Jan. Le.*

Corson, Hiram.   1828 *Pa.* ——.   Chaucerian and
Early English scholar.   Editor of Chaucer's Le-
gende of Goode Women, and author of a Thesau-
rus of Early English and a valuable Handbook of
Anglo-Saxon and Early English.   *Pub. Des. Ho.*

Cotton, John.   1585 *E.*-1652.   Puritan theologian.
His Meat for Strong Men and Milk for Babes had
great influence in its day.   *See Tyler's Am. Lit.
vol. 1.*

Coues [kōwz], Elliott.   1842 *N. H.* ——.   Scientist
of note.   Author Key to Am. Birds, Field Ornithology, Birds of the Northwest, Fur-Bearing Animals,
Birds of the Colorado Valley, New England Bird
Life, etc.   *Pub. Ba. Cass. Do. Est. Le.*

Cowles [kōlz], Henry.   1802 *Ct.*-1881.   Biblical commentator.   Author of a Series of Critical Notes on
the Old and New Testaments.   *Pub. Apl.*

Cox, Samuel Hanson.   1793 *N. J.*-1880.   Presbyterian theologian.   Author Quakerism not Christianity, Theopneuston, etc.   Style eccentric and
forcible.

Cox, Samuel Sylvester.   1824 *O.* ——.   Author of
Eight Years in Congress, Why We Laugh, etc.

Style humorous and entertaining. *Pub. Apl. Har. Put.*

Coxe, Arthur Cleveland. 1818 *N. Y.* ——. Bp. Western N. Y. Poet and religious writer. Son to S. H. Cox. Author Christian Ballads, Halloween, Thoughts on the Services, Apollos, or the Way of God, The Criterion, etc. A polished but opinionated writer. *Pub. Apl. Dut. Lip.*

Coxe, Tench. 1756 *Pa.*–1824. Political economist. A writer of excellent influence in his time.

Cozzens, Frederick Swartout. 1818 *N. Y.*–1869. Humorist. Author The Sparrowgrass Papers, Acadia, etc. A graceful writer, possessing genuine humor. *Pub. Lip.*

Cozzens, Samuel Woodworth. 1836 *Ms.*–1878. Author Nobody's Husband, Three Years in Arizona, etc. *Pub. Lip.*

Cranch, Christopher Pearse. 1813 *Va.* ——. Son to W. C. Poet and artist. Author of Satan : a Libretto, and an admirable translation of Virgil's Æneid. *Pub. Hou. Le. Rob.*

Cranch, Wm. 1769 *Ms.*–1855. Jurist. Author Cranch's Supreme Court Reports 1800–1815. *Pub. Jo.*

Crane, Jonathan Townley. 1819 *N. Y.* ——. Methodist religious writer. Author Methodism and its Methods, The Right Way, etc. *Pub. Phi.*

Crawford, Francis Marion. 1854 *Iy.* ——. Novelist. Author Mr. Isaacs, Dr. Claudius, A Roman Singer, To Leeward, etc. Style original and striking. *Pub. Hou. Mac.*

Crooks, George Richard. 1822 *Pa.* ——. Classical educational writer. *Pub. Clx. Phi.*

Crosby, Howard. 1826 *N. Y.* ——. Presbyterian religious writer. Author The Christian Preacher,

Notes on the New Testament, Life of Jesus, etc. *Pub. Ran. Scr.*

Cross, Mrs. Jane T. [Chinn] [Harding]. 1817 *Ky.* ——. Poet and novelist. Author Wayside Flowerets, Duncan Adair, a novel, etc.

Cummins, Maria S. 1827 *Ms.*–1866. Novelist. Author of The Lamplighter, a once famous work, El Fureidîs, and Mabel Vaughan. *Pub. Hou.*

Curtis, Benjamin Robbins. 1809 *Ms.*–1874. Legal writer of eminence. *See Memoir by G. T. Curtis. Pub. Lit.*

Curtis, George Ticknor. 1812 *Ms.* ——. Bro. to B. R. C. Legal writer. Author Treatises on the Law of Copyright, Rights and Duties of Merchant Seamen, etc., A Hist. Constitution of the U. S., Life of James Buchanan, Life of Daniel Webster, etc. *Pub. Har. Lit.*

Curtis, George Wm. 1824 *R. I.* ——. Journalist, novelist, and essayist. Editor of the Easy Chair department of Harper's Monthly. Author Nile Notes, Lotus Eating, Trumps, The Potiphar Papers, Prue and I, etc. A writer of wide influence, possessing a polished, persuasive, and delightful style. *See Century Mag. Feb. 1883. Pub. Har. Scr.*

Cushing, Caleb. 1800 *Ms.*–1879. Miscellaneous writer. Author Reminiscences of Spain, Hist. of Newburyport, The Treaty of Washington, etc. *See Am. Cyclopædia. Pub. Har.*

Cushing, Luther Stearns. 1803 *Ms.*–1856. Jurist of note. Author Massachusetts Reports 1848–1853, Parliamentary Law, etc. *Pub. Lit.*

Cuyler [ky′lẹr], **Theodore Ledyard.** 1822 *N. Y.* ——. Presbyterian religious writer. Author Stray Arrows, Cedar Christian, The Empty Crib, Wayside Springs, Right to the Point, etc. *Pub. A. T. S. Ca. Lo. Wd.*

Dabney, Richard. 1786 *Va.*–1825. Poet and scholar. Author of a volume of scholarly translations from the classic poets.

Daboll [da'bŏl], **Nathan.** c. 1750–1818. Mathematician.

Dall, Mrs. Caroline [Healey]. 1824 *Ms.* ——. Social reformer. Author College: Market and Court, Woman's Right to Labor, Essays on Confucius, Essays on Biblical Criticism, Patty Gray's Journey, etc. *Pub. Le. Rob.*

Dallas, Alexander James. 1759 *J.*–1817. Statesman and jurist. Author Address to Constitutional Republicans, Causes and Character of the Late War (1812), Reports of Cases, etc. *See Life and Writings of, by G. M. Dallas. Pub. Jo.*

Dalton [dawl'ton], **John Call.** 1825 *Ms.*–1889. Physiologist. Author Treatise on Human Physiology, Treatise on Physiology and Hygiene, etc. *Pub. Har. La.*

Dana, Charles Anderson. 1819 *N. H.* ——. Journalist. Editor New York Sun, and co-editor with George Ripley of the Am. Cyc.

Dana, James Dwight. 1813 *N. Y.* ——. Geologist. Author of numerous valuable scientific reports and a standard Manual of Geology. *See N. A. Rev. Oct. 1863. Pub. La. Wil.*

Dana, James Freeman. 1793 *N. H.*–1827. Chemist. Author Epitome of Chemical Philosophy.

Dana, Mrs. Mary S. B. See Shindler, Mrs.

Dana, Richard Henry. 1787 *Ms.*–1879. Poet. The Buccaneer is his chief poem; The Idle Man and ten Lectures on Shakespeare are his principal prose works. *See Atlantic Monthly, April, 1879, and Harper's Mag. April, 1879.*

Dana, Richard Henry, Jr. 1815 *Ms.*–1882. Son to

preceding. Jurist and miscellaneous writer. Author of numerous legal works, Letters on Italian Unity, To Cuba and Back, and the famous Two Years before the Mast. *Pub. Hou.*

Dana, Samuel Luther. 1795 *N. H.*–1868. Bro. to J. F. D. Agricultural writer. *See Am. Journal of Science, May, 1868.*

Dane, Nathan. 1752 *Ms.*–1835. Jurist. Author Abridgment and Digest of Am. Law [9 vols.].

Davidson, James Wood. 1829 *S. C.* ——. Littérateur. Author Living Writers of the South, etc.

Davidson, Lucretia Maria. 1808 *N.Y.*–1825. Poet. *See Memoir by S. F. B. Morse, and Life by C. M. Sedgwick.*

Davidson, Margaret Miller. 1823 *N. Y.*–1838. Sister to L. M. D. Poet. *See Memoir, by Washington Irving.*

Davies, Charles. 1798 *Ct.*–1876. Mathematical writer of note. *Pub. Bar.*

Davies, Samuel. 1724 *Del.*–1761. Presbyterian pulpit orator of note. Author of a number of hymns still in use, and numerous sermons. *See Sermons, 1851, N. Y., with Memoir by Albert Barnes.*

Davis, Andrew Jackson. 1826 *N. Y.* ——. Mystical writer. Author The Great Harmonia, Harmonial Man, Present Age and Inner Life, Philosophy of Spiritual Intercourse, etc.

Davis, Charles Henry. 1807 *Ms.*–1877. Hydrographer of note. Best known as editor of the Am. Nautical Almanac. *See Harvard Register, April, 1881.*

Davis, Edwin Hamilton. 1811 *O.* ——. Archæologist. Author Monuments of the Mississippi Valley.

Davis, Jefferson. 1808 *Ky.* ——. Pres. Confederate States. Author of The Rise and Fall of the

Confederate Gov't., an important work by reason of its personal character, but narrow and somewhat bitter in tone. *See Life by E. A. Pollard, and Prison Life of by Craven. Pub. Apl.*

Davis, L. Clarke. 1835 *Md.* ——. Novelist, essayist, and miscellaneous writer. Editor Philadelphia Inquirer. Author The Stranded Ship, etc. *Pub. Put.*

Davis, Matthew L. 1766 *N. Y.*-1850. Biographer. Author Life of Aaron Burr.

Davis, Mrs. Rebecca [Harding]. 1831 *W. Va.* ——. Wife to L. C. D. Novelist. Author Margret Howth, Waiting for the Verdict, Dallas Galbraith, A Law unto Herself, etc. *Pub. Lip.*

Dawes, Rufus. 1803 *Ms.*-1859. Author Nix's Mate: an Historical Romance, Miscellaneous Poems, etc.

Day, Henry Noble. 1808 *Ct.* ——. Neph. to J. D. Educational writer. Author The Art of Rhetoric, Elements of Logic, Art of Discourse, Science of Æsthetics, etc. *Pub. Bar. Put. Scr. Wils.*

Day, Jeremiah. 1773 *Ct.*-1867. Mathematician. Pres. Yale Col. *Pub. Pe.*

Deane, Charles. 1813 *Me.* ——. Author of numerous historical monographs of value.

Dearborn, Henry Alexander Scammell. 1783 *N. H.*-1851. Author Commerce of the Black Sea, Biography of Commodore Bainbridge, etc.

De Bow, James Dunwoody Brownson. 1820 *S. C.*-1867. Founder De Bow's Review. Author Industrial Resources of the South and West, and various statistical works.

De Costa, Benjamin F. 1831 *Ms.* ——. Historical writer. Author The Pre-Columbian Discovery of America, The Northmen in Maine, etc., and editor Hist. P. E. Church, etc. *Pub. Ran. Wi.*

Deems, Charles F. 1820 *Md.* ——. Methodist religious writer. Author Triumphs of Peace and Other Poems, Home Altar, Sermons, Life of Dr. Clarke, etc. *Pub. Cr. Fu.*

De Forest, John Wm. 1826 *Ct.* ——. Novelist. Author of Kate Beaumont, Honest John Vane, The Bloody Chasm, The Wetherel Affair, etc. *See Atlantic Monthly, Nov. 1873. Pub. Est. Har. Sh.*

De Kay, Charles. 1849 *D. C.* ——. Poet. Author Hesperus, Vision of Nimrod, Vision of Esther, etc. *Pub. Apl. Scr.*

De Koven, James. 1831 *Ct.*-1877. High Church theologian. Author Sermons, etc. An earnest writer, with ultra-ritualistic views. *Pub. Apl. Wh.*

De Mille, James. 1833 *N. B.*-1880. Humorous novelist. Author of the Cryptogram, The American Baron, Comedy of Terrors, The Dodge Club, The Lady of the Ice, etc., and the B. O. W. C., a series of boys' books. *Pub. Apl. Har. Le.*

Deming, Philander. 1829 *N. Y.* ——. Writer of sketches. Author of Adirondack Stories. Style direct and original. *Pub. Hou.*

Denison, Mrs. Mary [Andrews]. 1826 *Ms.* ——. Novelist. Author Opposite the Jail, That Husband of Mine, That Wife of Mine, Rothmell, etc. *Pub. Har. Le. Lip.*

Dennie, Joseph. 1768 *Ms.*-1812. Journalist. Author of The Lay Preacher, etc. In his day a popular but overrated writer.

De Peyster, John Watts. 1821 *N. Y.* ——. Historical writer. Author Life of Torstenson, The Dutch at the North Pole and the Dutch in Maine, Decisive Conflicts of the Late Civil War, etc.

Derby, George H., "John Phœnix." 1824 *Ms.*-1861. Humorist. Author Phœnixiana, etc. *Pub. Apl.*

De Vere, Maximilian Schele. 1820 *Sn.* ——. Philologist. Author Outlines of Comparative Philology, Studies in English, Americanisms, Wonders of the Deep, etc. *Pub. Lip. Put. Scr. Un.*

Dew, Thomas Roderick. 1802 *Va.*-1846. A Digest of the Hist. and Laws of Ancient and Modern Nations is his chief work. *Pub. Apl.*

Dewey, Chester. 1784 *Ms.*-1867. Botanist. Author of a noted series of papers on the Carices of N. A.

Dewey, Orville. 1794 *Ms.*-1882. Unitarian theologian. Author Unitarian Belief, Discourses on Human Life, The Old World and the New, etc. A strong and scholarly thinker. *See Autobiography, 1883.*

Dexter, Henry Martyn. 1821 *Ms.* ——. Religious historian. Author Congregationalism, Pilgrim Memoranda, The Verdict of Reason, etc. *Pub. C. P. S. Har. Loc.*

Diaz, Mrs. Abby [Morton]. 1821 *Ms.* ——. Humorous writer for the young. Author The William Henry Letters, William Henry and his Friends, Chronicles of the Stimpcett Family, etc. *Pub. Lo.*

Dickinson, Anna Elizabeth. 1842 *Pa.* ——. Lecturer. Author A Paying Investment, the novel What Answer, and several plays, among which is The Crown of Thorns. *Pub. Hou.*

Dickinson, John. 1732 *Md.*-1808. Political writer. Author Petition to the King, Letters from a Pennsylvania Farmer, Letters of Fabius, etc. Style clear, vigorous, and eloquent. *See Bancroft's Hist. U. S.*

Dickinson, Jonathan. 1688 *Ms.*-1747. Presbyterian theologian. Author Familiar Letters upon Important Subjects in Religion, etc. *See Tyler's Am. Lit. vol. 2. Pub. P. B.*

Dickson, Samuel Henry. 1798 *S. C.*-1872. Physician and essayist. Author Essays on Life, Sleep, Pain, On the Correlation of Forces, Æsthetics of Suicide, Elements of Medicine, etc. Style graceful and polished. *See Allibone's Dict. Pub. Wo.*

Didier [dy'deer], **Eugene L.** 18— *Md.* ——. Biographer and critic. Author Life of Poe, Life and Letters of Madame Bonaparte, Primer of Criticism, etc. As a critic his style is aggressive and fearless. *Pub. Scr.*

Diman, J. Lewis. 1831 *R. I.*-1881. Philosophical writer. Author Orations and Essays and The Theistic Argument. Style thoughtful and candid. *Pub. Hou.*

Dimitry, Charles. 1836 *D. C.* ——. Novelist. Author Guilty or Not Guilty, Angela's Christmas, etc.

Dinsmoor, Robert. 1757 *N. H.*-1836. Poet. Known as "The Rustic Bard." Author Incidental Poems. *See Whittier's Old Portraits and Modern Sketches.*

Dix, John Adams. 1798 *N. H.*-1879. Author Winter in Madeira, and A Summer in Spain and Florence. *See Memoir, by Morgan Dix. Pub. Apl.*

Dix, Morgan. 1827 *N. Y.* ——. Son to J. A. D. High Church theologian. Author Sermons, Lect. on the Calling of a Christian Woman, Memoir J. A. Dix, etc. An extremely conservative thinker. *Pub. Apl. Dut. Har. Hou. Yo.*

Doane, George Washington. 1799 *N. J.*-1859. Bp. N. J. Poet and religious writer. Author Songs by the Way, Sermons on Various Occasions, etc. The familiar hymn beginning "Softly now the light of day" is one of his most noted poems. *See Life and Writings of, by W. C. Doane. Pub. Dut.*

Doane, Wm. Croswell. 1832 *N. J.* ——. Son to G. W. D. Bp. Albany. Poet and religious writer.

Author Sermons, Mosaics, etc. The Sculptor Boy
is his best known poem. *Pub. Dut.*

Dod, Albert Baldwin. 1805 *N. J.*–1845. Presbyterian religious writer of much ability.

Dodge, Mary Abigail, "Gail Hamilton." 1838 *Ms.*
——. Miscellaneous writer. A New Atmosphere,
Gala-Days, Woman's Wrongs, Red-Letter Days,
Summer Rest, Battle of the Books, Twelve Miles
from a Lemon, Sermons to the Clergy, First Love
. is Best, and What Think ye of Christ? are her
chief works. Style witty and aggressive, but marred
by an occasional flippant handling of a subject.
Pub. Apl. Har.

Dodge, Mrs. Mary [Mapes]. 1838 *N. Y.* ——. Editor St. Nicholas. Author Hans Brinker, Donald
and Dorothy, and other excellent juvenile works,
Theophilus and Others, and Along the Way : a volume of Short Poems. *Pub. Rob. Scr.*

Doesticks, Q. K. Philander. See Thompson, Mortimer.

Donnelly, Ignatius. 1831 *Pa.* ——. Author Essay
on the Sonnets of Shakespeare, Atlantis : the An-
tediluvian World, and Ragnarok : the Age of Fire
and Gravel. *See Harper's Mag. May, 1882. Pub.
Apl.*

Dorgan, John A. 1836–1866. Poet. *See Manhat-
tan Mag. June, 1883.*

Dorr, Mrs. Julia Caroline [Ripley]. 1825 *S. C.* ——.
Novelist and poet. Author of the novels Lanmere,
Sibyl Huntington, and Expiation, and the poems
Vermont, Friar Anselmo, etc. *See Lit. World, Oct.
23, 1880. Pub. Lip. Ran. Scr.*

Douglas, Amanda Minnie. 1837 *N. Y.* ——. Nov-
elist. In Trust, Stephen Dane, Claudia, and With
Fate Against Him are among her best works.
Pub. Le.

Douglass, Frederick. 1817 *Md.* ——. Orator. Author My Bondage and My Freedom, etc. Style fervid, dramatic, and polished.

Dowling, John. 1807 *E.*-1878. Baptist religious writer. Author Vindication of the Baptists, Hist. of Romanism, etc.

Downing, Andrew Jackson. 1815 *N. Y.*-1852. Pomologist. Author Theory and Practice of Landscape Gardening, a work of much value, Fruit and Fruit Trees of America, Architecture of Country Houses, etc. A writer of much influence in his department. *Pub. Wil.*

Drake, Benjamin. 1794 *Ky.*-1841. Biographer. Author Lives of Black Hawk, Tecumseh, Harrison, etc.

Drake, Daniel. 1785 *N. J.*-1852. Bro. to B. D. Physician. Best known by his valuable work on The Diseases of the Interior Valley of North America. *Pub. Clx. Lip.*

Drake, Francis Samuel. 1828 *Ms.*-1885. Son to S. G. D. Author of A Dict. of American Biography. *Pub. Hou.*

Drake, Joseph Rodman. 1795 *N. Y.*-1820. Poet. Author The Culprit Fay, The American Flag, etc. Style delicate and imaginative. *Pub. Car.*

Drake, Samuel Adams. 1833 *Ms.* ——. Son to S. G. D. Author Around the Hub, The Heart of the White Mts., Old Landmarks and Historic Personages of Boston, Nooks and Corners of the New England Coast, Old Landmarks and Historic Fields of Middlesex, etc. *Pub. Har. Rob.*

Drake, Samuel Gardiner. 1798 *N. H.*-1875. Historian. Hist. and Antiquities of Boston, Indian Biography, Indian Captivities, Annals of Witchcraft in the U. S., and Hist. French and Indian War are some of his most important works.

Draper, John Wm. 1811 *E.*–1882. Historian and scientist. Author Hist. of the Civil War in America, Hist. Intellectual Development of Europe, The Future Civil Policy of America, Human Physiology, etc. A thinker of high authority, possessing a clear, logical style. *Pub. Apl. Har.*

Drayton, Wm. Henry. 1742 *S. C.*–1779. Author Hist. American Revolution.

Duane, Wm. 1760 *N. Y.*–1835. Political writer. Author Military Dict., etc.

Duane, Wm. John. 1780 *I.*–1865. Son to W. D. Legal writer. Author The Law of Nations Investigated, etc.

Dudley, Thomas Underwood. 1837 *Va.* ——. Bp. Ky. Author A Wise Discrimination The Church's Need, etc. *Pub. Wh.*

Duer, John. 1782 *N. Y.*–1858. Jurist of note. Author Duer's Reports, Laws and Practice of Marine Insurance, etc.

Duer, Wm. Alexander. 1780 *N. Y.*–1858. Bro. to J. D. Jurist. Author Constitutional Jurisprudence of the U. S., etc. *Pub. Har.*

Duffield, George. 1799 *Pa.*–1870. Presbyterian theologian. Author Dissertations on the Prophecies, etc.

Duffield, Samuel W. 1843 *L. I.*–1887. Grandson to G. D. Poet. Author Warp and Woof, and The Heavenly Land: the latter a translation of Bernard of Cluny's Hora Novissima. *Pub. Fu. Ran.*

Duganne, Augustine Joseph Hickey. 1823 *Ms.*–1884. Poet. Author of the tragedy The Lydian Queen, Home Poems, Parnassus in Pillory, etc., and several prose works. *Pub. De.*

Dugdale, Richard L. 1841 *F.*–1883. Writer on social science. Author of The Jukes, or Heredity in Crime. *Pub. Put.*

Dunglison [dŭng′glĭ-sǫn], **Robley.** 1798 *E.*-1869. Medical writer of note. Author of a valuable Medical Dict., Human Physiology, Elements of Hygiene, etc. *Pub. La.*

Dunlap, Wm. 1766 *N. Y.*-1839. Littérateur. Author Life of Geo. Frederick Cooke, Life of Chas. Brockden Brown, The Am. Theatre, Hist. of New York, etc. A popular writer in his day. *Pub. Har.*

Duponceau [du-pŏn′sō or dü′pon′so′], **Peter Stephen.** 1760 *F.*-1844. Philologist. Chiefly known by his Memoir on the Indian Languages of N. A.

Dupuy [dü-pwé], **Eliza Ann.** 18— *Va.*-1881. ˙ Sensational novelist. *See Lit. World, June 3, 1882. Pub. Pet.*

Durbin, John Price. 1800 *Ky.*-1876. Author Observations in Europe, Observations in Egypt, Palestine, Syria, and Asia Minor. *Pub. Har.*

Durivage, Francis Alexander. 1813 *Ms.*-1881. Neph. to Edw. Everett. Writer of stories and sketches.

Duyckinck [di′kiṇk], **Evart Augustus.** 1816 *N. Y.*-1878. Author Hist. War for the Union, etc.

Duyckinck, George Long. 1823 *N. Y.*-1863. Bro. to E. A. D., and co-author with him of a valuable Encyclopædia of Am. Literature. Sole author of Lives of George Herbert, Bishop Ken, and Jeremy Taylor. *Pub. Por.*

Dwight, Benjamin Woodbridge. ˙ 1816 *Ct.* ——. Grandson to Timothy D. Author The Higher Christian Education, Modern Philosophy, Modern Philology, Woman's Higher Culture, etc. *Pub. Scr.*

Dwight, John Sullivan. 1813 *Ms.* ——. Composer

and poet. Editor of Dwight's Musical Journal, and author of the poem God Save the State. A writer of high authority upon musical topics.

Dwight, Theodore. 1765 *Ms.*-1856. Bro. to succeeding. Journalist. Author Hist. of the Hartford Convention, Character of Thos. Jefferson, etc.

Dwight, Timothy. 1752 *Ms.*-1817. Congregationalist theologian. Pres. Yale Coll. Author Theology, a revision of Watt's version of the Psalms, and several satirical and epic poems. *Pub. Har.*

Dyer, Sidney. 1814 *N. Y.* ——. Song writer of note.

Earle, Thomas. 1791 *Ms.*-1849. Philanthropist. Author of several treatises on penal law and state rights.

Eastburn, James Wallis. 1797 *N. Y.*-1819. Poet. Co-author with R. C. Sands of the once noted poem Yamoyden. *See N. A. Rev. April, 1821.*

Eastman, Charles Gamage. 1816 *Me.*-1861. Poet and journalist. *Pub. Phin.*

Eastman, Mrs. Mary [Henderson]. 1818 *Va.* ——. Author Romance of Indian Life, and other works upon Indian character, and Aunt Phillis's Cabin, a reply to Uncle Tom's Cabin.

Eaton, Amos. 1776 *N. Y.*-1842. Naturalist. Author of a popular text-book on botany, Index to Geology of the Northern States, and numerous scientific works.

Eaton, Daniel Cady. 1834 *Mch.* ——. Botanist. Author The Ferns of North America. *Pub. Cass. Do.*

Edwards, Bela Bates. 1802 *Ms.*-1852. Congregationalist theologian. *See Memoir, by E. A. Parks. Pub. Dra.*

Edwards, Jonathan. 1703 *Ct.*-1757. Theologian and metaphysician of eminence. His chief work is the Inquiry into the Freedom of the Will. An acute, precise, and original thinker, whose influence on the thought of his age was very great. *See Lives by Dwight and S. Hopkins, Sparks's Am. Biog. vol. 8, Tyler's Am. Lit. vol. 2, and Duyckinck's Cyc. Am. Lit. vol. I. Pub. Scr.*

Edwards, Jonathan, Jr. 1745 *Ms.*-1801. Son to preceding. Congregationalist theologian. *See Memoir, by Tryon Edwards.*

Edwards, Tryon. 1809 *Ct.* ——. Grandson to preceding. Congregationalist theologian. Author Christianity a Philosophy of Principles, Self-Cultivation, etc.

Eggleston, Edward. 1837 *Ind.* ——. Novelist. Author of The Hoosier Schoolmaster, The End of the World, The Circuit Rider, Roxy, etc. Southern Indiana in pioneer days is the *locale* of several of his most popular stories. *Pub. Do. Scr.*

Eggleston, George Cary. 1839 *Ind.* ——. Bro. to E. E. Littérateur. Author How to Educate Yourself, A Man of Honor, A Rebel's Recollections, and several popular juvenile tales. *See Lit. World, Sept. 1878.. Pub. Do. Put.*

Eliot, Charles Wm. 1834 *Ms.* ——. Pres. H. U. Co-author with Storer of an Elementary Manual of Chemistry.

Eliot, John. 1604 *E.*-1690. Religious writer. Chiefly known by his famous translation of the Bible into the Indian language. *See Sparks's Am. Biog., and Life by R. B. Caverly.*

Eliot, John. 1754 *Ms.*-1813. Biographer. Author of the New England Biographical Dict., etc.

Eliot, Samuel. 1821 *Ms.* ——. Historian. Au-

thor Hist. of Liberty, Manual of U. S. Hist., Life
and Times of Savonarola, etc.

Eliot, Wm. Greenleaf. 1811 *Ms.*-1887. Unitarian
religious writer. Author Doctrines of Christianity,
Early Religious Education, Lect. to Young Men,
Lect. to Young Women, Discipline of Sorrow, etc.
Pub. A. U. A.

Ellet, Mrs. Elizabeth Fries [Lummis]. 1818 *N. Y.*-
1877. Historical writer. Author Domestic Hist.
of the Am. Revolution, Women of the Am. Revolution, Court Circles of the Republic, Queens of
Am. Society, etc. An industrious, careful writer,
whose works have a recognized value. *Pub. Har.
Lip. Por.*

Elliot, Wm. 1788 *S. C.*-1863. Political writer and
author of the tragedy of Fiesco.

Elliott, Charles Wyllys. 1817 *Ct.*-1883. Miscellaneous writer. Author of The Book of American
Interiors, Pottery and Porcelain, Remarkable Characters and Places in the Holy Land, etc. *Pub. Apl.
Hou.*

Ellis, George Edward. 1815 *Ms.* ——. Unitarian
theologian and historical writer. Author of A Half-
Century of the Unitarian Controversy, Evidences
of Christianity, The Red Man and the White, etc.
Pub. A. U. A. Lit. Loc.

Ellsworth, Erastus W. 1822 *Ct.* ——. Poet. *See
Poems, edition 1855.*

Embury, Mrs. Emma Catharine [Manly]. 1806
N. Y.-1863. Poet and writer of sketches. Author
Guido and Other Poems, Blind Girl and Other
Tales, The Waldorf Family, etc. Style quiet and
refined, with no very decided characteristics. *Pub.
Har.*

Emerson, George Barrell. 1797 *Me.*-1881. Educational writer. Author Lect. on Education, The School and the Schoolmaster, etc., and the noted and valuable report on the Trees and Shrubs of Massachusetts. *See Harvard Register, May, 1881. Pub. Lit.*

Emerson, Ralph Waldo. 1803 *Ms.*-1882. Poet and philosopher. Author Essays, Representative Men, Miscellanies, English Traits, Society and Solitude, Letters and Social Aims, Poems, and May-Day and Other Pieces. *See Scribner's Mag. Feb. 1879, Lit. World, May 22, 1880, Century Mag. April, 1883, Fraser's Mag. May, 1867, Harper's Mag. Feb. 1884, Conway's Emerson at Home and Abroad, Guernsey's Sketch of Emerson, Cooke's Study of Emerson, Benton's Emerson as a Poet, Holmes's Emerson in Am. Men of Letters, and Carlyle and Emerson. Pub. Hou.*

Emmet, Thomas Addis. 1764 *I.*-1827. Author Pieces of Irish History. *See Memoir, by C. G. Haynes.*

Emmons, Nathaniel. 1745 *Ct.*-1840. Congregationalist theologian of note. Style direct and forcible, with little or no ornament.

England, John. 1786 *I.*-1842. R. C. Bp. Charleston. Theologian. Style clear, shrewd, witty, and effective. *See Works, 8 vols. 1849.*

English, George Bethune. 1789 *Ms.*-1828. Author of several erratic religious works.

English, Thomas Dunn. 1819 *Pa.* ——. Poet and novelist. Best known by his song Ben Bolt.

Espy, James P. 1785 *Pa.*-1860. Meteorologist. Author The Philosophy of Storms.

Evans, Augusta J. See Wilson, Mrs. Augusta.

Evans, Hugh Davy. 1792 *Md.*-1868. Legal and theological writer. Author Essays on the Validity of Anglican Ordination, etc. *Pub. Hou.*

Evans [Iv'anz], **Thomas.** 1798–1868. Quaker controversialist.

Everett, Alexander Hill. 1792 *Ms.*–1847. Bro. to E. E. Statesman. His most important works are Europe : a General Survey, and America : a General Survey. An able writer, whose idiomatic style has been much admired. *See Allibone's Dict.*

Everett, Charles Carroll. 1829 *Me.* ——. Unitarian theologian. Author The Science of Thought.

Everett, Edward. 1794 *Ms.*–1865. Statesman and orator. Author Defence of Christianity, Orations and Speeches, Mt. Vernon Papers, and over one hundred articles for the N. A. Rev. *See Whipple's Character and Characteristic Men, Allibone's Dict., and Am. Cyc. Pub. Lit.*

Everett, Wm. 1839 *Ms.* ——. Son to E. E. Author College Essays, On the Cam : Lect. on Cambridge University, the poem Hesione, or Europe Unchained, School Sermons, etc. *See Lit. World, Mar. 11, 1882. Pub. Le. Rob.*

Ewbank, Thomas. 1792 *E.*–1870. Writer on mechanics. Author Thoughts on Matter and Force, Hydraulics, The World a Workshop, Life in Brazil, etc. *Pub. Har. Scr.*

Ewer, Ferdinand Cartwright. 1826 *Ms.*–1883. High Church theologian. Author The Failure of Protestantism, The Operations of the Holy Spirit, Grammar of Theology, etc. *See Am. Church Rev. Dec. 1883, and Sermons of, with Memoir by C. T. Congdon. Pub. Apl. Dut. Put. Yo.*

Fairchild, James H. 1817 *Ms.* ——. Pres. Oberlin Coll. Author of a noted treatise on Moral Philosophy, and other works. *Pub. Go. Sh.*

Fairfield, Sumner Lincoln. 1803 *Ms.*–1844. Poet

Author Abaddon and Other Poems. *See Gris-wold's Poets and Poetry of America.*

Farman, Ella. See Pratt, Mrs.

Farmer, John. 1789 *Ms.*-1838. Genealogist. Author of Farmer's Genealogical Register. *See Savage's edition, 1862, and Memorial by Le Bosquet.*

Farnham, Mrs. Eliza Woolson [Burhaus]. 1815 *N. Y.*-1864. Philanthropist. Author Life in Prairie-Land, My Early Days, etc. Woman and her Era is her most important work. *Pub. Har.*

Farquharson, Martha. See Finley, Martha.

Farrar, Mrs. Eliza Ware. 1791 *Bm.*-1870. Wife to J. F. Author Recollections of Seventy Years, The Children's Robinson Crusoe, The Young Lady's Friend, etc.

Farrar, John. 1779 *Ms.*-1853. Mathematical writer of note.

Fawcett, Edgar. 1847 *N. Y.* ——. Poet and novelist. Author Poems of Fantasy and Passion, the novels A Gentleman of Leisure, A Hopeless Case, An Ambitious Woman, etc. His verse presents a remarkable development of the quality of pure fancy. *Pub. Hou. Os.*

Fay, Theodore Sedgewick. 1807 *N. Y.* ——. Novelist. Norman Leslie is his best known work.

Featherstonehaugh [fĕth'er-ston-haw'], **George Wm.** —— 1866. Writer of travels.

Felt, Joseph Barlow. 1789 *Ms.*-1869. Author Annals of Salem, etc.

Felton, Cornelius Conway. 1807 *Ms.*-1862. Greek scholar of eminence. Author Lect. on Ancient and Modern Greece, etc. Of his many translations from the Greek, The Clouds and The Birds of Aristophanes are the most noted. *Pub. Al. Hou. Sev.*

Fern, Fanny. See Parton, Mrs. Sarah.

Fessenden, Thomas Green. 1771 *N. H.*-1837. Humorous poet. Author Country Lovers and The Terrible Tractoration. Best known as "Christopher Caustic." *See Hart's Am. Lit.*

Field, Henry Martyn. 1822 *Ms.* ——. Editor N. Y. Evangelist. Writer of travels. Author From the Lakes of Killarney to the Golden Horn, From Egypt to Japan, Hist. Atlantic Telegraph, Among the Holy Hills, etc. *Pub. Har. Scr.*

Fields, Mrs. Annie [Adams]. 1834 *Ms.* ——. Wife to J. T. F. Poet. Author Under the Olive, Memoir Jas. T. Fields, and How to Help the Poor. Her poems are mainly Greek in subject, Theocritus being one of the best. *Pub. Hou.*

Fields, James Thomas. 1816 *N. H.*-1881. Poet and publisher. Author of Yesterdays with Authors, Underbrush, and several volumes of graceful verse. *See Memoir, by Mrs. Fields. Pub. Hou.*

Finch, Francis Miles. 1827 *N. Y.* ——. Poet. Author of the well-known poem The Blue and the Gray.

Finley, Martha, "Martha Farquharson." 1828 *O.* ——. Novelist. Author Casella, Wanted — a Pedigree, and many volumes of religious tales for girls, Elsie Dinsmore being one of the best. *Pub. Do. Lip. P. B.*

Finney, Charles G. 1792 *Ct.*-1875. Revivalist preacher. Pres. Oberlin Coll. Author Lect. on Revivals, Systematic Theology, etc. *See Autobiography. Pub. Go. Rev.*

Fisher, Frances C., "Christian Reid." 18— *N. C.* ——. Novelist. Author Valerie Aylmer, Morton House, A Daughter of Bohemia, etc. *Pub. Apl. Sad.*

Fisher, George Park. 1827 *Ms.* ——. Congregationalist theologian. Author The Supernatural Origin of Christianity, The Reformation, The Beginnings of Christianity, Faith and Rationalism, Discussions in History and Theology, etc. *Pub. Scr.*

Fiske, John. 1842 *Ct.* ——. Philosopher. Author Myths and Myth-Makers, Outlines of Cosmic Philosophy, The Unseen World, Darwinism and Other Essays, Tobacco and Alcohol, Excursions of an Evolutionist, etc. An acute, versatile thinker and critic. *Pub. Ho. Hou. Mac.*

Fitzhugh, George. 1806 *Va.*-1881. Writer on social science. Author of Sociology for the South, and Cannibals All, or Slaves without Masters. An eccentric and extreme thinker.

Flagg, Edward. 1815 *Me.* ——. Author of several novels, and of an historical work entitled Venice : the City of the Sea.

Flagg, Wilson. 1805 *Ms.*-1884. Naturalist. Author Studies in the Field and Forest, Halcyon Days, A Year among the Trees, and A Year among the Birds. *Pub. Est.*

Fleming, George. See Fletcher, Julia.

Fletcher, James Cooley. 1823 *Ind.* ——. Co-author with D. P. Kidder of the noted work Brazil and the Brazilians. *Pub. Lit.*

Fletcher, Julia Constance. 185- *B.* ——. Dau. to J. C. F. Novelist. Author Kismet, The Head of Medusa, Mirage, Vestigia, etc. *Pub. Rob.*

Flint, Austin. 1812 *Ms.*-1886. Medical writer. Author Practice of Medicine, etc. *Pub. La. Wo.*

Flint, Austin, Jr. 1836 *Ms.* ——. Son to preceding. Medical writer. Author Text-Book of Human Physiology, etc. *See Popular Science Monthly, May, 1876. Pub. Apl.*

Flint, Timothy. 1780 *Ms.*-1840. His chief work,

Geography of the Mississippi Valley, materially advanced the settlement of that region.

Folger, Peter. 1618 *E.*–1690. Grandfather to Benj. Franklin. Author of A Looking-Glass for the Times, a curious, satirical doggerel poem in behalf of free speech. *See Tyler's Am. Lit. vol. 2.*

Follen, Charles. 1796 *G.*–1840. German scholar of note. *See Works, edited by Mrs. Follen.*

Follen, Mrs. Eliza Lee [Cabot]. 1787 *Ms.*–1859. Wife to C. F. Author Sketches of Married Life, Twilight Stories, a volume of excellent juvenile tales, and other works. *Pub. Le.*

Foote, Henry Wilder. 1838 *Ms.* ——. Author Annals of King's Chapel.

Foote, Wm. Henry. 1794 *Ct.*–1869. Historical writer. Author Sketches of North Carolina, Sketches of Virginia, and The Huguenots, or Reformed French Church. *Pub. Lip.*

Force, Peter. 1790 *N. J.*–1868. Historian. Author Historical Traits, American Archives, etc.

Ford, Mrs. Sallie [Rochester]. 1828 *Ky.* ——. Novelist. Author Grace Truman, Romance of Freemasonry, Raids and Romance of Morgan and his Men, etc. *Pub. Sh.*

Forestier, Auber. See Woodward, A. Aubertine.

Forney, John Weiss. 1817 *Pa.*–1881. Journalist. Editor The Philadelphia Press. Author Anecdotes of Public Men, The New Nobility, Letters from Europe, etc. *Pub. Apl. Har. Lip.*

Forester, Fanny. See Judson, Mrs.

Forrester, Francis. See Wise, David.

Forrester, Frank. See Herbert, Wm. H.

Foster, Mrs. Hannah. 1759 *Ms.*–1840. Author the once famous story The Coquette, or the Hist. of Eliza Wharton. *Pub. Pet.*

Foster, Randolph S. 1820 *O.* ——. Methodist theologian. Author Objections to Calvinism, etc. *Pub. Phi.*

Foster, Stephen Collins. 1826 *Pa.*–1864. Song writer. Author Suwanee River, My Old Kentucky Home, Nelly Bly, etc. *See Atlantic Monthly, Nov. 1867.*

Fowler, Orson Squire. 1809 *N. Y.*–1887. Phrenologist. Author several works on phrenology and physical culture. *Pub. Fow.*

Foxton, E. See Palfrey, Sarah.

Francis, Convers. 1796 *Ms.*–1863. Author Life of John Eliot, Historical Sketch of Watertown, Errors of Education, etc.

Francis, John Wakefield. 1789 *N. Y.*–1861. Physician. Author several valuable medical works, and a volume of pleasant reminiscences entitled Old New York. *See Life, by Tuckerman.*

Franklin, Benjamin. 1706 *Ms.*–1790. Statesman and philosopher. Author of numerous and valuable essays on politics, religion, commerce, science, and philosophy. A writer whose influence has been felt throughout the world. Style concise, witty, and vigorous. *See Autobiography, Edinburgh Rev. July, 1806, and Aug. 1817, Life and Times of by Parton, McMaster's Franklin in Am. Men of Letters, Life and Times of by J. Franklin and J. A. Headington, Contemporary Rev. July, 1879, and Harper's Mag. July, 1880.*

Fredet, Peter. 1801 *F.*–1856. Historian. Author Ancient Hist. and Modern Hist., works which have been extensively circulated. *Pub. Mur.*

French, Harry Willard. 1853 *Ct.* ——. Novelist and miscellaneous writer. Author the novels Ego and Castle Foam, Art and Artists in Connecticut,

Our Boys in China, Our Boys in India, etc. *Pub. Le.*

French, Mrs. L. Virginia [Smith]. 1830 *Va.*–1881. Poet. Author Wind Whispers, Legend of the South, etc.

Freneau [frē-nō´], Philip. 1752 *N. Y.*–1832. Poet. A versatile, witty, and satirical writer. *See Hart's Am. Lit. and Duyckinck's Cyc. Am. Lit.*

Frost, John. 1800 *Me.*–1859. A prolific writer and compiler. Author Pictorial Hist. U. S., Hist. of the World, and other works of indifferent merit. *Pub. Har. Le. Lip. Pott.*

Frothingham, Ellen. 1835 *Ms.* ——. Author of several fine metrical translations from Lessing, Auerbach, Goethe, and Grillparzer. *Pub. Rob.*

Frothingham, Nathaniel Langdon. 1793 *Ms.*–1870. Unitarian theologian and poet. A scholarly writer, whose hymns and metrical translations possess much merit.

Frothingham, Octavius Brooks. 1822 *Ms.* ——. Son to N. L. F. Radical theologian. Author Lives of Gerrit Smith, George Ripley, and Theodore Parker, Hist. New England Transcendentalism, etc. A leader of radical thought. *Pub. Hou. Put.*

Frothingham, Richard, Jr. 1812 *Ms.* ——. Journalist. Author of a masterly Hist. of the Siege of Boston, The Rise of the Republic of the U. S., Hist. of Charlestown, etc. *Pub. Lit.*

Fuller, Margaret. See Ossoli.

Fuller, Robert. 1808 *S. C.* ——. Baptist theologian of note. Author Argument on Baptist Close Communion, etc.

Furness, Mrs. Helen Kate [Rogers]. 1837–1883. Wife to H. H. F. Shakespearean scholar. Author of A Concordance to the Poems of Shakespeare. *Pub. Lip.*

Furness, Horace Howard. 1833 *Pa.* ——. Son to
W. H. F. Shakespearean scholar of eminence.
Author variorum editions of King Lear, Hamlet,
Macbeth, and Romeo and Juliet. *Pub. Lip.*
Furness, Wm. Henry. 1802 *Ms.* ——. Unitarian
theologian. Author The Unconscious Truth of the
Four Gospels, Jesus and his Biographers, Hist. of
Jesus, Thoughts on the Life and Character of Jesus,
The Power of Spirit, etc., and a much-admired trans-
lation of Schiller's Song of the Bell. *See N. A.
Rev. Oct. 1850. Pub. El. Lip.*

Gallagher [găl'a-ḡer], **Wm. D.** 1808 *Pa.* ——. Poet.
Author Miami Woods and Other Poems, etc. *See
Griswold's Poets and Poetry of America. Pub.
Clke.*
Gallatin, Albert. 1761 *Sd.*–1849. Financier. Author
Considerations on the Currency and Banking Sys-
tem of the U. S., Synopsis of the Indian Tribes,
etc. *Pub. Lip. See Life by H. Adams, and Gal-
latin by J. A. Stevens in Am. Statesmen. Pub.
Lip.*
Gallaudet [găl-aw-dĕt'], **Thomas Hopkins.** 1787
Pa.–1851. Educator of deaf mutes. Author The
Child's Book of the Soul, The Youth's Book of
Natural Theology, etc. *See Life, by H. Humphrey.*
Gannett, Ezra Stiles. 1801 *Ms.*–1871. Unitarian
theologian. *See Memoir, by W. C. Gannett.*
Gannett, Wm. Channing. 1840 *Ms.* ——. Son to E.
S. G. Poet and Unitarian religious writer. Author
of A Year of Miracle, Memoir of E. S. Gannett,
etc. *Pub. A. U. A. Rob.*
Garden, Alexander. c. 1685 *S.*–1756. Religious con-
troversialist. *See Tyler's Am. Lit. vol. 2.*
Garden, Alexander. 1730 *S.*–1791. Botanical writer.

Garden, Alexander. 1757 *S. C.*–1827. Son to pre‑ ceding. Author Anecdotes of the Revolutionary War, etc. *See 2 vol. edition, Brooklyn, 1865.*

Garfield, James Abram. 1831 *O.*–1881. Pres. U. S. Statesman. *See Complete Works. Pub. Os.*

Garrison, Wm. Lloyd. 1805 *Ms.*–1879. Antislavery writer. An author whose style is decided and un‑ compromising in its tone, but whose writings were of far-reaching influence. *See Johnson's Garrison and his Times, and Life, by his Sons.*

Gath. See Townsend, G. A.

Gay, Sydney Howard. 1814 *Ms.*–1888. Historian. Author Bryant's Hist. of the U. S., James Madison in Am. Statesmen, Edmund Quincy in Am. Men of 'Letters, etc. *Pub. Hou. Scr.*

Gayarré, Charles E. Arthur. 1805 *La.* ——. His‑ torian. Author Philip the Second, Hist. of Louis‑ iana, etc. *Pub. Arm. Wid.*

Gayler, Charles. 1820 *N. Y.* ——. Dramatist and novelist. Author The Gold Hunters, Taking the Chances, etc. *Pub. De.*

George, Henry. 1839 *Pa.* ——. Political econo‑ mist. Author Progress and Poverty, etc. *See Lit. World, Mar. 10, 1883, and N. A. Rev. Aug. 1883. Pub. Apl.*

Gerhart [gair′hart], **Emmanuel Vogel.** 1817 *Pa.* ——. German Ref. theologian. Author Philoso‑ phy and Logic, Monograph of the Ref. Church, etc.

Gibbes [gĭbz], **Robert Wilson.** 1809 *Ms.* ——. Author Documentary Hist. of the Am. Revolution, etc.

Gibbs, Josiah Willard. 1790 *Ms.*–1861. Philolo‑ gist. Author Philological Studies, etc.

Gibbs, Wolcott. 1822 *N. Y.* ——. Chemist.

Gibson, Wm. Hamilton. 1850 *Ct.* ——. Artist

and littérateur. Author Pastoral Days, Highways and Byways, etc. A writer who illustrates his delightful sketches with equally charming drawings. *Pub. Har.*

Giddings, Joshua Reed. 1795 *Pa.*–1864. Author essays and speeches, The Exiles of Florida, and The Rebellion: its Authors and its Causes.

Gihon, Albert Leary. 1833 *Pa.* ——. Littérateur. His sketch A Night in a Typhoon is well known.

Gilder, Richard Watson. 1844 *N. J.* ——. Poet. Editor The Century. Author The New Day and The Poet and his Master. The sonnet entitled What is a Sonnet? is one of his best poems. *Pub. Scr.*

Giles, Chauncey. 1809 ——. Swedenborgian theologian. Author Lect. on the Nature of Spirit, The Second Coming of the Lord, Perfect Prayer, etc. *Pub. Lip.*

Giles, Henry. 1809 *I.*–1882. Essayist and lecturer. Author Lect. and Essays, Christian Thought on Life, Illustrations of Genius, and Human Life in Shakespeare. His literary estimates are careful and discriminating, and his style is cultivated and thoughtful. *See Hart's Am. Lit. Pub. Le.*

Gillet [jĭl-lĕt′], Ezra Hall. 1823 *Ct.*–1875. Author Hist. Presb. Church in the U. S., Life of John Huss, God in Human Thought, The Moral System, etc. *Pub. P. B. Ran. Scr.*

Gilman, Arthur. 1837 *Il.* ——. Chaucerian editor. Author First Steps in Eng. Literature, Seven Historic Ages, First Steps in Eng. Hist., Hist. of the Am. People, etc., and editor the Riverside Chaucer. *Pub. Bar. Lo.*

Gilman, Mrs. Caroline [Howard]. 1794 *Ms.*–1888. Wife to S. G. Miscellaneous writer. Author Recollections of a Southern Matron, Recollections of

5

a New England Housekeeper, The Sibyl, Verses of a Lifetime, etc. *Pub. Le. Pott.*

Gilman, Daniel Coit. 1831 *Ct.* ——. Pres. Johns Hopkins Univ. Author James Monroe 'n Am. Statesmen. *Pub. Hou.*

Gilman, Samuel. 1791 *Ms.*–1858. Author Memoirs of a New England Choir, The Hist. of a Ray of Light, etc.

Gilmore, James R., " Edmund Kirke." 1823 *Ms.* ——. Novelist and miscellaneous writer. Author Among the Pines, My Southern Friends, Down in Tennessee, Life of Garfield, etc., and numerous war songs and ballads. *See Hart's Am. Lit. Pub. Fo. Har.*

Gladden, Washington. 1836 *Pa.* ——. Congregationalist religious writer. Author Seven Essays on the Lord's Prayer, The Christian League of Connecticut, Things New and Old, etc. *Pub. Hou. Loc.*

Gliddon, George Robins. 1808 *E.*–1857. Egyptologist. Author Ancient Egypt, etc., and co-author with Nott of Types of Mankind. His conclusions have met with much adverse criticism. *Pub. Lip.*

Glyndon, Howard. See Searing, Mrs. Laura.

Godfrey, Thomas. 1736 *Pa.*–1763. Poet. Author The Prince of Parthia. This was the first drama written in America, and is a work of considerable merit. *See Tyler's Am. Lit. vol. 2.*

Godkin, Edwin Laurence. 1831 *I.* ——. Editor The N. Y. Evening Post. Author Government in Am. Science Series. *Pub. Ho.*

Godman, John. 1794 *Md.*–1830. Physician and naturalist. Author Rambles of a Naturalist, Am. Natural Hist., and several medical works. *See Gross's Am. Medical Biography, and N. A. Rev. Jan. 1835.*

Godwin, Parke. 1816 *N. J.* ——. Journalist. Author Constructive Democracy, Handbook of Universal Biography, Hist. of France, Life Wm. Cullen Bryant, etc. *Pub. Apl.*

Goodale, Dora Reed. 1866 *Ms.* ——. Poet. **Goodale, Elaine.** 1863 *Ms.* ——. Sister to D. R. G. Poet. Authors of Verses from Sky-Farm, Apple Blossoms, In Berkshire with the Wild Flowers, etc. *Pub. Put.*

Goodale, George Lincoln. 1839 *Me.* ——. Botanist. Author The Wild Flowers of America. *Pub. Cass.*

Goodrich, Charles Augustus. 1790 *Ct.*–1862. Author Lives of the Signers of the Declaration of Independence, Hist. of the U. S., etc. *Pub. Cop.*

Goodrich, Chauncey Allen. 1790 *Ct.*–1860. Editor and reviser of Webster's Dict., and editor Select British Eloquence, with careful critical notes. *Pub. Har.*

Goodrich, Frank Boott. 1826 *Ms.* ——. Son to S. G. G. Author The Court of Napoleon, Man upon the Sea, Tri-Colored Sketches of Paris, etc. *Pub. Lip.*

Goodrich, Samuel Griswold, " Peter Parley." 1793 *Ct.*–1860. Bro. to Chas. A. G. Author of nearly two hundred volumes, mainly juvenile and educational, which have achieved a wide popularity. *See Allibone's Dict. Pub. Apl. Bu. Col.*

Gookin, Daniel. c. 1612 *E.*–1687. Colonial historian. Author Historical Collections of the Indians in New England, and an Account of the Doings and Sufferings of the Christian Indians in New England. A generous-minded, tolerant writer. *See Tyler's Am. Lit. vol. I.*

Gould [goold], **Augustus Addison.** 1805 *N. H.*–1866. Naturalist. Author System of Natural History, and several valuable works on conchology. *Pub. Lit.*

Gould, Benjamin Apthorp. 1824 *Ms.* ——. Astronomer. Author of numerous valuable astronomical works.

Gould, Edward S. 1808 *Ct.*–1885. Littérateur. Author of The Sleep Rider, The Very Age, Good English, etc. *Pub. Arm.*

Gould, Hannah Flagg. 1789 *Vt.*–1865. Poet. The Snow Flake and The Frost are among her most quoted poems. Style simple and not unpleasing. *See N. A. Rev. Oct. 1835.*

Gould, James. 1770 *Ct.*–1830. Jurist. Author Principles of Pleading in Civil Actions. *Pub. Jo.*

Graham, Sylvester. 1794 *Ct.*–1851. Vegetarian. Author Lect. on the Science of Human Life.

Grant, Robert. 1852 *Ms.* ——. Satirical poet and novelist. Author The Little Tin Gods on Wheels, The Lambs, Yankee Doodle, and the novels Confessions of a Frivolous Girl and An Average Man. *Pub. Cu. Os. Sev.*

Gray, Albert Zabriskie. 1840 *N. Y.*–1889. Episcopal religious writer. Author The Land and the Life, Jesus Only, Mexico as it Is, etc. *Pub. Dut. Ran.*

Gray, Asa. 1810 *N. Y.*–1889. Botanist. Author Elements of Botany, How Plants Grow, Structural and Systematic Botany, etc. A high authority in his department. *See Harvard Book, vol. 1. Pub. Iv. Scr.*

Gray, Barry. See Coffin, R. B.

Gray, Francis Calley. 1790 *Ms.*–1856. Reviewer and author of several volumes of prose and poetry.

Gray, George Zabriskie. 1838 *N. Y.* ——. Bro. to A. Z. G. Episcopal theologian. Author The Scripture Doctrine of Recognition, The Crusade of the Children in the XIII. Century, etc. *Pub. Hou. Wh.*

Graydon, Alexander. 1752 *Pa.*–1818. Autobiographer. Author Memoirs of a Life, a curious and entertaining work.

Greeley, Horace. 1811 *N. H.*–1872. Journalist. Founder and editor of the N. Y. Tribune. Author What I Know About Farming, The Am. Conflict, Recollections of a Busy Life, etc. *See Life by Parton, 1868, and Memorial pub. by Tribune Association, 1873. Pub. Por.*

Green, Anna Katharine. 185– *L. I.*——. Novelist. Author The Sword of Damocles, The Leavenworth Case, A Strange Disappearance, Hand and Ring, etc. Her works are all sensational in character, but display much inventive power. *Pub. Put.*

Green, Ashbel. 1762 *N. J.*–1848. Presbyterian theologian. Pres. Princeton Coll. Author Hist. Presbyterian Missions, etc. *See Autobiography and Memoir by J. H. Jones.*

Green, Joseph. 1706 *Ms.*–1780. Humorous poet. *See Tyler's Am. Lit. vol. 2, and Hart's Am. Lit.*

Greene, Samuel Stillman. 1810 *Ms.*–1883. Author several valuable treatises on Eng. Grammar.

Green, Wm. Henry. 1825 *N. J.* ——. Presbyterian theologian. Author The Pentateuch Vindicated, etc.

Greene, Albert Gorton. 1802 *R. I.*–1868. Author Canonchet, etc. Old Grimes is his best known poem.

Greene, Asa. 1788 *Ms.*–1837. Humorist. Author Life and Adventures of Dr. Dodimus Duckworth, etc.

Greene, George Washington. 1811 *R. I.*–1883. Historian. Historical Studies, The German Element in the Am. War of Independence, Short Hist. of Rhode Island, Historical View of the Am. Revolution, and Life Gen. Nathanael Greene are some of his numerous and valuable works. His style has been greatly admired. *See Lit. World, Feb. 10, 1883. Pub. Hou. Re.*

Greenleaf, Benjamin. 1786 *Ms.*–1864. Mathematical writer of note. *Pub. Da.*

Greenleaf, Simon. 1783 *Ms.*–1853. Jurist. His greatest work is a Treatise on the Laws of Evidence. *Pub. Lit.*

Greenough [green'o], Henry. 1807 *Ms.*–1883. Artist. Author of the novels Ernest Carroll, Apelles and his Contemporaries, and of various essays on art.

Greenough, Mrs. Richard. See Greenough, Mrs. Sarah.

Greenough, Mrs. Sarah Dana [Loring]. 1827–1885. Novelist and poet. Author In Extremis, Arabesques, Mary Magdalene, a poem, etc. Style original and striking. *Pub. Os. Pet. Rob.*

Greenwood, Francis Wm. Pitt. 1797 *Ms.*–1843. Unitarian theologian. Author Sermons, Essays, Lives of the Apostles, etc. *Pub. A. U. A.*

Greenwood, Grace. See Lippincott, Mrs. Sarah J.

Greey [gree], Edward. 1835 *E.*–1888. Littérateur. Author the plays Vendome and Mirah, the novel Blue Jackets, several works relating to Japan, — The Golden Lotus, Young Americans in Japan, The Wonderful City of Tokio, The Bear Worshippers of Yezo, etc., — and one of the translators of the Japanese romance The Loyal Ronins. *Pub. Le. Put.*

Griffis, Wm. Elliot. 1843 *Pa.* ——. Writer of works on Japan. Author The Mikado's Empire, Japanese

Fairy World, Corea: the Hermit Nation, The Tokio Guide, The Yokohama Guide, etc. *Pub. Har.*

Grimshaw, Wm. 1782 *I.*–1852. Author of a once popular series of school histories. *Pub. Lip.*

Griswold, Alexander Viets. 1766 *Ct.*–1843. Bp. Mass. Religious writer. *See Memoirs, by J. S. Stone. Pub. Dut. Wh.*

Griswold, Mrs. Harriet [Tyng]. 1842 *Ms.* ——. Poet. Author Apple Blossoms. Under the Daisies and several other poems of hers have been widely popular. *See Lit. World, Oct. 6, 1883. Pub. Ja.*

Griswold, Rufus Wilmot. 1815 *Vt.*–1857. Compiler. Chiefly known by his Female Poets of America, Prose Writers of America, and Poets and Poetry of America. A writer who has done good service to literature without possessing much original talent. *Pub. Apl. Por.*

Gross, Samuel D. 1805 *Pa.*–1884. Physician. Author Am. Medical Biography, etc. *Pub. Lip.*

Guernsey, Alfred Hudson. 1825 *Vt.* ——. Author The Spanish Armada, The World's Opportunities, etc. *Pub. Apl. Har.*

Guild, Curtis. 1828 *Ms.* ——. Journalist. Founder and editor of the Boston Commercial Bulletin. Author Over the Ocean, a popular book of travels, Abroad Again, etc. *Pub. Le.*

Guild, Reuben Aldridge. 1822 *Ms.* ——. Librarian and local historian. Author Librarian's Manual, Rhode Island in the Continental Congress, etc.

Guyot [g̃e-o'], Arnold Henry. 1807 *Sd.*–1884. Geographer of note. Author Earth and Man, and several valuable text-books on geography. *Pub. Iv.*

Habberton, John. 1842 *L. I.* ——. Littérateur. Author of Other People's Children, The Barton Experiment, etc. Helen's Babies is his most noted book. *Pub. Car. Har. Ho. Put.*

Hackett, Horatio Balch. 1808 *Ms.*–1875. Baptist biblical scholar. Editor of Smith's Bible Dict. A Commentary on the Original Text of the Acts of the Apostles is his chief work. *Pub. Apl.*

Hackley, Charles. 1808 *N. Y.*–1861. Mathematical writer. *Pub. Bar. Har.*

Hadley, James. 1821 *N. Y.*–1872. Philologist. Author Lect. on Roman Law, a valuable Greek grammar, and numerous scientific and other papers. *Pub. Apl. Ho. Me.*

Hageman, Samuel Miller. 1848 *N. J.* ——. Poet. Author Vesper Voices. Silence is one of his best poems.

Hague, Wm. 1805 *N. Y.*–1887. Baptist theologian. Author Christianity and Statesmanship, etc. *Pub. Lo.*

Haldeman [hŏl'de-man], **Samuel Stehman.** 1812 *Pa.*–1880. Philologist and naturalist. Author Zoological Contributions, Analytical Orthography, Word Building, etc. *Pub. Lip.*

Hale, Edward Everett. 1822 *Ms.* ——. Son to N. H. Littérateur. Widely known as the author of the short stories The Man Without a Country, My Double, Ten Times One is Ten, In His Name, and The Brick Moon. Author of the novel Philip Nolan's Friends, the volumes of sketches entitled His Level Best and The Ingham Papers, and several volumes of sermons. *See Harvard Register, May, 1881. Pub. El. Fu. Rob. Scr.*

Hale, Horatio. 1817 *R. I.* ——. Son to S. J. B. H. Philologist. Author Ethnology and Philology, a work of great value and the fruit of infinite labor and research, and editor the Iroquois Book of Rites. *Pub. Br.*

Hale, Lucretia P. 1820 *Ms.* ——. Dau. to N. H. Humorous writer for young people. Author of the famous Peterkin Papers. *Pub. Os. Rob.*

Hale, Nathan. 1784 *Ms.*–1863. Journalist of note.

Hale, Mrs. Sarah Josepha [Buell]. 1790 *N. H.*– 1879. Editor of The Lady's Book for forty years. Of her numerous books her Woman's Record, a large biographical work, is the most important. *Pub. Har. Rob.*

Hall, Charles Francis. 1821 *N. H.*–1871. Arctic explorer. Author The Arctic Regions, etc. *Pub. Har.*

Hall, James. 1793 *Pa.*–1868. Miscellaneous writer. A Hist. of the Indian Tribes (with McKinney) is his chief work. *See Complete Works, 4 vols. 1856. Pub. Clke.*

Hall, Mrs. Louisa Jane [Park]. 1802 *Ms.* ——. Author of Miriam, a dramatic poem, Joanna of Naples, a tale, and the Life of Elizabeth Carter. *See Griswold's Female Poets of America.*

Hall, Wm. W. 1810 *Ky.*–1876. Physician. Founder of Hall's Journal of Health. Author Health and Good Living, etc. *Pub. Hou.*

Halleck, Fitz-Greene. 1790 *Ct.*–1867. Poet. Fanny, Alnwick Castle, and Marco Bozzaris are among his best poems. His verse has grace and sweetness, but is wanting in the higher qualities of poetry. *See Life and Letters, by Grant Wilson. Pub. Apl.*

Halleck, Henry Wager. 1816 *N. Y.*–1872. Author Elements of Military Art and Science, Treatise on International Law, etc. *Pub. Clx. Lip.*

Halpine, Charles Graham, "Miles O'Reilly." 1829 *I.*–1868. Poet. Author Poems, Miles O'Reilly Papers, etc. *Pub. Har.*

Hamilton, Alexander. 1757 *W. I.*–1804. Statesman.

Principal contributor to .The Federalist, and author
of numerous political essays. *See Lives, by Renwick, J. C. Hamilton, and J. T. Morse; also N. A.
Rev. April, 1858, McMaster's Hist. People of the
U. S., Hamilton by H. C. Lodge in Am. Statesmen,
and Shea's Historical Study of Hamilton. Pub.
Lip.*

Hamilton, Gail. See Dodge, Abigail.

Hamilton, John Church. 1792 *Pa.*-1882. Son to
A. H. Author Memoirs of Alex. Hamilton, Hist.
of the Republic, etc., and editor Works of Alex.
Hamilton.

Hammond, Wm. Alexander. 1828 *Md.* ——. Physician. Author Military Hygiene, Physiological
Essays, Sleep and its Derangements, Nervous Derangements, etc. *Pub. Apl. Lip. Put.*

Harbaugh [har'baw], **Henry.** 1817 *Pa.*-1867. Ger-
man Reformed theologian. Author Fathers of the
German Ref. Church in Europe and America, The
Heavenly Home, etc.

Hardy, Arthur Sherburne. 1847 *Ms.* ——. Novelist and mathematician. Author But Yet a Woman,
etc. *See Lit. World, May 5, 1883, and London
Academy, June 30, 1883. Pub. Gi. Hou. Lip. Mac.*

Harland, Marion. See Terhune, Mrs.

Harney, Will Wallace. 1831 *Ia.* ——. Journalist
and littérateur. Author of numerous graceful poems and sketches, Adonais being one of his finest
poems. *See Coggeshall's Western Poets.*

Harper, Robert Goodloe. 1765 *Va.*-1825. Legal
writer. Style able and profound.

Harris, Joel Chandler. 1848 *Ga.* ——. Author Uncle Remus : his Songs and his Sayings, and Nights
with Uncle Remus ; unique works and valuable ad-
ditions to the literature of folk lore. *Pub. Apl.*

Harris, Mrs. Miriam [Coles]. 1834 *L. I.* ——. Novelist. Author of Rutledge, Richard Vandermarck, and other novels, and The Rosary for Lent. *Pub. Car. Dut. Hou.*

Harris, Samuel. 1814 *Me.* ——. Congregationalist theologian. Author of Zaccheus, or the Scriptural Plan of Benevolence, The Kingdom of Christ on Earth, The Philosophical Basis of Theism, etc. *See Andover Rev. Feb. 1884. Pub. A. T. S. Dra. Scr.*

Harris, Samuel Smith. 1841 *Al.*-1888. Bp. Michigan. Religious writer. Author Christianity and Civil Society. *Pub. Wh.*

Harris, Thaddeus Mason. 1768 *Ms.*-1842. Author Natural Hist. of the Bible, etc.

Harris, Thaddeus Wm. 1795 *Ms.*-1856. Son to T. M. H. Entomologist. Chiefly known by his valuable work Insects of Massachusetts Injurious to Vegetation. *Pub. Cass.*

Harris, Thomas Lake. 1823 *E.* ——. Spiritualistic poet. Author Epics of the Starry Heavens, etc. *See Am. Cyc.*

Harris, Wm. Torrey. 1835 *Ct.* ——. Speculative philosopher. Translator of Hegel and editor The Journal of Speculative Philosophy.

Harrison, Mrs. Constance [Cary]. 18— *Mi.* ——. Author Story of Helen Troy, Woman's Handiwork in Modern Homes, etc. *Pub. Har. Scr.*

Harrison, James Albert. 1848 *Mi.* ——. Philologist and traveler. Author Greek Vignettes, Spain in Profile, The Rhine, French Syntax, etc. *See Lit. World. vol. 10, and Southern World, June 1, 1883. Pub. Gi. Ho. Hou. Lip. Lo. Pott.*

Hart, John Seely. 1810 *Ms.*-1877. Educational writer. Author Manuals of Eng. and Am. Literature, Composition and Rhetoric, etc., and an appreciative Essay upon Spenser and The Faërie Queene. *Pub. Clx. Eld. P. B. Ze.*

Harte, Francis Bret. 1837 *N. Y.* ——. Poet and novelist. Author of the novel Gabriel Conroy, the play Two Men of Sandy Bar, East and West Poems, Echoes of the Foot Hills, and the volumes of short stories entitled The Luck of Roaring Camp, Drift from Two Shores, Tales of the Argonauts, Thankful Blossom, The Story of a Mine, Flip and Found at Blazing Star, Twins of Table Mountain, Mrs. Skaggs's Husbands, and Condensed Novels. Dow's Flat, Her Letter, and A Newport Romance are among his best poems. *See Complete Works, 5 vols., and Haweis's Am. Humorists. Pub. Hou.*

Hassard, John R. G. 1836 *N. Y.*–1888. Littérateur. Author Life Archbishop Hughes, Life Pope Pius Ninth, A Pickwickian Pilgrimage, Bayard Taylor in Am. Men of Letters, etc. *Pub. Cath. Hou. Os.*

Haven, Mrs. Alice [Bradley] [Neal]. 1828 *N. Y.*–1863. Writer of juvenile tales. Author No Such Word as Fail, Contentment Better than Wealth, Patient Waiting No Loss, and other excellent stories. *See Memoir, and Harper's Mag. Oct. 1863. Pub. Apl.*

Haven, Erastus Otis. 1820 *Ms.*–1881. Methodist religious and educational writer. Pres. Univ. of Michigan. Author Pillars of Truth, Young Man Advised, Rhetoric, etc. *Pub. Har. Phi.*

Haven, Gilbert. 1821 *Ms.*–1880. Methodist religious writer. Author Sermons, The Pilgrim's Wallet, Our Next-Door Neighbor, or Mexico of To-Day, etc. *See Monograph, by E. Wentworth. Pub. Har. Le. Phi.*

Haven, Joseph. 1816 *Ms.*–1874. Philosophical writer. Author Mental Philosophy, Moral Philosophy, Hist. of Ancient and Modern Philosophy.

Hawes, Joel. 1789 *Ms.*–1867. Moralist. Author Lect. to Young Men, etc.

Hawks, Francis Lister. 1798 *N. C.*–1866. Ecclesiologist and miscellaneous writer. Author Hist. P. E. Church in Virginia, Hist. P. E. Church in Maryland, The Romance of Biography, Cyclopædia of Biography, Egypt and its Monuments, etc.

Hawthorne, Julian. 1846 *Ms.* ——. Son to N. H. Novelist. Author Bressant, Garth, Dust, Idolatry, Fortune's Fool, Beatrix Randolph, Saxon Studies, etc. *Pub. Apl. Hou.*

Hawthorne, Nathaniel. 1804 *Ms.*–1864. Romancer. Twice-Told Tales, Mosses from an Old Manse, The Scarlet Letter, The House of the Seven Gables, The Blithedale Romance, The Marble Faun, and Our Old Home are his chief works. The fragmentary works, Septimius Felton, The Dolliver Romance, and The Ancestral Footstep, appeared posthumously, as did also the English, American, and Italian Note-Books. Among the most characteristic of his shorter sketches are The Snow Image, The Great Stone Face, and Ethan Brand. A master of the purest English, and the greatest of American prose writers. *See N. A. Rev. July, 1837, July, 1850, Jan. 1852, Blackwood's Mag. Nov. 1863, Atlantic Monthly, May, 1860, Lathrop's Study of Hawthorne, James's Hawthorne in English Men of Letters, The Hawthorne Index, and Lowell's Fable for Critics. Pub. Hou.*

Hay, John. 1839 *Il.* ——. Poet. Author Pike County Ballads and Other Poems, and Castilian Days, a delightful volume of travels. Of his dia-

lect poems, Jim Bludsoe and Little Breeches are
best known. *Pub. Hou.*

Hayes, Isaac Israel. 1832 *Pa.*–1881. Arctic ex-
plorer. Author The Open Polar Sea, An Arctic
Boat Journey, Cast Away in the Cold, etc. *Pub.
Car. Hou. Le.*

Hayne, Paul Hamilton. 1831 *S. C.*–1886. Lyric
poet. Author Legends and Lyrics, Sonnets and
Other Poems, etc. His verse is spirited and original, his sonnets, in particular, taking high rank.
*See complete edition, 1883, and Lit. World, Mar.
10, 1883. Pub. Lip. Lo.*

Hazard, Rowland Gibson. 1801 *R. I.*–1888. Essayist. Author Essays on Finance, Essay on the
Resources of the U. S., Freedom of the Mind in
Willing, Causation, Man a Creative First Cause,
etc. *Pub. Hou. Le.*

Hazard, Samuel. 1784 *Pa.*–1870. Annalist. Author Annals of Pennsylvania, etc.

Hazewell, Charles Creighton. 1814 *R. I.*–1883.
Critic of eminence. A keen, able writer, possessing a vigorous, compact style. Author of the Review of the Week in the Boston Traveller for many
years.

Headley, Joel Tyler. 1814 *N. Y.* ——. Historical
writer. Napoleon and his Marshals, The Old
Guard of Napoleon, and Life of Oliver Cromwell
are some of his numerous works. His style is
graphic and entertaining, but the merit of his books
is much impaired by the partisan spirit in which
they are conceived. *Pub. Scr.*

Heard, Franklin Fiske. 1825 *Ms.* ——. Jurist. Author Criminal Law, Criminal Pleading, Civil Pleading, Shakespeare as a Lawyer, etc. *Pub. Lit.*

Hecker, Isaac Thomas. 1819 *N. Y.*–1888. Founder

of the Society of the Paulists. Author Questions
of the Soul, etc. *Pub. Cath.*

Hedge, Frederick Henry. 1805 *Ms.* ——. Son to
L. H. Unitarian theologian. Author Reason in
Religion, The Primeval World of Hebrew Tradi-
tion, A Christian Liturgy, Prose Writers of Ger-
many, etc. A strong, keen, and original thinker.
Pub. Por. Rob. Scr.

Hedge, Levi. 1767 *Ms.*-1843. Author of a noted
System of Logic. *Pub. Arm.*

Helper, Hinton Rowan. 1829 *N. C.* ——. Author
The Impending Crisis of the South, a once famous
work, Nojoque, and The Negroes in Negroland.
Style reckless and views iconoclastic. *See Davidson's Living Writers of the South.*

Henry, Caleb Sprague. 1804 *Ms.*-1884. Translator of Guizot's Hist. of Civilization and other works,
and author of Essays, Satan as a Moral Philosopher, About Men and Things, etc. *Pub. Dut. Wh.*

Henry, Joseph. 1797 *N. Y.*-1878. Scientist of eminence. Secretary of the Smithsonian Institute,
and author of many scientific monographs of value.

Henry, Patrick. 1736 *Va.*-1799. Statesman. Known
to literature by his speeches, which possess much
artistic finish.

Henshaw, J. Sidney. 1814 *Ms.*-1859. Author Philosophy of Human Progress, etc.

Hentz, Mrs. Caroline Lee [Whiting]. 1804 *Ms.*-
1856. Novelist. Author of many sensational romances of slight merit. Rena, The Planter's
Northern Bride, and Linda are among the best.
Pub. Pet.

Hepworth, George Hughes. 1833 *Ms.* ——. Religious and miscellaneous writer. Author ! ! !,
Rocks and Shoals, etc. *Pub. A. U. A. Har.*

Herbert, Henry Wm., " Frank Forrester." 1807 *E.-*
1858. Miscellaneous writer. Author of novels,
poems, etc., but best known by his Deer Stalkers,
Field Sports of the U. S., and other sporting works.
Pub. Lip. Pet. Por.

Hickok [hĭk'ŏk], **Laurens Perseus.** 1798 *Ct.-*1888.
Metaphysician. Author Logic of Reason, Moral
Science, Empirical Psychology, etc. Style involved
and somewhat obscure. *Pub. Apl. Iv.*

Hicks, Elias. 1748 *L. I.-*1830. Quaker controversialist, and founder of the sect of the Hicksite Qua-
kers. *See Journal of his Life and Religious Labors.*

Higginson, Francis. 1588 *E.-*1630. Puritan clergy-
man. Author True Relation of the Last Voyage
·to New England, and New England's Plantation.
Style vivid and picturesque. *See Tyler's Am. Lit.
vol. 1.*

Higginson, John. 1616 *E.-*1708. Son to F. H.
Puritan theologian. His most noted work is the
Attestation to Cotton Mather's Magnalia. Style
able and clear. *See Tyler's Am. Lit. vol. 2.*

Higginson, Thomas Wentworth. 1823 *Ms.* ——.
Descendant of preceding. Littérateur. Malbone,
a romance, Out-Door Papers, Army Life in a Black
Regiment, Atlantic Essays, Sympathy of Religions,
and Young Folks' Hist. of the U. S. are his chief
works. *Pub. Hou. Le.*

Hildreth, Richard. 1807 *Ms.-*1865. Historian.
Hist. of the U. S. from the Discovery of the Continent to the Close of the 16th Congress in 1820 is
his chief work. Its style is cold and dry, but its
general merit is unquestioned. *Pub. Har.*

Hildreth, Samuel Prescott. 1783 *Ms.-*1863. Historical writer. Author Pioneer Hist. of Ohio Valley, 1848, Biography and Historical Memoranda of
Early Settlers of Ohio, etc.

Hill, Daniel Harvey. 1824 *S. C.* ——. Essayist and mathematician. *Pub. Lip.*

Hill, Thomas. 1818 *N. J.* ——. Mathematician of note, and Unitarian theologian. Author Geometry and Faith, Essays on Curves, Jesus the Interpreter of Nature, etc. *Pub. Dra. Le. Put. Wa.*

Hillhouse, James Abram. 1789 *Ct.*–1841. Dramatic poet. His dramas, Percy's Masque, Hadad, and Demetria, were once extravagantly praised, but are now little read. Style strained, ambitious, and heavy. *See N. A. Rev. Jan. 1840.*

Hilliard, Francis. 1808 *Ms.*–1878. Jurist. Author The Law of Taxation, The Law of Vendors and Purchasers, Treatises on Mortgages, Torts, etc. *Pub. Clx. Jo. Lip. Lit.*

Hillard, George Stillman. 1808 *Me.*–1879. Lawyer and littérateur. Author Six Months in Italy, Eulogy on Daniel Webster, etc., and editor of Spenser. Style scholarly and refined. *Pub. Har. Hou.*

Hirst, Henry B. 1813 *Pa.*–1874. Poet. Author Endymion, The Penance of Roland, etc.

Hitchcock, Edward. 1793 *Ms.*–1864. Geologist of note. Religion of Geology, Illustrations of Surface Geology, and Fossil Footprints in the U. S. are some of his most valuable works. *Pub. Iv.*

Hobart, John Henry. 1775 *Pa.*–1830. Bp. N. Y. Controversialist. Author Companion for the Altar, State of Departed Spirits, Festivals and Fasts, etc. A writer to whose influence the present character of the American church is largely due. *Pub. Dut.*

Hodge, Archibald Alexander. 1823 *N. J.*–1886. Son to C. H. Presbyterian theologian. Author Outlines of Theology, Life of Chas. Hodge, etc. *Pub. P. B. Scr.*

Hodge, Charles. 1797 *Pa.*–1878. Presbyterian the-

6

ologian of eminence. Author Systematic Theology, Commentaries on the Epistles, Constitutional Hist. of the Presb. Church in the U. S., etc. Style clear, earnest, and scholarly. *See Life, by A. A. Hodge. Pub. P. B. Scr.*

Hoffman, Charles Fenno. 1806 *N. Y.*–1884. Poet and novelist. Author Grayslaer and other novels, and several volumes of poems. He excelled as a song-writer, his best known songs being Sparkling and Bright, and The Myrtle and Steel. *Pub. Por.*

Hoffman, David. 1784 *Md.*–1854. Legal writer. Author of A Course of Legal Study, Legal Outlines, Legal Hints, Miscellaneous Thoughts on Men and Things, etc.

Holcombe, James P. 1820 *Va.*–1873. Legal writer. Author Law of Debtor and Creditor, Literature in Letters, etc. *Pub. Apl.*

Holcombe, Wm. H. 1825 *Va.* ——. Physician and Swedenborgian writer. Bro. to J. P. H. Author of Our Children in Heaven, Lost Truths of Christianity, The Other Life, Southern Voices, etc. *Pub. Lip.*

Holland, Josiah Gilbert, " Timothy Titcomb." 1819 *Ms.*–1881. Poet and novelist. Author Kathrina, Bitter Sweet, The Mistress of the Manse, and The Marble Prophecy; the novels Arthur Bonnicastle, Sevenoaks, Miss Gilbert's Career, and Nicholas Minturn ; and Timothy Titcomb's Letters, Goldfoil, and minor works. His work has met with severe criticism from a literary point of view, but remains widely popular. As editor of Scribner's Monthly he exercised a wide and excellent influence. *See Century Mag. Dec. 1881. Pub. Scr.*

Holley, Marietta, "Josiah Allen's Wife." 18—— ——. Humorist. Author My Opinions and Betsey

Bobbet's, My Wayward Pardner, Josiah Allen's
Wife as a P. A. and a P. I., etc. *Pub. Wor.*

Holmes, Abiel. 1763 *Ct.*–1837. Annalist. Author
Hist. Cambridge, American Annals, Memoir of the
French Protestants, etc.

Holmes, Mrs. Mary Jane [Hawes]. 18— *Ms.* ——.
Novelist. A voluminous author of well-meaning
and popular fiction of slight literary pretension.
Lena Rivers and Tempest and Sunshine are among
the best of her novels. *See Lit. World, June 3,
1882. Pub. Car.*

Holmes, Nathaniel. 1814 *N. H.* ——. Author of
a noted work on The Authorship of Shakespeare,
in which the Baconian theory of the authorship of
Shakespeare's plays is stoutly advocated. *Pub.
Hou.*

Holmes, Oliver Wendell. 1809 *Ms.* ——. Son to
A. H. Physician, poet, novelist, and essayist.
Author of the novels Elsie Venner and The Guar-
dian Angel, several valuable medical works, The
Autocrat of the Breakfast Table, The Professor at
the Breakfast Table, The Poet at the Breakfast
Table, Mechanism in Thought and Morals, Mem-
oir of Motley, and other prose works. Songs in
Many Keys, Songs of Many Seasons, and The Iron
Gate are some of his volumes of verse. Among his
finest poems are The Chambered Nautilus, The
Voiceless, The Last Leaf, The Parting of the Ways,
and Under the Violets. The One Hoss Shay is
his most noted humorous poem. *See Life by W.
Kennedy, Harvard Register, April, 1881, Haweis's
Am. Humorists. Pub. Hou.*

Holt, John Saunders. 1826 *Al.* ——. Novelist.
Author Abraham Page, etc. Style original and
realistic. *Pub. Lip.*

Hooker, Herman. 1804 *Vt.*-1857. Devotional writer. Author Family Book of Devotion, The Uses
of Adversity, etc.

Hooker, Thomas. 1586 *E.*-1647. Puritan theologian. A writer of great influence in New England
during the seventeenth and eighteenth centuries.
See Tyler's Am. Lit. vol. 1.

Hooker, Worthington. 1806 *Ms.*-1867. Physician.
Author of several medical works and a valuable
series of text-books in natural history and physiology. *Pub. Har. Pe. Sh.*

Hooper, Lucy. 1816 *Ms.*-1841. Poet. *See Griswold's Female Poets of America.*

Hooper, Mrs. Lucy Hamilton [Jones]. 1835 *Pa.*
——. Poet and littérateur. Author Poems, Under
the Tri-Color, etc. *Pub. Lip.*

Hopkins, John Henry. 1792 *I.*-1868. Bp. Vt. High
Church controversialist of note. Author Hist. of
the Confessional, The End of Controversy Con-
troverted, etc. *See Life, by his son.*

Hopkins, John Henry. 1820 *Pa.* ——. Son to
preceding. Episcopal religious writer. Founder
The Church Journal. Author Carols: Hymns and
Songs, Poems by the Wayside, Life of Bishop Hopkins, etc., and translator of Goethe's Autobiography.

Hopkins, Mrs. Louisa [Payson]. 1812 *Me.*-1862.
Religious writer. *See Sewall's Memoirs of Albert
Hopkins, and Life of Elizabeth Prentiss.*

Hopkins, Mark. 1802 *Ms.*-1887. Moral and relig-
ious writer. Pres. Williams Coll. Author Lect. on
Moral Science, The Law of Love and Love as a
Law, Discourses and Essays, etc. *Pub. Do. Scr.*

Hopkins, Samuel. 1721 *Ct.*-1803. Congregationalist theologian. The founder of what has been

called Hopkinsian Divinity. The System of Doctrine contained in Divine Revelation is his principal work. *See Life, by Park, and Mrs. Stowe's Minister's Wooing.*

Hopkins, Samuel. 1807 *Ms.*–1887. Cousin to M. H. Historian. Author The Puritans and Queen Elizabeth, Lessons at the Cross, and Youth of the Old Dominion. *Pub. Ran.*

Hopkinson, Francis. 1737 *Pa.*–1791. Political Humorist. Author of the famous poem The Battle of the Kegs. A witty, daring writer of much service to his generation. *Pub. Ran.*

Hopkinson, Joseph. 1770 *Pa.*–1842. Son to F. H. Chiefly known as the author of the poem Hail Columbia.

Hosack, David. 1769 *N. Y.*–1835. Medical writer of note.

Hosmer, James Kendall. 1834 *Ms.* ——. Author The Color Guard, a narrative of personal experience, The Thinking Bayonet, a novel, and A Short Hist. of German Literature. *Pub. Jon.*

Hosmer, Mrs. Margaret. 1830 *Pa.* ——. Novelist and writer of Sunday-school tales. Author Blanche Gilroy, Chinaman in California, etc. *Pub. Lip. P. B. Por.*

Hosmer, Wm. Henry Cuyler. 1814 *N. Y.*–1877. Poet. His verse is quiet in tone, relating mainly to Indian legends. See his Hall of Tecumseh, Legends of the Senecas, etc. *See Griswold's Poets and Poetry of America.*

Houghton [ho'ton]**, George Washington Wright.** 1850 *Ms.* ——. Poet. Author St. Olaf's Kirk, Niagara, etc. *See London Lit. World, March 31, 1883. Pub. Est. Hou.*

Hovey, [hŭv'ĭ]**, Alvah.** 1820 *N. Y.* ——. Baptist

theologian. Author The Miracles of Christ, The Scriptural Law of Divorce, etc. *Pub. Lo.*

Howard, Blanche Willis. 1847 *Me.* ——. Novelist. Author One Summer, Aunt Serena, Guenn, etc. *Pub. Hou. Os.*

Howe, John Badlam. 1813 *Ms.*–1883. Writer on finance. Author Monetary and Industrial Fallacies, Mono-Metalism and Bi-Metalism, The Political Economy of Gt. Britain, The U. S. and France in the Use of Money, etc. A clear, earnest thinker. *Pub. Hou.*

Howe, Mrs. Julia Ward. 1819 *N. Y.* ——. Wife to S. G. H. Poet. Author of Passion Flowers, Hippolytus, From the Oak to the Olive, Later Lyrics, etc. The Battle Hymn of the Republic is her most familiar poem. *Pub. Le. Rob.*

Howe, Samuel Gridley. 1801 *Ms.*–1876. Philanthropist. Author Historical Sketch of the Greek Revolution. *See J. F. Clarke's Memorial and Biographical Sketches.*

Howells, Wm. Dean. 1837 *O.* ——. Poet and novelist. Author Poems, Venetian Life, Italian Journeys, Suburban Sketches, Their Wedding Journey, A Foregone Conclusion, The Lady of the Aroostook, The Undiscovered Country, A Modern Instance, A Woman's Reason, etc., and the comedies Out of the Question, A Counterfeit Presentment, The Parlor Car, The Sleeping Car, etc. *See Century Mag. March, 1882. Pub. Hou. Os.*

Howison, Robert Reid. 1820 *Va.* ——. Historian. Author Hist. of Virginia, Hist. Am. Civil War, etc. *Pub. We.*

Hoyt, Ralph. 1810 *N. Y.*–1878. Poet. Author of The Chant of Life and Other Poems, etc.

Hubbard, Wm. 1621 *E.*–1701. Colonial historian.

Author Hist. New England. *See Tyler's Am. Lit.
vol. 2, and edition 1815, pub. Mass. Historical
Society.*

Hudson, Frederick. 1819 *Ms.*–1875. Author Hist.
of Journalism, etc. *Pub. Har.*

Hudson, Henry Norman. 1814 *Vt.*–1886. Shakespearean scholar of eminence. Author Sermons,
Lect. on Shakespeare, etc., and editor the Harvard and the University editions of Shakespeare.
An able, enthusiastic, but somewhat dogmatic critic,
whose comments are of much value, æsthetically
considered. *Pub. Gi. Lit.*

Hudson, Mrs. Mary [Clemmer]. 1839 *N. Y.*–1884.
Novelist and poet. Author Eirene, His Two Wives,
Poems of Life and Nature, Memorials of Alice and
Phœbe Cary, etc. Best known by her brilliant
Woman's Letters from Washington in The Inde-
pendent. *Pub. Hou. Put.*

Hughes, John. 1797 *I.*–1864. R. C. Abp. N. Y.
Religious controversialist. *See Life, by Hassard.
Pub. Cath.*

Hunt, Freeman. 1804 *Ms.*–1858. Founder Hunt's
Merchants' Magazine, and author Lives of Am.
Merchants.

Hunt, Helen. See Jackson, Mrs. Helen.

Hunt, Thomas Sterry. 1826 *Ct.* ——. Geologist.
Author Chemical and Geological Essays, etc. *Pub.
Cass.*

Huntington, Frederic Dan. 1819 *Ms.* ——. Bp.
Central N. Y. Theologian. Author Christian Be-
lieving and Living, Sermons for the People, Christ
in the Christian Year, etc. *Pub. Dut. Wh.*

Huntington, Jedediah Vincent. 1815 *N. Y.*–1862.
Poet and romancer. Author America Discovered:
a Poem, Alban, or the Hist. of a Young Puritan,
etc. Style careful and polished.

Huntington, Wm. Reed. 1838 *Ms.* ——. Broad Church theologian. Author The Church Idea, Conditional Immortality, etc. Style thoughtful and strong. *Pub. Dut.*

Hurlburt, Wm. Henry. 1827 *S. C.* ——. Journalist of note. Style brilliant and forcible. *See Galaxy Mag. Jan. 1869, and Hart's Am. Lit.*

Hurst, John Fletcher. 1834 *Md.* ——. Author Hist. of Rationalism, etc., and translator of Hagenbach's Hist. of the Church. *Pub. Ran. Scr.*

Hutchinson, Thomas. 1711 *Ms.*-1780. Colonial historian. Author Hist. of the Colony of Massachusetts Bay. The work begins with the year 1628 and closes with the year 1774.

Hyatt, Alpheus. 1838 *D. C.* ——. Curator Boston Society of Natural Hist., and author of numerous valuable zoölogical monographs. *Pub. Gi.*

Ingersoll, Charles Jared. 1782 *Pa.*-1862. Political writer of note. Author Hist. of the War of 1812–15, etc. Style able and energetic, but rough and unpolished. *See Duyckinck's Cyc. Am. Lit.*

Ingersoll, Ernest. 1852 *Mch.* ——. Naturalist. Author Friends Worth Knowing, Natural Hist. of Insects, Knocking Around the Rockies, etc. *Pub. Ba. Cass. Har. Lo.*

Ingersoll, Robert Green. 1833 *N. Y.* ——. Freethinker. Author of several works attacking Christianity. Style forcible and plausible.

Ingraham, Joseph H. 1809 *Me.*-1866. Author of sensational and religious romances. Lafitte: the Pirate of the Gulf, and The Prince of the House of David, are among his most noted works. *Pub. Rob.*

Innsley, Owen. See Jennison, Lucia.

Irving, John Treat. 1778 *N. Y.*–1838. Bro. to Wn.
I. Poetical political satirist.

Irving, John Treat, Jr. c. 1810 ——. Son to preceding. Novelist. Author The Attorney, Harry Harson, etc. *Pub. De.*

Irving, Peter. 1771 *N. Y.*–1838. Bro. to Wn. I. Journalist.

Irving, Pierre Munroe. c. 1802 *N. Y.*–1874. Neph. to Wn. I. Biographer. Author Life of Washington Irving. *Pub. Put.*

Irving, Theodore. 1809 *N. Y.*–1880. Neph. to Wn. I. Author Conquest of Florida, etc. *Pub. Put.*

Irving, Washington. 1783 *N. Y.*–1859. Historian and writer of tales and sketches. Author The Sketch Book, Bracebridge Hall, Wolfert's Roost, Knickerbocker's Hist. of New York, Life and Voyages of Columbus, The Alhambra, Mahomet, Life of Washington, etc. The most popular of the earlier American writers. *See Life and Letters of by Pierre Irving, Atlantic Monthly, Nov. 1860, and June, 1864, Haweis's Am. Humorists, Lippincott's Mag. May, 1869, and Irving by C. D. Warner in Am. Men of Letters. Pub. Lip. Mac. Put.*

Irving, Wm. 1766 *N. Y.*–1821. Poet. Bro. to preceding. Author of the poetical portion of Salmagundi.

Ives, Levi Silliman. 1797 *Ct.*–1867. Bp N. C. Afterwards a Roman Catholic theologian. Author Trials of a Mind in its Progress to Catholicism, The Obedience of Faith, etc.

Jackson, Mrs. Helen [Fiske] [Hunt], " H. H." 1831 *Ms.*–1885. Poet and littérateur. The highest quality of her verse is imagination. Tides, October, and Poppies on the Wheat are some of her finest poems. Bits of Travel, Bits of Talk, Ramona, and A Century of Dishonor are her principal prose works. *Pub. Har. Rob.*

Jackson, Henry Rootes. 1820 *Ga.* ——. Author of Tallulah and Other Poems. *See Griswold's Poets and Poetry of America.*

Jacobus, Melancthon Williams. 1816 *N. J.*-1876. Presbyterian biblical commentator. *Pub. Ca. P. B.*

James, Henry. 1811 *N. Y.*-1882. Swedenborgian theologian and metaphysician. Author Remarks on the Gospels, Moralism and Christianity, The Nature of Evil, Substance and Shadow, The Secret of Swedenborg, etc. A writer of keen, delicate perceptions, possessing a clear, graceful style. *See Lit. World, Jan. 13, 1883. Pub. Hou.*

James, Henry, Jr. 1843 *N. Y.* ——. Son to preceding. Novelist and critic. Author the novels Roderick Hudson, The American, The Europeans, Confidence, Washington Square, and The Portrait of a Lady ; the novelettes The Pension Beaurepas, Daisy Miller, An International Episode, etc.; A Passionate Pilgrim and Other Tales, Transatlantic Sketches, French Poets and Novelists, Portraits of Places, and Hawthorne in Eng. Men of Letters. The strength of his books is mainly in the delineation of character, and not in their plots, which are usually slight, while a prominent defect is the absence of the sympathetic quality. *See Hazeltine's Chats About Books. Pub. Hou. Mac.*

James, Henry Ammon. 1854 *Md.* ——. Author of Communism in America, a work of much value. *Pub. Ho.*

James, Thomas Chalkley. 1766 *Pa.*-1835. Poet. *See Gross's Am. Medical Biography.*

Janeway, Jacob. 1774 *N. Y.*-1858. Ref. Dutch

theologian. Author Exposition of the Acts, Romans, and Hebrews, Natural Evidences of the Holy Bible, etc. *See Life, by J. A. James.*

Janney, Samuel M. 1801 *Va.*–1880. Religious historian. Author Lives of Wm. Penn and George Fox, a valuable Hist. of the Religious Society of Friends from its Rise to 1628, etc.

Jarves, James Jackson. 1818 *Ms.*–1888. Writer on art. Author A Glimpse at the Art of Japan, Art Hints, The Art Idea, Art Thoughts, Italian Rambles, etc. A writer whose conclusions and opinions are of much value. *Pub. Har. Hou. Put.*

Jarvis, Samuel Farmer. 1787 *Ct.*–1851. Episcopal theologian. Author The Church of the Redeemed, On the Religion of the Indian Tribes of N. A., etc.

Jay, John. 1745 *N. Y.*–1829. Statesman. One of the authors of The Federalist. Of his state papers, the Address to the People of Gt. Britain is the most celebrated. *See Life, by Wm. Jay.*

Jay, Wm. 1789 *N. Y.*–1858. Son to J. J. Philanthropist. Author Life of John Jay, War and Peace, Causes and Consequences of the Mexican War, etc.

Jefferson, Thomas. 1743 *Va.*–1826. Pres. U. S. Statesman. Author Notes on Virginia, Rights of British America, Manual of Parliamentary Practice, and numerous state papers. His literary monument is the famous Declaration of Independence, known to the whole world. *See Lives by Tucker, Rayner, Dwight, Biddle, Randall, and Parton, Domestic Life of by Randolph, Edinburgh Rev. July, 1830, and Oct. 1837, N. A. Rev. April, 1830, and Jan. 1835, Harper's Mag. Aug. 1871, and Jefferson by J. T. Morse, Jr., in Am. Statesmen. Pub. Clk. Lip.*

Jeffrey, Mrs. Rosa Griffith [Vertner] [Johnson.]
1826 *Mi.* ——. Novelist and poet. Author Wood-
. burn, Florence Vale, The Crimson Hand and Other
Poems, etc. *Pub. Clx. Lip.*

Jennison, Lucia, "Owen Innsley." 1850 *Ms.* ——.
Poet. Author Love Songs and Sonnets. *Pub. Cu.*

Jewett, Charles Coffin. 1816 *Me.*-1868. Bibliographer. Author Facts and Considerations Rela-
tive to Duties on Books, and works of a similar
character.

Jewett, Sarah Orne. 1849 *Me.* ——. Writer of
short stories. Author Old Friends and New, Play-
Days, Country By-Ways, Deephaven, and The
Mate of the Daylight. The possessor of an ex-
quisitely simple, natural, and graceful style. *See
Lit. World, Nov. 19, 1881. Pub. Hou.*

Johnson, Alexander Bryan. 1786 *E.*-1857. Miscellaneous writer. Author Treatise on Banking,
The Philosophy of Human Knowledge, Religion
in its Relations to the Present Life, The Physiol-,
ogy of the Senses, The Meaning of Words, etc.
Pub. Apl. Har.

Johnson, Edward. 1600 *E.*-1682. Colonial historian. His Wonder-Working Providence is a valuable hist. of New England "from the English
planting in 1628 till 1652," and is an accurate re-
flection of the spirit of the writer's day. *See Tyler's
Am. Lit. vol. 1.*

Johnson, Mrs. Helen [Kendrick]. 1843 *N. Y.* ——.
Wife to Rossiter J. Editor Our Familiar Songs,
Tears for the Little Ones, etc., and author of the
charming juvenile stories Roddy's Romance, Rod-
dy's Ideal, and Roddy's Reality. *Pub. Ho. Hou.
Put. Rou.*

Johnson, Oliver. 1809 *Vt.* ——. Biographer. Author Garrison and his Times, etc. *Pub. Hou.*

Johnson, Reverdy. 1796 *Md.*–1876. Legal writer.
Johnson, Mrs. Rosa V. See Jeffrey, Mrs.
Johnson, Rossiter. 1840 *N. Y.* ——. Poet and littérateur. Author Idler and Poet, Hist. of the War of 1812–15, etc., and editor Famous Single Poems, Play-day Poems, the Little Classics, and Appleton's Annual Cyclopædia. *Pub. Do. Ho. Hou. Os.*
Johnson, Samuel. 1696 *Ct.*–1772. Episcopal theologian. A writer of much influence in his day. *See Life and Correspondence, by E. E. Beardsley.*
Johnson, Samuel. 1822 *Ms.*–1882. Author Oriental Religions, and Lectures : Essays and Sermons. Style devout, candid, and thoughtful. *See Memoir, by S. Longfellow. Pub. Hou.*
Johnson, Mrs. Sarah [Barclay]. 1837 *Va.* ——. Author of the popular work The Hadji in Syria.
Johnson, Virginia Wales. 1847 *L. I.* ——. Novelist. Author Joseph the Jew, A Sack of Gold, The Calderwood Secret, Two Old Cats, Miss Nancy's Pilgrimage, A Foreign Marriage, The Neptune Vase, An English Daisy Miller, etc. The possessor of a graceful, original style. *See Lit. World, June 3, 1882. Pub. Clx. Est. Har. Loc.*
Johnson, Walter Rogers. 1794 *Ms.*–1852. Writer on geology.
Johnson, Sir Wm. 1715 *E.*–1774. Author of a work on the Customs and Languages of the Am. Indians.
Johnston, Richard Malcolm. 1822 *Ga.* ——. Humorist. Author The Dukesborough Tales and Old Mark Langston. *Pub. Har.*
Jones, George. 1801 *Me.*–1870. Author Sketches of Naval Life, Life Scenes from the Gospels, etc.
Jones, Joel. 1795 *Ct.*–1860. Jurist and theologian.

Author Manual of Pennsylvania Land Law, Jesus and the Coming Glory, etc. *Pub. Jo.*

Jones, John B. 1810 *Md.*-1866. Author A Rebel War Clerk's Diary, Wild Western Scenes, etc. His works have been very popular, in spite of their absence of literary merit. *Pub. Clx. Lip.*

Jones, Joseph Huntington. 1797 *Ct.*-1868. Bro. to J. J. Author The Effects of Physical Causes on Christian Experience, etc. *Pub. P. B.*

Jones, Wm. Alfred. 1817 *N. Y.* ——. Critic and essayist. Author The Analyst, Essays upon Authors and Books, Characters and Criticisms, etc. A careful, discriminating writer.

Joyce, Robert Dwyer. 1813 *I.*-1883. Poet, novelist, and journalist. Author Ballads Romances and Songs, Deirdrè, Blanid, and the historical novel The Squire of Castleton. He has been called " The Scott of Ireland." *Pub. Rob.*

Judd, Sylvester. 1813 *Ms.*-1853. Best known as the author of Margaret: a Tale of the Real and the Ideal, a work of great but unequal power. *See Darley's illustrated edition, and Lowell's Fable for Critics. Pub. Arm. Rob.*

Judson, Mrs. Emily [Chubbuck], " Fanny Forester." 1817 *N. Y.*-1854. Author essays, sketches, and poems. Alderbrook is her chief work. Style pleasing, but not strong.

Junkin, D. X. 1808 *Pa.*-1880. Presbyterian religious writer. Author The Good Steward, Life of Gen. Hancock, etc. Style scholarly and dignified. *Pub. Apl.*

Junkin, George. 1790 *Pa.*-1868. Bro. to D. X. J. Presbyterian theologian. Author Commentary on Hebrews, Political Fallacies, The Great Apostasy, etc. *See Biography, by D. X. Junkin. Pub. P. B.*

Junkin, Margaret. Dau. to G. J. See Preston, Mrs.

Kane, Elisha Kent. 1820 *Pa.*–1857. Arctic explorer. Author Arctic Explorations, etc. *See Lives by Elder and Schmucker.*

Kellogg, Elijah. 1813 *Me.* ——. Writer of juvenilê works. Author Lion Ben of Elm Island, etc., but best known as the author of the Address of Spartacus to the Gladiators. *Pub. Le.*

Kemble, Mrs. Frances Anne. 1811 *E.* ——. Autobiographer and poet. Author Residence on a Georgian Plantation, Records of a Girlhood, Records of Later Life, etc. *See Living Age, Dec. 7, 1878, and Sept. 22, 1880, and La Jeunesse de Fanny Kemble, by Madame Craven. Pub. Har. Ho.*

Kendrick, Asahel Clark. 1809 *Vt.* ——. Greek scholar. Editor of editions of the Greek classics, and author of several religious works. *Pub. Apl. Os. Sh.*

Kennedy, John Pendleton. 1795 *Md.*–1870. Novelist. Author Swallow Barn, Horse-Shoe Robinson, Rob of the Bowl, Life of Wm. Wirt, etc. His novels, written in an easy, pleasant style, are of value as careful historical studies. *See Life, by H. T. Tuckerman. Pub. Lip. Put.*

Kenrick, Francis Patrick. 1797 *I.*–1863. R. C. Abp. Baltimore. Theologian. Author Dogmatic Theology, Moral Theology, etc. His style is cultivated and logical. *Pub. Pi.*

Kent, James. 1763 *N. Y.*–1847. Jurist of eminence. Author Commentaries on Law, a work of the highest rank in its department, and of much literary merit. *See Duer's Discourse on Life of Kent. Pub. Lit.*

Kerr, Orpheus C.   See Newell, R. H.

Key, Francis Scott.   1779 *Md.*-1843.   Poet.   The Star-Spangled Banner is his only poem of note.

Kidder, Daniel Parrish.   1815 *N. Y.* ——.   Methodist theologian.   Author Homiletics, The Christian Pastorate, etc., and co-author with J. C. Fletcher of Brazil and the Brazilians.   *Pub. Phi.*

Kimball, Richard Burleigh.   1816 *N. H.* ——.   Novelist and littérateur.   Author St. Ledger, Undercurrents, Letters from Cuba, etc.   *Pub. Car.*

King, Clarence.   1843 *Ct.* ——.   Author Mountaineering in the Sierra Nevada, etc.   *Pub. Os.*

King, Edward.   1848 *Ms.* ——.   Novelist and littérateur.   Author The Gentle Savage, The Golden Spike, French Leaders, My Paris, or French Character Sketches, Kentucky's Love, The Great South, Echoes from the Orient, a volume of poems, etc. *Pub. Le. Os. Put.*

King, Mrs. Sue [Petigru].   See Bowen, Mrs.

King, Thomas Starr.   1824 *N. Y.*-1864.   Unitarian religious writer.   Author Substance and Show, Christianity and Humanity, and The White Hills. *See Memoir, by E. P. Whipple.   Pub. Hal. Hou. Lo.*

Kingsley, James Luce.   1778 *Ct.*-1852.   Author Life of Ezra Stiles, and of various educational works.   *Pub. Clk.*

Kinney, Coates.   1826 *N. Y.* ——.   Poet.   The Rain upon the Roof is his most familiar poem.

Kinney, Mrs. Elizabeth Clementine [Dodge] [Stedman].   1810 *N. Y.* ——.   Poet.   Author Felicitá, Poems, Bianca Capello : a Tragedy, etc.   The Italian Beggar-Boy is one of her finest poems. *See Griswold's Female Poets of America.   Pub. Put.*

Kip, Wm. Ingraham.   1811 *N. Y.* ——.   Bp. California. Theologian. Author Double Witness of the Church, Lenten Fasts, Early Conflicts of Christianity, Christmas Holidays in Rome, Catacombs of Rome, etc. *Pub. Apl. Dut. Put. Ran. Wh.*

Kirk, Edward Norris. 1802 *N. Y.*–1874. Presbyterian religious writer. Author Sermons, The Parables of our Lord, etc.

Kirk, Mrs. Ellen W. [Olney]. 1842 *Ct.* ——. Wife to J. F. K. Novelist. Author Through Winding Ways, A Midsummer Madness etc.

Kirk, John Foster. 1824 *N. B.* ——. Historian. Editor Lippincott's Magazine. Author of a standard Hist. of Charles the Bold, and historical essays and reviews. *Pub. Lip.*

Kirkbride, Thomas S. 1809 *Pa.*–1883. Physician. Author Appeal for the Insane, Essays on Insanity, Hospitals for the Insane, etc. *Pub. Lip.*

Kirke, Edmund. See Gilmore, J. R.

Kirkland, Mrs. Caroline Matilda [Stansbury]. 1801 *N. Y.*–1864. Writer on domestic and social topics. Author of A New Home Who'll Follow? Western Clearings, Fireside Talks on Morals and Manners, etc. Her books are uniformly excellent, and their style is picturesque and graceful. *See Hart's Am. Lit. Pub. Scr.*

Kirkland, John Thornton. 1770 *N. Y.*–1840. Biographer. Pres. Harvard Univ. Author Life of Fisher Ames, etc.

Kirwan. See Murray, Nicholas.

Knapp, Samuel Lorenzo. 1784 *Ms.*–1838. Author American Biography, etc.

Knight, Edward Henry. 1824 *E.*–1883. Author Am. Mechanical Dictionary. *Pub. Hou.*

Krauth [krawth], **Charles Philip.** 1797 *Pa.*–1867. Lutheran theologian.

7

Krauth, Charles Porterfield. 1823 *Va.*–1883. Son to preceding. Lutheran theologian of note. Author an annotated translation of the Augsburg Confession, The Evangelical Mass and the Romish Mass, Sketch of the Thirty Years' War, etc. The Conservative Reformation and its Theology is his greatest work, and one marked by careful, temperate views. *Pub. Lip.*

Krebs, John Michael. 1804 *Md.*–1867. Presb. religious writer. Author Righteousness and National Prosperity, etc.

Kurtz, Benjamin. 1795 *Pa.*–1865. Lutheran theologian. Editor The Lutheran Observer. Author Lutheran Prayer-Book, Year Book of the Reformation, etc.

Ladd, George Trumbull. 1842 *O.* ——. Congregationalist theologian. Author Principles of Church Polity and The Doctrine of Sacred Scripture. *Pub. Scr.*

Lamb, Mrs. Martha Joan Reade [Nash]. 1829 *Ms.* ——. Historian. Editor Magazine of Am. Hist. The Hist. of the City of New York, her chief work, is one of enduring excellence and the result of many years' patient labor and research. *Pub. Apl. Bar. Lo.*

Lance, Wm. 1791 *S. C.*–1840. Political writer. Author of a Latin Life of Washington.

Lanier [la-neer'], Clifford Anderson. 1844 *Ga.* ——. Novelist. Author Thorn-Fruit, etc.

Lanier, Sidney. 1842 *Ga.*–1881. Bro. to C. A. L. Poet and littérateur. Author of a Centennial Ode, Poems, Tiger Lilies, a novel, The Science of English Verse, The English Novel and its Development, Florida : its Scenery, History, and Climate, etc., and editor The Boys' Percy, The Boys' Mabinogion, The Boys' King Arthur, etc. *See Century Mag. April, 1884. Pub. Lip. Scr.*

Lanman, Charles. 1819 *Mch.* ——. Artist and littérateur. Author Essays for Summer Hours, Summer in the Wilderness, Private Life of Daniel Webster, Dict. of Congress, etc. Style entertaining and picturesque. *See Lit. World, Jan. 15, 1881. Pub. Un.*

Lapham [lăp'ạm], **Increase Allen.** 1811 *N. Y.*-1875. Scientist. Author Antiquities of Wisconsin, Wisconsin: its Geography Topography Hist. Geology and Mineralogy, etc. *See Popular Science Monthly, April, 1883.*

Larcom, Lucy. 1826 *Ms.* ——. Poet. Author An Idyl of Work, Childhood Songs, Wild Roses of Cape Ann, etc. Best known by the pathetic poems Skipper Ben and Hannah Binding Shoes. *Pub. Hou.*

Lathrop, George Parsons. 1851 *Sh.* ——. Novelist. Author An Echo of Passion, In the Distance, Newport, A Study of Hawthorne, Spanish Vistas, etc. *Pub. Har. Hou. Os.*

Lawrence, Eugene. 1823 *N. Y.* ——. Historical writer. Author Lives of the British Historians, Historical Studies, Essays and Papers, Literature Primers, etc. *Pub. Har.*

Lawrence, Wm. Beach. 1800 *N. Y.*-1881. Jurist of eminence. Author Letters on the Treaty of Washington, an edition of Wheaton's Elements of International Law, and of many other legal works. A high authority on international jurisprudence. *See Am. Annual Cyc. 1881.*

Lawson, John. 16— *E.*-1712. Colonial historian. Author Hist. of North Carolina, a work of considerable merit. *See Tyler's Am. Lit. vol. 2.*

Lazarus, Emma. 1849 *N. Y.*-1887. Poet. Author
Alide, Poems, Admetus and Other Poems, Songs
of a Semite, and Poems and Ballads translated
from Heine. *Pub. A. H. C. Lip. Wor.*

Lea, Henry Carey. 1825 *Pa.* ——. Son to I. L.
Publisher and ecclesiastical historian. Author Su-
perstition and Force, Hist. Sacerdotal Celibacy,
Studies in Church Hist., etc. A thorough, careful scholar. *Pub. Hou. La. Lip.*

Lea, Isaac. 1792 *Del.*-1886. Publisher and naturalist. Author Contributions to Geology, etc., and of
many scientific monographs of value. *Pub. Clx.
La.*

Le Conte [le-kŏnt], **John.** 1818 *Ga.* ——. Naturalist and physicist.

Le Conte, John Eaton. 1784 *N. J.*-1861. Naturalist of note.

Le Conte, John Lawrence. 1825 *N. Y.*-1883. Son
to preceding. Entomologist. A writer of the highest rank in his department.

Le Conte, Joseph. 1823 *Ga.* ——. Bro. to J. L. C.
Scientist. Author Elements of Geology, Sight, etc.
Pub. Apl.

Lee, Alfred. 1807 *Ms.*-1887. Bp. Delaware. Religious writer. Author The Harbinger of Christ, etc.
Pub. Lip. Ran.

Lee, Mrs. Eliza [Buckminster]. 1794 *N. H.*-1864.
Littérateur. Author Life of Richter, Sketches of
a New England Village, Naomi, etc.

Lee, Mrs. Hannah F. [Sawyer]. 1780 *Ms.*-1865.
Author Grace Seymour and other novels, Luther
and his Times, Sculpture and Sculptors, etc. A
versatile writer, whose works were very popular
when first issued.

Lee, Mary Elizabeth. 1813 *S. C.*-1849. Poet and

translator. Author of numerous translations from
the French, German, and Italian poets.

Leeser, Isaac. 1806 *G.*–1868. Jewish theologian.
Author The Jews and the Mosaic Law, etc.

Legaré [leh-gree'], **Hugh Swinton.** 1797 *S. C.*–1843.
Jurist and essayist. Author Constitutional Hist. of
Greece, Essay on Classical Learning, Essay on
Roman Literature, etc.

Leggett, Wm. 1802 *N. Y.*–1840. Journalist. Author
Sketches of the Sea, Tales by a Country Schoolmaster, etc. *See Memoir, by T. Sedgwick.*

Leidy [lī'dĭ], **Joseph.** 1823 *Pa.* ——. Scientist of
note. *Pub. Lip.*

Leighton [lī'tǫn], **Wm.** 1833 *Ms.* ——. Poet. Au-
thor the dramas The Sons of Godwin and At the
Court of King Edwin, Shakespeare's Dream,
Change, The Subjection of Hamlet, etc. *Pub.
Lip.*

Leland, Charles Godfrey. 1824 *Pa.* ——. Poet.
Author the Hans Breitmann Ballads, etc., and of
several prose works, among which are The English
Gypsies and their Language, Origin of the Gypsies,
The Gypsies, etc. His best poem is The Music
Lesson of Confucius. *Pub. Ho. Hou. Mac. Pet.*

Leland, Henry Perry. 1828 *Pa.*–1868. Bro. to C.
G. L. Littérateur. Author The Americans in
Rome, etc.

Lesley, John Peter. 1819 *Pa.* ——. Geologist. Author Man's Origin and Destiny from the Platform
of the Sciences, etc. *Pub. El.*

Leslie, Eliza. 1787 *Pa.*–1857. Writer of tales and
sketches. Author Mrs. Washington Potts, The
Behavior Book, Pencil Sketches, etc. A writer of
excellent aims, who has been deservedly popular.
See Hart's Am. Lit.

Leslie, Madeline. See Baker, Mrs.

Lester, Charles Edwards. 1815 *Ct.* ——. Miscellaneous writer. Author Artists of America, The Glory and Shame of England, My Consulship, Samuel Houston and his Republic, etc.

Leverett, Frederick Percival. 1803 *Ms.*–1836. Classical lexicographer. *Pub. Da. Lip.*

Le Vert, Mrs. Octavia [Walton]. 1820 *Ga.*–1877. Author of the noted Souvenirs of Travel.

Lewis, Alonzo. 1794 *Ms.*–1861. Poet. Called "The Lynn Bard." Author Forest Flowers and Sea Shells, etc. *See works edited by Ion Lewis, 1883. Pub. Cu.*

Lewis, Dio. 1823 *N. Y.*–1886. Writer on physical training. Author The New Gymnastics, Our Girls, Our Digestion, etc. *Pub. Har. Hou.*

Lewis, Elisha J. 1820 *Pa.* ——. Author Hints to Sportsmen, The Am. Sportsman, etc. *Pub. Lip.*

Lewis, Enoch. 1776 *Pa.*–1856. Mathematician. Author of valuable treatises on algebra and trigonometry, Life of Wm. Penn, etc. *Pub. Por.*

Lewis, Mrs. Estelle Anna [Robinson], "Stella." 1824 *Md.*–1880. Poet. Sappho is her most famous book; others are Records of the Heart, Child of the Sea, Myths of the Minstrel, etc.

Lewis, Tayler. 1802 *N. Y.*–1877. Theologian and classical scholar. Author The Platonic Theology, The Bible and Science, Six Days of Creation, Religion and the State, etc. *Pub. Ca. Har.*

Lieber [lee'ber], Francis. 1800 *P.*–1872. Political philosopher. Author Manual of Political Ethics, Laws of Property, Civil Liberty and Self-Government, Legal and Political Hermeneutics, etc. *See Life and Letters, by T. S. Perry. Pub. Lip. Th.*

Lincoln, Abraham. 1809 *Ky.*–1865. Pres. U. S.

Statesman. Known to literature by his orations, which reveal a masterly use of English. His Gettysburg Oration is the most famous. *See Lives by Raymond and Holland.*

Lincoln, Mrs. Almira. See Phelps, Mrs. A. H.

Lincoln, John Larkin. 1817 *Ms.* ——. Classical scholar. Editor editions of Livy, Horace, and Cicero. *Pub. Apl.*

Linton, Wm. James. 1812 *E.* ——. Poet and engraver. Author Claribel, Life Thos. Paine, a valuable Hist. of Wood Engraving, etc. *See Stedman's Victorian Poets, and Atlantic Monthly, Feb. 1883. Pub. Est. Le.*

Lippard, George. 1822 *Pa.*-1854. Novelist. Author Blanche of Brandywine and other sensational romances of slight merit. *Pub. Pet.*

Lippincott, Mrs. Sarah Jane [Clarke], "Grace Greenwood." 1823 *N. Y.* ——. Littérateur. Author Greenwood Leaves, Record of Five Years, Poems, Life of Queen Victoria, etc. *Pub. An.*

Livermore, Abiel Abbot. 1811 *N. H.* ——. Unitarian theologian. Lect. to Young Men, Discourses and Commentaries on the Gospels, Acts, and Romans, are some of his works. *Pub. A. U. A. Loc.*

Livermore, Mrs. Mary Ashton. 1821 *Ms.* ——. Lecturer. Author Superfluous Women and Other Lectures, Pen Pictures, Thirty Years Too Late: a temperance tale, etc. *Pub. Le.*

Livingston, Edward. 1764 *N. Y.*-1836. Jurist. Author of a valuable System of Penal Law. *See Life, by Chas. Hunt, 1864.*

Livingston, Wm. 1741 *N. Y.*-1790. Jurist and poet. Author of a poem called Philosophical Solitude, etc. *See Memoir by T. Sedgwick, and Tyler's Am. Lit. vol. 2.*

Locke, David Ross, " Petroleum V. Nasby." 1833
N. Y.-1888. Political humorist. A satirist of wide
influence. Author A Paper City, Swinging Round
the Circle, The Moral Hist. of America's Life
Struggle, etc. *Pub. Le.*

Lodge, Giles Henry. 1805 *Ms.* ——. Physician
and translator. Best known as the author of a
scholarly translation of Winckelmann's Hist. of
Ancient Art. *Pub. Os.*

Lodge, Henry Cabot. 1850 *Ms.* ——. Neph. to G.
H. L. Littérateur. Author Essay on Anglo-Saxon
Land Law, Life and Letters of Geo. Cabot, Short
Hist. of the Eng. Colonies in America, Lives of
Webster and Hamilton in Am. Statesmen, etc.
*See Harvard Register, June, 1881, and Atlantic
Monthly, Oct. 1883. Pub. Har. Hou. Le. Lit.*

Logan, Cornelius A. 1800 *Md.*-1853. Dramatist
and actor. Author The Wool Dealer, Yankee Land,
etc.

Logan, James. 1674 *I.*-1751. Author Duties of Man,
Defence of Aristotle, and many scientific papers.
Founder of the Loganian Library at Philadelphia.

Logan, Olive. See Sikes, Mrs. Dau. to C. A. L.

Long, John Davis. 1838 *Me.* ——. Author of a fine
blank verse translation of the Æneid. *Pub. Loc.*

Longfellow, Henry Wadsworth. 1807 *Me.*-1882.
Poet. Author of the Spanish translation Coplas
de Manrique, 1833 ; Outre-Mer, a prose vol. of
travels, 1835; Hyperion, a prose romance, 1839;
Voices of the Night, 1839; Ballads and Other
Poems, 1841 ; Poems on Slavery, 1842 ; The Span-
ish Student, 1843; The Belfry of Bruges and
Other Poems, 1846; Evangeline, 1847; Kavanagh,
a prose tale, 1849 ; Seaside and Fireside, 1850 ;
The Golden Legend, 1851 ; Hiawatha, 1855; The

Courtship of Miles Standish, 1858; Tales of a Wayside Inn, 1st series, 1863; Flower de Luce, 1867; New England Tragedies, 1868; Dante's Divina Commedia: a translation, 1867-1870; The Divine Tragedy, 1872; Three Books of Song, 1872; Aftermath, 1874; The Masque of Pandora, 1875; Kéramos, 1878; Ultima Thule, 1880; In the Harbor, 1882; and Michael Angelo, 1883. *See Lives by Stoddard and Underwood, Austin's Longfellow his Work, Life, and Friendships, Atlantic Monthly, Dec. 1863, and June, 1882, Scribner's Mag. Nov. 1878, Harper's Mag. June, 1882, Lit. World, Feb. 26, 1881, Living Age, Nov. 4, 1882, Fortnightly Rev. Jan. 1883, Century Mag. Oct. 1883, and Hazeltine's Chats About Books. Pub Hou.*

Longfellow, Samuel. 1819 *Me.* ——. Bro. to H. W. L. Poet. Author of several hymns of great beauty. *Pub. Hou.*

Longstreet, Augustus Baldwin. 1790 *S. C.*-1870. Miscellaneous writer. Chiefly known by his Georgia Scenes, a book of genuine though broad humor.

Loomis, Elias. 1811 *Ct.* ——. Astronomer and mathematician of note. *Pub. Har.*

Lord, John. 1811 *Me.* ——. Historical lecturer. Author Hist. of the U. S., Modern Hist., Points of Hist., etc. *Pub. Bar. Clx. Des. Loc.*

Lorimer, George C. 1837 *S.* ——. Baptist religious writer. Author Isms Old and New, Under the Evergreens, The Great Conflict, Jesus : the World's Saviour, etc. *Pub. Gri. Le.*

Loring, Frederic Wadsworth. 1848 *Ms.*-1871. Poet and littérateur. Author of the novel Two College Friends, etc.

Lossing, Benson John. 1813 *N. Y.* ——. Historian. Author Pictorial Field Books of the Revolution,

War of 1812 and the Civil War, Life of Philip
Schuyler, etc. The literary merit of these books
is considerable, and their value as collections of
facts, incidents, etc., is very great. *Pub. Har. Por.
Put. Sh.*

Lothrop, Amy. See Warner, Anna.

Lounsbury, Thomas R. 18— ——. Author of a
Hist. of the English Language, and a masterly Life
of Cooper in Am. Men of Letters. *See Atlantic
Monthly, April, 1883. Pub. Gi. Ho. Hou.*

Lowell, James Russell. 1819 *Ms.* ——. Poet and
critical essayist. His prose is comprised chiefly in
the volumes entitled Among my Books, Fireside
Travels, and My Study Windows. The Vision of
Sir Launfal, Three Memorial Poems, The Biglow
Papers, The Cathedral, and Under the Willows in-
clude his principal volumes of verse. Among his
finest single poems are Columbus, Agassiz, The
Commemoration Ode, Sir Launfal, Above and Be-
low, and Lines on the Death of a Friend's Child.
A high English authority rests the fame of Lowell
on his Biglow Papers mainly, but American critics
have not so decided. As a whole, the verse of
Lowell represents the highest reach of American
poetry. *See Lippincott's Mag. June, 1871, Century Mag. May, 1882, Underwood's Sketch of Lowell, 1882, and Haweis's Am. Humorists. See complete works, 5 vols. Pub. Hou.*

Lowell, Mrs. Maria [White]. 1821 *Ms.*–1855. Wife
to J. R. L. Poet. Her best known poem is the ex-
quisite lyric The Alpine Sheep.

Lowell, Robert Traill Spence. 1816 *Ms.* ——. Bro.
to J. R. L. Poet and novelist. The spirited Defence of Lucknow is his most familiar poem. The
New Priest in Conception Bay, Fresh Hearts that

Failed Three Thousand Years Ago, and Antony Brade, a book for boys, are his principal prose works. *See Atlantic Monthly, Dec. 1858. Pub. Rob.*

Ludlow, Fitzhugh. 1837 *N. Y.*–1870. Littérateur. Author The Hasheesh Eater, The Opium Habit, The Heart of the Continent, and The Little Brother. Style brilliant and witty.

Lunt, George. 1807 *Ms.*–1885. Poet. Author The Age of Gold and Other Poems, Lyric Poems : Sonnets, and Miscellanies, Poems (1883), Old New England Traits, etc. *Pub. Cu.*

Lyman, Theodore. 1792 *Ms.*–1849. Political writer. Author The Diplomacy of the U. S. with Foreign Nations, etc.

Lynch, Anne C. See Botta, Mrs.

Lynch, Wm. F. 1805 *Va.*–1865. Author Narrative of the U. S. Exploring Expedition to the River Jordan and the Dead Sea, a work of great interest and scientific value.

Macclurg, James. 1747 *Va.*–1825. Physician. Author of several medical works, and co-author with Tucker of a once famous poem, The Belles of Williamsburg.

MacDowell, Mrs. Katherine Sherwood Bonner. 1849 *Mi.*–1883. Humorous writer. Author Dialect Tales, Suwanee River Tales, and Like unto Like. *Pub. Har. Rob.*

Mace, Mrs. Frances [Laughton]. 1836 *Me.* ——. Poet. Author Legends Lyrics and Sonnets. Style graceful and delicate. *Pub. Cu.*

MacKellar, Thomas A. 1812 *N. Y.* ——. Poet. Author Rhymes Atween Times, etc. *Pub. Lip.*

Mackenzie, Alexander Slidell. 1803 *N. Y.*–1848.

Biographer. Author Lives of John Paul Jones, Com. Decatur, and Com. Perry, A Year in Spain, etc. *Pub. Har.*

Mackenzie, Robert Shelton. 1809 *I.*–1881. Littérateur. Author Lays of Palestine, Lives of Dickens, Scott, and Guizot, Titian : an art novel, etc. An industrious author, possessing a lively, entertaining style. *Pub. Arm. Har. Lip. Por.*

Mackey [măk′ee], **Albert Gallatin.** 1809 *S. C.*–1881. Masonic writer of note. Author Text-Book of Masonic Jurisprudence, Lexicon of Freemasonry, etc. *Pub. Clk.*

Mackie, John Milton. 1813 *Ms.* ——. Littérateur. Author Cosas de España, Lives of Leibnitz, Schamyl, etc.

Macleod, Xavier Donald. 1821 *N. Y.*–1865. Author Life of Mary, Queen of Scots, Hist. of the Devotion to the Blessed Virgin Mary in North America, etc. *See Memoir, by Abp. Purcell. Pub. Arm. Pi.*

Madison, James. 1751 *Va.*–1836. Pres. U. S. Statesman. His Reports of the Debates in the National Convention of 1788 are of much historic value. Style clear and logical. *See Bancroft's Hist. of the U. S., Lives by Rives and J. Q. Adams, Living Age, July 13, 1878, and Madison by S. H. Gay in Am. Statesmen. Pub. Clx. Lip.*

Magoon, Elias Lyman. 1810 *N. H.*–1886. Baptist preacher of note. Author Proverbs for the People, Orators of the Am. Revolution, Republican Christianity, etc. *Pub. Arm. Har.*

Mahan [mạ-hăn′], **Asa.** 1800 *N. Y.*–1889. Philosopher. Author Critical Hist. of Philosophy, The Science of Intellectual Philosophy, Science of Moral Philosophy, The Doctrine of the Will, etc. *Pub. Bar. Gri. Har. Phi.*

Malcom, Howard. 1799 *Pa.*–1879. Baptist theologian of note. Author Nature and Extent of the Atonement, Bible Dict., Christian Rule of Marriage, Travels in South Eastern Asia, etc. *Pub. Lip. Sh.*

Mann, Horace. 1796 *Ms.*–1859. Writer on education. Author Lect. on Education, An Educational Tour, Thoughts for a Young Man, etc. *See Life, by Mrs. Mann. Pub. Bard. Le.*

Manning, Jacob M. 1824 *N. Y.*–1882. Congregationalist religious writer. Author Helps to a Life of Prayer, Half Truths and the Truth, Not of Man but of God, etc. *Pub. Le.*

March, Francis Andrew. 1825 *Ms.* ——. Anglo-Saxon scholar. Author Comparative Grammar of the Anglo-Saxon Language, etc. A high authority in his department. *Pub. Har.*

Marsh, George Perkins. 1801 *Vt.*–1882. Philologist of note. Author Lect. on the English Language, Man and Nature, Icelandic Grammar, etc. A writer of wide culture and profound scholarship. *See Lit. World, Oct. 21, 1882. Pub. Scr.*

Marsh, James. 1794 *Vt.*–1842. Philosopher and scholar. *See Remains with Memoir (Boston), 1843.*

Marsh, Othniel Charles. 1831 *N. Y.* ——. Palæontologist. Author of many valuable scientific monographs.

Marshall, John. 1755 *Va.*–1835. Chief Justice of the U. S. Author The Life of Washington, a valuable but somewhat heavy work.

Marvel, Ik. See Mitchell, D. G.

Mason, John. 1600 *E.*–1672. Colonial historian. Author Hist. of the Pequot War, a vigorous narration, of value for its personal character rather than for intrinsic literary merit.

Mason, John Mitchell. 1770 *N. Y.*–1829. Pulpit orator. Remembered for his famous Oration on the Death of Alex. Hamilton.

Mason, Lowell. 1792 *Ms.*–1872. Composer. Author of many works of value on musical subjects. *See Ritter's Music in America. Pub. Gi.*

Mather, Cotton. 1663 *Ms.*–1728. Son to I. M. Puritán theologian. Author Wonders of the Invisible World, Magnalia Christi Americana, Christian Philosopher, Psalterium Americanum, etc. A writer of great learning, possessing a pedantic, weighty, and fantastic style. *See Life by S. Mather, N. A. Rev. July, 1840, and Tyler's Am. Lit. vol. 2.*

Mather, Increase. 1639 *E.*–1723. Son to R. M. Puritan theologian. Remarkable Providences is his most noted work. Style energetic and terse. *See Tyler's Am. Lit. vol. 2.*

Mather, Moses. 1719 *Ct.*–1806. Congregationalist theologian. Author Systematic View of Divinity, etc.

Mather, Richard. 1596 *E.*–1669. Puritan theologian. *See Life by I. Mather, and Tyler's Am. Lit. vol. 2.*

Mather, Samuel. 1706 *Ms.*–1785. Son to C. M. Congregationalist theologian. One of his works is an attempt to prove the Japhetic origin of the primary inhabitants of the American continent.

Mathews, Cornelius. 1817 *N. Y.*–1889. Littérateur. Author the plays, The Politicians and Witchcraft, Money-Penny: a romance, etc.

Mathews, Wm. 1818 *Me.* ——. Essayist. Author Hours with Men and Books, Getting on in the World, The Great Conversers, etc. *Pub. Gri.*

Matthews, James Brander. 1852 *La.* ——. Dramatist. Author French Dramatists of the 19th Cent., The Theatres of Paris, the comedy Margery's Lovers, etc. *Pub. Scr.*

Maturin [măt′yoo-rĭn], **Edward.** 1821 *I.*–1881. Historical novelist. Author Bianca, Montezuma, Benjamin: the Jew of Grenada, etc. *Pub. Har.*

Maury [maw′rĭ or mŭr-rĭ], **Matthew Fontaine.** 1806 *Va.*–1873. Hydrographer of note. Author Treatise . on Navigation, Physical Geography of the Sea, Wind and Current Charts, etc. *See North British Rev. May, 1858. Pub. For. Har. Un.*

May, Sophie. See Clarke, R. S.

Mayer, Brantz. 1809 *Md.*–1879. Archæologist. Author Mexico as it Was and as it Is, Mexico: Aztec Spanish and Republican, Observations on Mexican Hist. and Archæology, Mexican Antiquities, Twenty Years of an African Slaver, etc.

Mayhew, Jonathan. 1720 *Ms.*–1766. Congregationalist controversialist. Author Christian Sobriety, Sermon on the Repeal of the Stamp Act, etc. A bold, original thinker.

Mayo, Amory Dwight. 1823 *Ms.* ——. Unitarian religious writer. Author Graces and Powers of the Christian Life, Symbols of the Capitol, etc.

Mayo, Mrs. Sarah C. [Edgarton]. 1819 *Ms.*–1848. Wife to A. D. M. Miscellaneous writer.

Mayo, Wm. Starbuck. 1812 *N. Y.* ——. Novelist. Author Kaloolah, The Berber, Never Again, etc. *Pub. Put.*

McCabe, James D., Jr. 1840 *Va.* ——. Littérateur. A Life of Gen. R. E. Lee is his chief work. Style clear and careful. *Pub. Le. Lip. Sto.*

McClellan, George Brinton. 1826 *Pa.*–1885. Author The Armies of Europe, Organization and Campaigns of the Army of the Potomac, etc. *Pub. Lip.*

McClintock, John. 1814 *Pa.*–1870. Methodist theologian of note. Co-author with Dr. Strong of a valuable Theological and Biblical Cyclopædia. *Pub. Har. Phi.*

McCord, Mrs. Louisa S. [Cheves]. 1810 *S. C.*–1879. Author Caius Gracchus, a tragedy, My Dreams, a volume of poems, and several monographs on political economy.

McCosh, James. 1811 *S.* ——. Metaphysician. Pres. Princeton Coll. A profound thinker, whose contributions to philosophical literature are of great value. Among the chief are Laws of Discursive Thought, Christianity and Positivism, Scottish Philosophy, Mill's Philosophy, and Method of the Divine Government. *Pub. Ca. Scr.*

McGill, John. 1809 *Pa.*–1872. R. C. Bp. Richmond. Author Life of John Calvin, etc. *Pub. Pi.*

McIlvaine [mak-il-vān'], Charles Pettit. 1798 *N. J.*–1873. Bp. Ohio. Low Church theologian. Evidences of Christianity is his most noted work. *See Memorials edited by Wm. Carus. Pub. Ca.*

McIntosh, Maria J. 1803 *Ga.* ——. Novelist. Author Praise and Principle, Conquest and Self-Conquest, Violet, etc. The tone of her books is quiet and domestic, and the style graceful and easy. *Pub. Apl. Har.*

McKeever, Harriet B. 1807 *Pa.* ——. Poet and religious fictionist. *Pub. Clx. L. P. S. Por. P. B.*

McLean, Sarah Pratt. 1855 *Ct.* ——. Novelist. Author Cape Cod Folks, Towhead and Some Other Folks. *Pub. Cu.*

McLellan, Isaac. 1810 *Me.* ——. Poet. Author The Year and Other Poems, The Fall of the Indian, etc. Style quiet and meditative.

McMaster, Guy Humphrey. 1829 *N. Y.*–1887. Poet. Author of the spirited lyric Carmen Bellicosum.

McMaster, John Bach. 1852 *L. I.* ——. Historian. Author Hist. of the People of the U. S., etc. An able writer, possessing an easy, graphic style. *Pub. Apl. Hou.*

McSherry, James. 1819 *Md.*–1869. Historian and littérateur. Author of a popular Hist. of Maryland.

McSherry, Richard. 1817 *W. Va.*–1885. Physician and essayist. Author Early Hist. of Maryland and Other Essays, El Puchero, etc. *Pub. Apl. Pi.*

Mead, Edwin Doak. 1849 *N. H.* ——. Critic and lecturer. Author Martin Luther: a Study of the Reformation, The Philosophy of Carlyle, etc. *Pub. El. Hou.*

Meade, Wm. 1789 *Va.*–1862. Bp. Va. Author Family Prayers, Old Churches of Virginia, etc. *Pub. Lip.*

Meigs [mĕgs], **James Atkins.** 1829 *Pa.* ——. Naturalist. Author Cranial Characteristics, etc.

Mellen, Grenville. 1799 *Me.*–1841. Poet. His verse was once popular, but is now forgotten. *See Griswold's Poets and Poetry of America.*

Melville, Herman. 1819 *N. Y.* ——. Novelist. Author of several tales of adventure, of which Typee, Omoo, White Jacket, and Redburn are the chief. Style breezy and forcible. *Pub. Har.*

Menken, Adah Isaacs. 1835 *La.*–1868. Poet. Author Infelicia, etc. Her verse is morbid and unhealthy in tone. *See Every Saturday, Sept. 12, 1868. Pub. Lip.*

Meriwether, Mrs. Elizabeth [Avery]. 1832 *Tn.* ——. Novelist. Author The Master of Red Leaf, Black and White, The Ku Klux Klan, My First and Last Love, etc. Style entertaining, but somewhat melodramatic. *Pub. Ha.*

8

Miles, George H. 1824 *Md.*–1871. Poet. Author of the dramas Mahomet and De Soto, and of several stirring war songs.

Miller, Cincinnatus Hiner, "Joaquin Miller." 1841 *Ind.* ——. Poet. Author Songs of the Sierras, The Ship in the Desert, Songs of the Sunlands, the novels The Danites in the Sierras, Shadows of Shasta, Memorie and Rime, etc. Style luxurious and sensuous. His Sunrise in Venice and portions of Walker in Nicaragua nearly reach the high-water mark of American poetry. *See Wide Awake Mag. July, 1878. Pub. Jan. Rob.*

Miller, Joaquin. See Miller, C. H.

Miller, Samuel. 1769 *Del.*–1850. Presbyterian theologian of note. Author Life of Jonathan Edwards, Presbyterianism the Truly Primitive and Apostolic Constitution of the Church of Christ, Letters on Clerical Habits and Manners, etc. *See Life, by his son. Pub. P. B.*

Milligan, Robert. 1814 *I.* ——. Campbellite theologian. Style scholarly and earnest.

Mitchel, Ormsby MacKnight. 1810 *Ky.*–1862. Astronomer. Author Planetary and Stellar Worlds, Astronomy of the Bible, etc. *See Headley's Old Stars and Popular Science Monthly, March, 1884. Pub. Arm.*

Mitchell, Donald Grant, "Ik Marvel." 1822 *Ct.* ——. Littérateur. Author Dream Life, Reveries of a Bachelor, My Farm at Edgewood, Dr. Johns, an excellent novel, Rural Studies, etc. *Pub. Scr.*

Mitchell, Henry. 1830 *Ms.* ——. Hydrographer of eminence. Author of numerous and valuable scientific reports.

Mitchell, John Kearsley. 1796 *W. Va.*–1858. Physician. Author of several medical works of value,

Indecision and Other Poems, St. Helena: a poem, etc. *Pub. Clx. Lip.*

Mitchell, Maria. 1818 *Ms.* ——. Sister to H. M. Astronomer of note. *See Mrs. Hale's Woman's Record.*

Mitchell, S. Weir. 1829 *Pa.* ——. Son to J. K. M. Physician, novelist, poet. Author of several valuable professional works, the novels Hephzibah Guinness and In War Time, The Hill of Stones and Other Poems, etc. *Pub. Hou. Lip.*

Mitchell, Walter. 1826 *Ms.* ——. Novelist and magazinist. Author Bryan Maurice, a novel, and of numerous sermons and poems. *Pub. Clx. Lip.*

Mitchill, Samuel Latham. 1764 *L. I.*–1831. Scientist and littérateur. *See Reminiscences of, by J. W. Francis, 1859.*

Moffat, James Clement. 1811 *S.* ——. Ecclesiologist. Author Comparative Hist. of Religions, Life of Dr. Chalmers, etc. *Pub. Do. Ran. Wils.*

Monroe, James. 1758 *Va.*–1831. Pres. U. S. Statesman. Author State Papers, Tour of Observation in 1817, The People: the Sovereigns, etc. Style scholarly and discreet. *See Monroe, by D. C. Gilman, in Am. Statesmen. Pub. Clx. Lip.*

Monti, Luigi. 1830 *Sy.* ——. Littérateur. Author An American Consul Abroad, Leone, a novel, etc. He appears in Longfellow's Tales of a Wayside Inn as "The Young Sicilian." *Pub. Le. Os.*

Moore, Clement Clarke. 1779 *N. Y.*–1863. Author of a Hebrew-Eng. Lexicon, but more widely known as the author of the famous poem The Visit of St. Nicholas. *Pub. Por.*

Moore, Frank. 1828 *N. H.* ——. Son to J. B. M. Historical compiler. Editor Cyc. of American Eloquence, The Rebellion Record, etc. Author Women of the War, etc.

Moore, George Henry. 1823 *N. H.* ——. Son to
J. B. M. Historical writer. Author Hist. of the
Jurisprudence of N. Y., Treason of Chas. Lee, etc.

Moore, Jacob Bailey. 1797 *N. H.*-1853. Political
writer. Author Laws of Trade in the U. S., etc.

Morford, Henry. 1823 *N. J.*-1884. Novelist and
dramatist. Author Shoulder Straps, Days of
Shoddy, etc. His style has little literary value.*
Pub. Pet.

Morris, Edward Joy. 1817 *Pa.*-1881. Traveler.
Author Tour Through Turkey, etc., The Turkish
Empire, and several translations from the German.

Morris, George P. 1802 *Pa.*-1864. Lyric poet. My
Mother's Bible, Woodman Spare that Tree, are
among his most noted poems. Style simple and
direct.

Morse, Jedidiah. 1761 *Ct.*-1826. Geographer of
note. Author Elements of Geography, Am. Gazetteer, Annals of the American Revolution, etc.

Morse, John Torrey, Jr. 1840 *Ms.* ——. Author
J. Q. Adams and Thos. Jefferson in Am. Statesmen,
Life of Alex. Hamilton, Banks and Banking, Arbi-
tration and Award, Famous Trials, etc. *Pub. Hou.*
Lit.

Morton, Nathaniel. 1612 *E.*-1685. Colonial annalist. Author New England's Memorial, a work of
much historic value. *See Tyler's Am. Lit. vol. 1.*

Morton, Samuel George. 1799 *Pa.*-1851. Ethnologist. Author Crania Americana, Crania Egyptica,
etc. *Pub. Lip.*

Morton, Thomas. c. 1590 *E.*-1646. Author of The
New English Canaan. Style able and humorous.

Motley, John Lothrop. 1814 *Ms.*-1877. Historian.
Author The Rise of the Dutch Republic, The Hist.
of the United Netherlands, Life of John Barneveld

etc. Style brilliant and sympathetic. *See Life, by
O. W. Holmes. Pub. Har.*

Moulton, Mrs. Ellen Louise [Chandler]. 1835 *Ct.*
——. Poet and littérateur. Author of Poems,
Some Women's Hearts, Random Rambles, Bed-
Time Stories, etc. Style finished and delicate.
Pub. Har. Rob.

Mountford, Wm. 1816 *E.*-1885. Unitarian religious writer. Author Martyria, Euthanasy, or Happy
Talk toward the End of Life, etc. The tone of his
works is quiet and reverent, and the style is one of
much beauty. *Pub. Hou.*

Mowatt, Mrs. A. C. See Ritchie, Mrs.

Mudge, Zechariah Atwell. 1813 *Me.*-1888. Miscellaneous writer. Author The Christian Statesman,
Views from Plymouth Rock, Witch Hill, Life of
Abraham Lincoln, Footprints of Roger Williams,
etc. *Pub. Lo. Phi.*

Muhlenberg, Wm. Augustus. 1796 *Pa.*-1877. Poet
and religious writer. His hymn " I would not live
alway " is widely known. *See Life, by Anne Ayres,
and Atlantic Monthly, Oct. 1880. Pub. Ran. Wh.*

Mulford, Elisha. 1833 *Pa.*-1885. Philosopher. Author The Nation: the Foundations of Civil Order
and Political Life in the U. S., and The Republic
of God. A clear, masterly thinker. *See Lit. World,
March 26, 1881. Pub. Hou.*

Mullany, Patrick F., " Brother Azarias." 1847 ——.
Educational writer. Author The Development of
Eng. Literature: Old Eng. Period. Philosophy of
Literature, Psychological Aspects of Education,
Address on Thinking, etc. *Pub. Apl. Clx. Ste.*

Munford, Wm. 1775 *Va.*-1825. Poet. Author of a
scholarly blank verse translation of the Iliad. *See
Griswold's Poets and Poetry of America.*

Munger, Theodore Thornton. 1830 *N. Y.* ——.
Congregationalist theologian. Author On the
Threshold and The Freedom of Faith. A thinker
of much force and originality. *See Atlantic
Monthly, July, 1883. Pub. Hou.*

Murdock, James. 1776 *Ct.*–1856. Congregationalist
theologian. Translator of Mosheim's Eccl. Hist.
Pub. Ca.

**Murphy, Lady Blanche Elizabeth Mary Annun-
ciata [Noel].** 1846 *E.*–1881. Writer of excellent
stories and sketches.

Murray, Lindley. 1745 *Pa.*–1826. Grammarian of
note. Author of a famous Grammar of the Eng.
Language, and several religious works. *Pub. Da.
Lip. Mur. Sa. Ze.*

Murray, Nicholas, "Kirwan." 1802 *I.*–1861. Con-
troversialist. Author Letters by Kirwan to Bishop
Hughes, etc. Style lively and keen. *See Life, by
Prime. Pub. Har. P. B.*

Nasby, Petroleum V. See Locke, D. R.

Neal, Alice B. See Haven, Mrs.

Neal, John. 1793 *Me.*–1876. Littérateur. A prolific
writer of novels, plays, poems, and essays, none of
which possess high merit. Wandering Recollections of a Somewhat Busy Life (1870) was his latest
work. *See Duyckinck's Cyc. Am. Lit. Pub. Rob.*

Neal, Joseph Clay. 1807 *N. H.*–1848. Humorist.
Author of the once popular Charcoal Sketches,
Peter Ploddy, etc. *See Griswold's Am. Prose
Writers.*

Nelson, David. 1793 *Ind.*–1844. Presbyterian theologian. Cause and Cure of Infidelity is his chief
work, and has been widely read.

Nevin, John Williamson. 1803 *Pa.*–1886. German

Ref. theologian. Pres. Franklin and Marshall Coll. The founder of the "Mercersburgh Theology." Author of many theological works of profound learning and much vigor of style. See Hist. and Genesis of the Heidelberg Catechism, etc.

Nevin, Wm. Wilberforce. 1836 *Pa.* ——. Son to J. W. N. Journalist. Author Vignettes of Travel, a work of much interest. *Pub. Lip.*

Newcomb, Harvey. 1803 *Ms.*–1863. Congregationalist religious writer. Author of more than a hundred moral and religious works, mainly juvenile in character. *Pub. Scr.*

Newcomb, Simon. 1835 *N. S.* ——. Astronomer. Author mathematical text-books of much value. *Pub. Apl. Har. Ho.*

Newell, Robert Henry, "Orpheus C. Kerr." 1836 *N. Y.* ——. Humorist. Author Versatilities : poems patriotic, sentimental, and humorous, etc. *Pub. Le.*

Newton, Reginald Heber. 1840 *Pa.* ——. Son to R. N. Broad Church theologian. Author Womanhood, The Morals of Trade, The Right and Wrong Uses of the Bible, The Book of the Beginnings, etc. A clear, bold thinker, whose views have attracted much attention. *Pub. Put. Ran. Wh.*

Newton, Richard. 1812 *E.*–1887. Low Church religious writer. Author The King's Highway, The Great Pilot, etc. *Pub. Ca.*

Newton, Wm. Wilberforce. 1843 *Pa.* ——. Son to R. N. Episcopal religious writer. Author of several religious works and a fine historical novel, The Priest and the Man, or Abelard and Héloise. Style strong and masterly. *Pub. Ca. Cu. Ran. Wh.*

Nichols, George Ward. 1831 *Me.*–1885. Littérateur. Author The Story of the Great March, Art

Education Applied to Industry, Pottery, etc. *Pub.
Har. Put.*

Niles, Hezekiah. 1777 *Del.*–1839. Journalist.
Founder of Niles's Register.

Niles, John Milton. 1787 *Ct.*–1856. Biographer.
Author Lives of Perry, Laurence, Pike, etc.

Noah, Mordecai Manuel. 1785 *Pa.*–1851. Journalist. Author of numerous essays and plays.

Noble, Annette Lucile. 1844 *N. Y.* ——. Novelist.
Author Uncle Jack's Executors, Eunice Lathrop:
Spinster, etc., and of numerous juvenile tales. *Pub.
A. T. S. Ho. Lo P. B. Put.*

Nordhoff, Charles. 1830 *P.* ——. Littérateur. Au-
thor Cape Cod and All Along Shore, California,
Communistic Societies of the U. S., Politics for
Young Americans, God and the Future Life, etc.
An able and versatile writer. *Pub. Apl. Do. Har.*

Norton, Andrews. 1786 *Ms.*–1853. Unitarian theologian. Historical Evidences of the Genuineness
of the Gospels is his chief work. The possessor
of a clear, scholarly style. *Pub. A. U. A.*

Norton, Charles Eliot. 1827 *Ms.* ——. Son to A.
N. Author of Historical Studies of Church Building in the Middle Ages, Notes of Travel and Study
in Italy, etc., and translator of Dante's Vita Nuova.
Pub. Har. Hou.

Norton, John. 1606 *E.*–1663. Puritan theologian.
The Life of John Cotton is his best known work.

Norton, John. 1651 *Ms.*–1716. Neph. to preceding.
Poet. Author of an Elegy on Anne Bradstreet, a
poem of some force and merit. *See Tyler's Am.
Lit. vol. 2.*

Norton, Sidney Andrews. 1835 *O.* ——. Author
Elements of Physics and other scientific text-
books. *Pub. Vab.*

Nott, Eliphalet. 1773 *Ct.*–1866. Presbyterian preacher. Pres. Union Coll. Author Counsels to Young Men and Lect. on Temperance.

Nott, Josiah Clark. 1804 *S. C.* ——. Ethnologist. Author The Physical Hist. of the Jewish Race, and co-author with Gliddon of the once famous Types of Mankind. *Pub. Lip.*

Noyes, George Rapall. 1798 *Ms.*–1868. Unitarian biblical scholar of note. Author annotated translations of the Psalms, Job, Ecclesiastes, Canticles, and the Prophets. *See N. A. Rev. Oct. 1832. Pub. A. U. A.*

Noyes, James O. 1829 *N. Y.* ——. Physician and journalist. Author Roumania, The Gypsies : their Hist., Origin, and Manner of Life.

Nuttall [nŭt′al], **Thomas.** 1786 *E.*–1859. Botanist. Author Manual of the Ornithology of the U. S. and Canada, etc.

Oakes, Urian. 1631 *E.*–1680. Puritan theologian. Chiefly remembered for a pathetic elegiac poem on his friend Thos. Shepard. *See Tyler's Am. Lit. vol. 2.*

O'Brien, Fitz James. c. 1828 *I.*–1862. Littérateur. *See Tales, Poems, and Sketches, with Memoir by Wm. Winter. Pub. Os.*

Odenheimer, Wm. Henry. 1817 *Pa.*–1879. Bp. N. J. Religious writer. Author Origin of the Prayer-Book, Essay on Canon Law, etc. A high authority on canon law and hymnology. *See Sermons, with Memoir. Pub. Dut. Ran.*

Oliver, Peter. 1821 *N. H.*–1855. Historian. Author Hist. of the Puritan Commonwealth. *Pub. Lit.*

Olmstead [ŭm′sted or ŏm′sted], **Denison.** 1791 *Ct.*–

1859. Scientist. Author Letters on Astronomy, Compendium Natural Philosophy, etc. *Pub. Clk. Col. Har.*

Olmsted, Frederick Law. 1822 *Ct.* ——. Author Walks and Talks of an Am. Farmer, Journey in the Seaboard Slave States, etc.

Onderdonk, Henry Ustick. 1789 *N. Y.*–1858. Bp. Pa. Religious writer. Author Episcopacy Tested by Scripture, a much-criticised work, Family Devotions, etc.

Optic, Oliver. See Adams, W. T.

O'Reilly, John Boyle. 1844 *I.* ——. Poet. Author Songs Legends and Ballads, Moondyne, The Statues in the Block and Other Poems, etc. *Pub. Rob.*

O'Reilly, Miles. See Halpine, C. G.

Orton, James. 1830 *N. Y.*–1877. Naturalist. Author Comparative Zoölogy, The Andes and the Amazon, etc. *Pub. Bai. Har.*

Osborn, John. 1713 *Ms.*–1753. Song writer. His Whaling Song was long popular among sailors.

Osborn, Laughton. 1806 *N. Y.*–1878. Novelist. Author Confessions of a Poet, Sixty Years of the Life of Jeremy Levis, etc. A writer of some power, whose works have been criticised as of questionable morality.

Osgood, Mrs. Frances Sargent [Locke]. 1812 *Ms.*–1850. Poet. Her verse is graceful and pleasing, and was once popular, but lacks enduring qualities.

Osgood, Kate Putnam. 1841 *Me.* ——. Poet and writer of sketches. Driving Home the Cows is her most popular poem.

Osgood, Samuel. 1812 *Ms.*–1880. Unitarian (later Episcopal) religious writer. Author Studies in

Christian Biography, God With Men, Mile-Stones in our Life-Journey, etc. *Pub. Dut. Har.*

Osmun, Thomas Embley, " Alfred Ayres." 18— *O.* ——. Orthoepist. Author The Verbalist, The Orthoepist, and an edition of Cobbett's Grammar. *See Lit. World, June 17, 1882. Pub. Apl. Fu.*

Ossoli [ŏs'o-lee], **Sarah Margaret [Fuller], Mar- ·chioness d'Ossoli.** 1810 *Ms.*–1850. Essayist and critic. A writer of rare gifts and wide learning, whose personality was greater than her writings. Author Woman in the Nineteenth Century, Art Literature and the Drama, etc. *See Memoir, by Emerson, W. H. Channing, and J. F. Clarke, Margaret Fuller Ossoli by Higginson in Am. Men of Letters, Mrs. J. W. Howe's Margaret Fuller in Famous Women, and Galaxy Mag. May, 1878.*

Otis, Harrison Gray. 1765 *Ms.*–1845. Son to J. O. Orator of eminence. Author Orations and Addresses.

Otis, James. 1725 *Ms.*–1783. Political writer. Author Rights of the British Colonies Asserted and Approved, Vindication of the British Colonies, etc. A writer of great vigor and force. *See Life, by G. Tudor.*

Owen, John J. 1803 *N. Y.*–1869. Author of several popular Greek text-books and biblical commentaries. *Pub. Apl. Scr.*

Owen, Robert Dale. 1801 *S.*–1877. Author Footfalls on the Boundary of Another World, Wrongs of Slavery, Beyond the Breakers, a novel, etc. A noted advocate of Spiritualism. *Pub. Car. Clx. Lip.*

Packard, Alpheus Spring, Jr. 1839 *Me.* ——. Naturalist. Editor The Am. Naturalist. Author Zoöl-

ogy, Outlines of Comparative Embryology, Guide
to the Study of Insects, Half-Hours with Insects,
etc. *Pub. Cass. Ho.*

Paige, Lucius Robinson. 1802 *Ms.* ——. Universalist biblical commentator. Author Commentary
on the New Testament, and a Hist. of Cambridge
1630–1877, with Genealogical Register. *Pub. Hou.*

Paine, Martyn. 1794 *Vt.*–1877. Physician. Author
Medical and Physiological Commentaries, Institutes of Medicine, etc. *Pub. Har.*

Paine, Robert Treat, Jr. 1773 *Ms.*–1811. Poet.
His verse in general has little merit, but his political song Adams and Liberty has preserved his
memory.

Paine, Thomas. 1737 *E.*–1809. Political and deistical writer. His pamphlet Common Sense (1776)
was of great influence in spreading republican
ideas. The Rights of Man was equally popular.
The Age of Reason is a deistical argument, of
little strength or scholarship. *See Lives by Chat-
ham, Carlile, G. Chalmers, G. Vale, and W. T.
Sherwin. Also Atlantic Monthly, July, Nov., and
Dec. 1859, Nineteenth Cent. March, 1879, McMaster's Hist. People of the U. S., and Watson's Men
and Times of the Revolution.*

Palfrey [pawl'frĭ], **Francis Winthrop.** 1831 *Ms.* ——.
Son to J. G. P. Author Antietam and Fredericks-
burg in Scribner's Campaigns of the Civil War,
Memoir Wm. Francis Bartlett, etc. *Pub. Hou. Scr.*

Palfrey, John Gorham. 1796 *Ms.*–1881. Historian.
His chief production is the Hist. of New England.
The work extends to the year 1765, and is an en-
during specimen of accurate scholarship. *Pub.
Lit. Os.*

Palfrey, Sarah Hammond, "E. Foxton." 18— *Ms.*–

——. Dau. to J. G. P. Novelist and poet. Author of the novels Katharine Morne and Herman, and several volumes of poems. *Pub. Le. Lip.*

Palmer, Mrs. Henrietta [Lee]. 1834 *Md.* ——. Wife to J. W. P. Author of The Stratford Gallery, Home Life in the Bible, etc. *Pub. Os.*

Palmer, John Williamson. 1825 *Md.* ——. Author The Queen's Heart: a comedy, and several translations, etc.

Palmer, Ray. 1808 *R. I.*–1887. Religious poet. His hymn "My Faith looks up to Thee " is that by which he is best known. *Pub. Bar. Ca. Ran.*

Palmer, Wm. Pitt. 1805 *Ms.*–1884. Poet. Author Light, Echoes of Half a Century, etc. *Pub. Put.*

Pansy. See Alden, Mrs.

Park, Edwards Amasa. 1808 *R. I.* ——. Congregationalist theologian. Of his numerous works, the Discourses and Treatises on the Atonement are the chief. *Pub. Dra.*

Parker, Joel. 1795 *N. H.*–1875. Jurist. Author legal works on The War Power of Congress, The Right of Secession, etc.

Parker, Joel. 1799 *Vt.*–1873. Presbyterian religious writer. Author of several popular religious works. *Pub. Har.*

Parker, Theodore. 1810 *Ms.*–1860. Unitarian radical theologian. His Sermons and other works, edited by Frances Power Cobbe, fill twelve vols. *See Life by John Weiss, Atlantic Monthly, Oct. 1860, N. A. Rev. April, 1864, and The Story of Theodore Parker by Miss Cobbe. Pub. Put.*

Parkman, Francis. 1823 *Ms.* ——. Historian. Author of The Oregon Trail, Conspiracy of Pontiac, Pioneers of France in the New World, The Jesuits in North America, The Old Régime in Canada,

Count Frontenac and New France, etc. His works all exhibit a thorough scholarship, the finest of literary art, and are of absorbing interest. He is also known as a high authority on the culture of roses. *See Atlantic Monthly, Nov. 1874. Pub. Lit.*

Parsons, Theophilus. 1750 *Ms.*–1813. Jurist. Chief Justice Mass. Author Commentaries on the Law of the U. S. *See Memoir, by his son.*

Parsons, Theophilus. 1797 *Ms.*–1882. Jurist and Swedenborgian theologian. Author of numerous legal works of value, The Ministry of Sorrow, Deus Homo, The Infinite and the Finite, etc. *Pub. Lip. Lit. Rob.*

Parsons, Thomas Wm. 1819 *Ms.* ——. Poet and physician. Author of a much-admired translation of Dante's Inferno. Of his poems, the Lines on the Death of Webster and On a Bust of Dante are the best. The latter, in fact, is one of the finest of modern poems. *Pub. Lit.*

Partington, Mrs. See Shillaber.

Parton, James. 1822 *E.* ——. Biographer. A prolific writer. Author of attractive biographies of Greeley, Aaron Burr, Andrew Jackson, Benj. Franklin, Jefferson, and Voltaire, Famous Americans, etc. His Life of Voltaire is his most important work. *Pub. Har. Hou.*

Parton, Mrs. Sarah Payson [Willis] [Eldridge], "Fanny Fern." 1811 *Me.*–1872. Wife to J. P. Sister to N. P. Willis. Essayist and novelist. Author Ruth Hall, Fern Leaves, Folly as it Flies, etc. Style pithy and vivacious.

Paul, John. See Webb, C. H.

Paulding, James Kirke. 1779 *Md.*–1860. Novelist and littérateur. Author John Bull and Brother

Jonathan, John Bull in America, The Dutchman's Fireside, Lay of the Scotch Fiddle, Westward Ho, etc. Style humorous and attractive. *See Life, by his son. Pub. Har. Scr.*

Payne, John Howard. 1792 *N. Y.*-1852. Dramatist. Author Brutus, Virginius, Charles II., etc. In Clari, the Maid of Milan, occurs the famous song, Home sweet home, his chief claim to remembrance. *See Lit. World, June 16, 1883, and Am. Magazine of Hist. May, 1881.*

Peabody, Andrew Preston. 1811 *Ms.* ——. Unitarian theologian. Author Sermons of Consolation, Lect. on Christian Doctrine, Christianity the Fruit of Nature, Moral Philosophy, Faults and Graces of Conversation, etc. The general excellence of his style is very marked. *Pub. A. U. A. Bar. Hou. Le. Rob. Sh.*

Peabody, Elizabeth Palmer. 1804 *Ms,* ——. Educational writer. Author Chronological Hist. U. S., Record of a School, Kindergarten Guide, etc. *Pub. Rob. Ste.*

Peabody, Ephraim. 1807 *N. H.*-1856. Unitarian religious writer and poet. Author Christian Days and Thoughts, etc.

Peabody, Oliver Wm. Bourne. 1799 *N. H.*-1848. Reviewer and Shakespearean editor.

Peabody, Wm. Bourne Oliver. 1799 *N. H.*-1847. Twin bro. to preceding. Poet and reviewer. Monadnock, Hymn of Nature, and Winter Night are some of his best poems.

Peale, Charles Wilson. 1741 *Md.*-1827. Artist and miscellaneous writer. *See Tuckerman's Book of the Artists.*

Peale, Rembrandt. 1778 *Pa.*-1860. Son to C. W. P. Artist. Author Notes on Italy, Portfolio of an

Artist, Graphics, etc. *See Tuckerman's Book of the Artists. Pub. For.*

Peck, George. 1797 *N. Y.*-1876. Methodist theologian. Author Christian Perfection, Early Methodism, etc. *See Life and Times of, by himself. Pub. Phi.*

Peck, Wm. Henry. 1830 *Ga.* ——. A prolific writer of inartistic, sensational novels. *See Davidson's Living Writers of the South.*

Peirce [pêrss], Benjamin. 1809 *Ms,*-1880. Mathematician of note. Author Ideality in the Physical Sciences, Hist. Harvard Univ., etc. A thinker of great analytical powers. *Pub. Le. Lit. Sev.*

Peirce, James Mill. 1834 *Ms.* ——. Son to B. P. Mathematical writer. *Pub. Gi.*

Penhallow, Samuel. 1665 *E.*-1726. Colonial historian. Author Hist. of the Wars of New England with the Eastern Indians. Style vivid and forcible. *See Tyler's Am. Lit. vol. 2.*

Percival, James Gates. 1795 *Ct.*-1856. Poet. and geologist. Author Prometheus, etc. Seneca Lake and the Coral Grove are his most familiar poems. His verse was once admired, but it lacks the finish which he seems to have had the genius but not the disposition to bestow upon it. *See Life and Letters, by Julius H. Ward.*

Percy, Florence. See Allen, Mrs.

Perkins, Charles C. 1823 *Ms.*-1886. Writer on art. Author Raphael and Michael Angelo, Tuscan Sculptors, Italian Sculptors, Historical Handbook of Italian Sculpture, etc. *Pub. Hou. Scr.*

Perkins, George Roberts. 1812 *N. Y.*-1876. Astronomical and mathematical writer. *Pub. Apl.*

Perkins, James Handasyd. 1810 *Ms.*-1849. Historical writer. Author Annals of the West, etc.

Perry, Arthur Lapham. 1830 *N. H.* ——. Political economist. Author Elements of Political Economy, etc. *Pub. Scr.*

Perry, Mary Alice. 1854 *Ms.*–1883. Novelist. Author Esther Pennefather, More Ways Than One, etc. *Pub. Har. Lo.*

Perry, Nora. 18—*R. I.* ——. Poet. Author After the Ball and Other Poems, Her Lover's Friend and Other Poems, The Tragedy of the Unexpected and Other Stories, etc. Her verse is graceful and musical. The Romance of a Rose is one of her finer poems. *Pub. Hou. Lo. Os.*

Perry, Thomas Sergeant. 1845 *R. I.* ——. Littérateur. Author English Literature in the Eighteenth Cent., Life of Lieber, etc. *See The American, April 28, 1883. Pub. Har. Os. Rob.*

Perry, Wm. Stevens. 1832 *R. I.* ——. Bp. Iowa. Historiographer. Author The Centennial Hist. of the American Episcopal Church, etc. The leading authority upon the history of the American Church. *Pub. Os. Wh.*

Peters, Mrs. Phillis [Wheatley]. 1754 *Sl.*–1784. Poet. Of African race. Her Poems on Various Occasions, Religious and Moral, appeared in London in 1772, and won a fleeting popularity. *See Griswold's Female Poets of America.*

Peters, Samuel. 1735 *Ct.*–1826. Author of a General Hist. of Connecticut, a curious work, full of satirical misrepresentations. *Pub. Apl.*

Peterson, Charles J. 1818 *Pa.*–1887. Novelist. Editor Peterson's Magazine. Author Kate Aylsford, Cruising in the Last War, Military Heroes of the U. S., etc.

Peterson, Henry. 1818 *Pa.* ——. Poet. Editor Saturday Evening Post. Author The Modern Job

9

and Other Poems. The Modern Job is a work of much thought and originality. *Pub. Clx. Lip.*

Peyton, John Lewis. 1824 *Va.* ——. Historical writer. Author Adventures of my Grandfather, Hist. of Augusta Co., Va., The American Crisis, etc. Style graphic and vigorous. *See Men of the Times, 10th ed. Pub. Sa. Wn. Yt.*

Phelps, Mrs. Almira [Hart] [Lincoln]. 1793 *Ct.* 1884. Educational writer of note. Author Familiar Lect. on Botany, Hours with my Pupils, etc. *See Mrs. Hale's Woman's Record. Pub. Bar. Clx. Lip.*

Phelps, Austin. 1820 *Ms.* ——, Congregationalist theologian. Author The Still Hour, The New Birth, The Theory of Preaching, English Style in Public Discourse, etc. Style logical, compact, and positive. *See London Lit. World, March 31, 1882. Pub. Dra. Lo. Ran. Scr.*

Phelps, Mrs. Elizabeth [Stuart]. 1815 *Ms.*–1852. Wife to A. P. Author Sunnyside, A Peep at No. 5, etc., works which were once widely popular. *Pub. Sh.*

Phelps, Elizabeth Stuart. 1844 *Ms.* ——. Dau. to two preceding. Novelist and poet. Author Gates Ajar, Hedged In, The Silent Partner, Sealed Orders, Men Women and Ghosts, Friends: a Duet, Dr. Zay, Beyond the Gates, Poetic Studies, etc. Style intense, emphatic, and always strikingly original. *Pub. Hou.*

Phillips, Wendell. 1811 *Ms.*–1884. Orator of eminence. *Pub. Le.*

Phœnix, John. See Derby, George.

Piatt [pē-ăt'], John James. 1835 *O.* ——. Poet. Author Landmarks, Western Windows, Poems of House and Home, etc. His verse is always graceful and tender, his finest poem being The Morning

Street. He has been styled "The poetic voice of Ohio." *See Atlantic Monthly, May, 1866. Pub. Clke. Hou.*

Piatt, Mrs. Sarah Morgan [Bryan]. 1836 *Ky.* ——. Wife to J. J. P. Poet. Author of A Woman's Poems, A Voyage to the Fortunate Isles, That New World, Dramatic Persons and Moods, etc. Her poetry is strongly dramatic in tone and exquisitely tender and pathetic in sentiment. Love Stories, The Black Princess, The Favorite Child, and Sometime, are some of her most striking poems. *See Wide Awake Mag. Nov. 1876, and Atlantic Monthly, Jan. 1877. Pub. Hou. Lo.*

Pickering, Charles. 1805 *Pa.*-1878. Naturalist. Author Races of Men and their Geographical Distribution, Geographical Distribution of Animals and Men, and Chronological History of Plants.

Pickering, Edward Charles. 1846 *Ms.* ——. Son to C. P. Author Elements of Physical Manipulation. *Pub. Hou.*

Pickering, John. 1777 *Ms.*-1846. Linguist. His most important work, a Greek and English Lexicon, still continues popular. *Pub. Lip.*

Pierpont, John. 1785 *Ct.*-1866. Poet and educational writer. Author Airs of Palestine, etc. Passing Away is one of his best known poems. *See Atlantic Monthly, Dec. 1866. Pub. Lip.*

Pike, Albert. 1809 *Ms.* ——. Poet. Author Hymns to the Gods, etc. *See Griswold's Poets and Poetry of America.*

Pinckney, Henry Laurens. 1794 *S. C.*-1863. Political writer.

Pinkney, Edward Coate. 1802 *E.*-1828. Poet. Some of his lyrics possess much beauty. *See Griswold's Poets and Poetry of America.*

Pise [pize], **Charles Constantine.** 1802 *Md.*–1866. R. C. ecclesiologist. Author Hist. of the Church to the Reformation, The Acts of the Apostles in Blank Verse, etc.

Plumer, Wm. Swan. 1802 *Pa.*–1880. Presbyterian theologian. Author Pastoral Theology, Jehovah-jireh, Studies in the Book of Psalms, etc. *Pub. Clx. Har. Lip. P. B. Ran.*

Poe, Edgar Allan. 1809 *Ms.*–1849. Poet and ro-mancer. Author of The Bells, The Raven, Annabel Lee, etc., and numerous powerful sketches : The Gold Bug, The Fall of the House of Usher, etc. His prose style is ingenious, original, and morbid. His verse possesses wonderful melody, and shows great mastery of metrical technicalities. As to this last, however, some few critics, including Henry James, Jr., and Edgar Fawcett, have dissented. *See Memoirs by Stoddard, Didier, and Ingram, Fortnightly Rev. July, 1880, Lit. World, Dec. 16, 1882, Poe and his Critics by Mrs. Whitman, Essay on Poe's Poetry by Andrew Lang, Critical Essay on by Stedman, and Poe by G. E. Woodberry in Am. Men of Letters. Pub. Arm. Os. Por. Wid.*

Pollard, Edward A. 1833 *Va.*–1872. His most important work is The Lost Cause, a history of the Civil War from a Southern standpoint. *Pub. Lip.*

Pollard, Josephine. 18— *N. Y.* ——. Poet and miscellaneous writer. Author of The Decorative Sisters, The Boston Tea-Party, etc. *Pub. Ran.*

Pond, Enoch. 1791 *Ms.*–1882. Congregationalist theologian. Author Text-Book of Eccl. Hist., Pas-toral Theology, etc. *See Autobiography. Pub. C. P. S. Dra.*

Poole, Wm. Frederick. 1821 *Ms.* ——. Author of

an invaluable Index to Subjects in Reviews and Periodicals, Anti-Slavery Opinions before 1800, etc. *Pub. Clke. Os.*

Poore, Benjamin Perley. 1820 *Ms.*–1887. Journalist. Author Rise and Fall of Louis Philippe, Political Register 1776–1878, etc. *Pub. Hou.*

Porter, Ebenezer. 1772 *Ct.*–1834. Educational and religious writer. His Rhetorical Reader reached its 300th edition.

Porter, Noah. 1811 *Ct.* ——. Psychologist. Author The Human Intellect, Books and Reading, etc. *See Allibone's Dict. Pub. Do. Scr.*

Potter, Alonzo. 1800 *N. Y.*–1865. Bp. Pa. Educational and religious writer. Author Religious Philosophy, Political Economy, etc. Co-author with G. B. Emerson of The School and the Schoolmaster. Style earnest and popular. *See Memoirs of. Pub. Har. Lip.*

Potter, Henry Codman. 1835 *N. Y.* ——. Son to A. P. Asst. Bp. N. Y. Broad Church religious writer. Author Sermons of the City, The Gates of the East, etc. *Pub. Dut.*

Powell, Thomas. 1809 *E.*–1887. Dramatist. Author True at Last, The Shepherd's Well, etc. Tales from Boccaccio, Florentine Tales, etc.

Powers, Horatio Nelson. 1826 *N. Y.* ——. Poet and critic. Author Early and Late, Through the Year, a vol. of religious essays, etc. Deukalion and Ariss are among his finer poems. *See Lit. World, Dec. 1, 1883. Pub. Jan. Rob.*

Pratt, Mrs. Ella [Farman]. 18— *N. Y.* ——. Editor of The Wide Awake. Author Good-for-Nothing Polly, A Girl's Money, and other excellent and helpful juvenile tales. *Pub. Lo.*

Pray, Isaac. 1813 *Ms.* ——. Dramatist and poet.

Co-author with Boucicault of The Corsican Brothers.

Prentice, George Denison. 1802 *Ct.*-1870. Journalist and poet. Editor The Louisville Journal 1831–1870. His prose style is witty and satirical. Some of his poems are excellent, among the best being The Flight of Years. *See Poems with Memoir by J. J. Piatt, also Lippincott's Mag. Nov. 1869, and Harper's Mag. Jan. 1875. Pub. Clke.*

Prentiss, Mrs. Elizabeth [Payson]. 1818 *Me.*-1878. Religious fictionist. Author Pemaquid, The Home at Graylock, etc. Stepping Heavenward, her most noted book, has been widely popular. *See Life, 1882. Pub. Ran.*

Prescott, Wm. Hickling. 1796 *Ms.*-1850. Historian. Author Hist. Reign of Ferdinand and Isabella, The Conquest of Mexico, The Conquests of Peru, Robertson's Charles V., Hist. Philip II., and Biographical and Critical Miscellanies. Style clear, picturesque, and tolerant. *See Life by Geo. Ticknor, and Allibone's Dict. See Kirk's edition, 15 vols. Pub. Lip.*

Preston, Harriet Waters. 18— *Ms.* ——. Poet and littérateur. Author Aspendale, Love in the Nineteenth Century, Troubadours and Trouvères, and numerous translations from the Latin, French, and Provençal. A high authority upon Provençal literature. *Pub. Rob.*

Preston, Mrs. Margaret [Junkin]. 1838 *Va.* ——. Poet. Author Old Song and New, Beechenbrook, Cartoons, etc. A writer of much grace and power of expression. *Pub. Lip.*

Preston, Thomas Scott. 1824 *Ct.* ——. Roman Catholic theologian. Author Protestantism and the Bible, Reason and Revelation, Christ and the Church, etc. *Pub. Cath. Cod.*

Prime, Benjamin Young. 1733 *L. I.*-1791. Poet and physician. Author The Patriot Muse, etc.

Prime, Edward Dorr Griffin. 1814 *N. Y.* ——. Son to N. S. P. Traveler. Author Around the World, Letters of Eusebius, etc. *Pub. Ca. Har.*

Prime, Nathaniel Scudder. 1785 *L. I.*-1856. Son to B. Y. P. Author Hist. Long Island, etc.

Prime, Samuel Irenæus. 1812 *N. Y.*-1885. Son to N. S. P. Presbyterian religious writer. Editor N. Y. Observer. Author Five Years of Prayer, Irenæus Letters, etc. *Pub. Apl. Ca. Har. Ran. Scr.*

Prime, Wm. Cowper. 1825 *N. Y.* ——. Son to N. S. P. Littérateur. Author Boat Life in Egypt, Tent Life in the Holy Land, Pottery and Porcelain, etc. *Pub. Har.*

Prince, Thomas. 1687 *Ms.*-1758. Annalist. Author Chronological Hist. of New England. *See Tyler's Am. Lit. vol. 2.*

Proctor, Edna Dean. 18— *N. H.* ——. Author Poems, A Russian Journey, etc. Style graceful and piquant. *Pub. Hou.*

Pumpelly, Raphael. 1837 *N. Y.* ——. Geologist. Author Geological Researches in China, Across America and Asia, Notes of a Five Years' Journey Around the World, etc. *Pub. Ho.*

Punchard, George. 1806 *Ms.*-1881. Ecclesiologist. Author Hist. Congregationalism from A. D. 250. *Pub. C. P. S. Dra.*

Putnam, Mrs. Mary [Lowell]. 1810 *Ms.* ——. Sister to J. R. Lowell. Author Records of an Obscure Man, Tragedy of Errors, Tragedy of Success, etc.

Pynchon, Thomas Ruggles. 1823 *Ct.* ——. Scientist. Author Heat Light and Electricity.

Quackenbos, George Payn. 1826 *N. Y.*–1881. Educational writer. Author of numerous popular text-books on rhetoric, grammar, and history. *Pub. Apl.*

Quincy, Edmund. 1808 *Ms.*–1877. Son to Pres. J. Quincy. Essayist. Author of Wensley, a novel, etc., and an admirable biography of his father. *See Edmund Quincy, by S. H. Gay, in Am. Men of Letters. Pub. Os.*

Quincy, Josiah, Jr. 1744 *Ms.*–1775. Orator and political essayist. Author of Observations on the Boston Port Bill. *See Life, by his son.*

Quincy, Josiah. 1772 *Ms.*–1864. Son to preceding. Political and historical writer. Pres. Harvard Univ. Author Hist. Harvard Univ., Speeches and Orations in Congress, Hist. of Boston, etc. *See Life by E. Quincy, and Duyckinck's Cyc. Am. Lit. vol. 1. Pub. Lit.*

Quincy, Josiah. 1802 *Ms.*–1882. Son to preceding. Author Figures of the Past. *Pub. Rob.*

Quincy, Josiah Phillips. 1830 *Ms.* ——. Poet and littérateur. Author The Protection of Majorities and Other Papers, etc. *Pub. Rob.*

Ramsay, David. 1749 *Pa.*–1815. Historian. Author Hist. Am. Revolution, Hist. U. S., Life of Washington, etc. A writer of great industry and careful research. *See Tuckerman's Sketch of Am. Lit.*

Randall, James Ryder. 1839 *Md.* ——. Lyric poet. Author of the famous song Maryland, my Maryland.

Randall, Samuel S. 1809 *N. Y.* ——. Educational writer. Author Popular Education, Walks with the Poets and Philosophers, Conduct and Charac-ter, etc. *Pub. Har.*

Randolph, Anson Davies Fitz. 1820 *N. J.* ——.
Poet and publisher. Author Hopefully Waiting,
etc. *Pub. Scr.*

Raphall, Morris Jacob. 1798 *Sn.*-1868. Jewish
theologian of note. Author Post-Biblical Hist. of
the Jews, Literature of the Jews in Spain, Social
Condition of the Jews, etc. *Pub. Apl.*

Ray, Isaac. 1807 *Ms.*-1881. Physician. Author
Medical Jurisprudence of Insanity, etc. *Pub. Lit.*

Ray, Joseph. 1807 *Va.*-1855. Mathematical writer.
Pub. Va.

Raymond, Henry Jarvis. 1820 *N. Y.*-1869. Journalist. Founder of the N. Y. Times. Author Life
of Lincoln, etc. *See Maverick's Raymond and the
N. Y. Press.*

Read, Thomas Buchanan. 1822 *Pa.*-1872. Poet and
artist. Author The New Pastoral, The House by
the Sea, The Wagoner of the Alleghanies, etc.
Sheridan's Ride and Drifting are his most famous
poems. The Closing Scene, though less known, is
one of the finest American poems. He was a poet
of delicate fancy, whose fame is not equal to his
deserts. *See Lit. World, Oct. 21, 1882. See complete edition 1882. Pub. Lip.*

Realf, Richard. 1834 *E.*-1878. Poet. Indirection
and Nil Nisi Bonum are among his most striking
poems. *See Lippincott's Mag. Feb. 1879.*

Redden, Laura C. See Searing, Mrs.

Reed, Henry. 1808 *Pa.*-1854. Critic and lecturer.
Author Lect. on English Hist., Lect. on English
Literature, Lect. on the British Poets, etc. Style
scholarly and discriminating. *See Memoir, by Wm.
B. Reed. Pub. Clx.*

Reed, Wm. Bradford. 1806 *Pa.*-1876. Bro. to
H. R. Critic and biographer.

Reese, David Meredith. 1800 *Pa.*–1861. Educational and miscellaneous writer. *Pub. Bar.*

Reid, Christian. See Fisher, Frances.

Reid, Whitelaw. 1839 *O.* ——. Journalist. Editor N. Y. Tribune. Author Newspaper Tendencies, etc. *See Hart's Am. Lit. Pub. Ho.*

Renwick, James. 1792 *N. Y.*–1863. Scientific writer of note. *Pub. Har.*

Requier, Augustus Julian. 1825 *S. C.* ——. Author of the dramas Marco Bozzaris and The Spanish Exile, and of romances and poems.

Richardson, Mrs. Abby [Sage]. 18— ——. Wife to A. D. R. Littérateur. Author Familiar Talks on English Literature, Stories from Old English Poetry, Hist. of Our Country, Abelard and Héloise, etc. *Pub. Hou. Jan. Os.*

Richardson, Albert D. 1833 *Ms.*–1869. Journalist. Author Beyond the Mississippi, etc. Style graphic and fluent. *See Memoir.*

Richardson, Charles Francis. 1851 *Me.* ——. Littérateur. Author Primer of Am. Literature, etc., and co-editor with H. A. Clark of The College Book. *See Lit. World, Oct. 1878. Pub. Hou.*

Riddle, Albert Gallatin. 1816 *Ms.* ——. Novelist. Author The House of Ross, Bart Ridgely, Alice Brand, etc. Style realistic and original. *See Lit. World, April 23, 1881. Pub. Apl. Hal.*

Rideing, Wm. Henry. 1853 *E.* ——. Littérateur.

Riley, James Whitcomb. 1854 *Ind.* ——. Poet. Author The Old Swimmin' Hole and 'Leven More Poems.

Ripley, George. 1802 *Ms.*–1880. Chief editor of the Am. Cyc., and literary editor of the N. Y. Tribune. A critic of wide culture and extended influence. *See Modern Rev. July, 1883, and Frothingham's Ripley in Am. Men of Letters.*

Ripley, Henry Jones. 1798 *Ms.*-1875. Baptist theologian. Author Notes on the Gospels, etc. *Pub.*
Sh.

Ritchie, Mrs. Anna Cora [Ogden][Mowatt]. 1822
F.-1870. Actress and littérateur. Author the dramas Fashion and Armand, the novels The Fortune
Hunter, The Mute Singer, etc., and the noted Autobiography of an Actress, which see.

Rittenhouse, David. 1732 *Pa.*-1796. Scientist of
note. *See Life by Renwick, and Harper's Mag.*
May, 1882.

Ritter, Frederick Louis. 1834 *F.* ——. Writer on
music. Author Music in England, Music in America, Hist. of Music in the Form of Lectures, and
Student's Hist. of Music. *Pub. Scr.*

Rivers, Wm. James. 1822 *S. C.* ——. Historian.
Author Hist. of South Carolina to the Close of the
Proprietary Government.

Rives [reevz], Wm. Cabell. 1793 *Va.*-1868. Biographer. Author Lives of John Hampden, James
Madison, etc.

Robbins, Chandler. 1810 *Ms.*-1882. Unitarian religious writer. Author Liturgy for the Use of a
Christian Church, etc. *Pub. A. U. A.*

Robbins, Royall. 1787 *Ct.*-1861. Historical writer.
Author Outlines of Ancient Hist., The World Displayed, etc. *Pub. Bro.*

Robinson, Edward. 1794 *Ct.*-1863. Biblical schol-
ar. Author Biblical Researches in the Holy Land,
Harmony of the Four Gospels, etc. *See London*
Quarterly Rev. Dec. 1841, N. A. Rev. April,
1851, and Life by R. D. Hitchcock. Pub. Har.
Hou.

Robinson, Horatio Nelson. 1806 *N. Y.*-1867.
Mathematical writer. *Pub. Iv.*

Robinson, John Hovey. 1825 *Me.* ——. Physician and sensational novelist.

Robinson, Mrs. Martha Harrison. 18– *Va.* ——. Author of several excellent translations from the French and the novel Helen Erskine. *Pub. Lip.*

Robinson, Solon. 1803 *Ct.*–1880. Agricultural writer of note, but once best known by his sensational novel Hot Corn.

Robinson, Stuart. 1816 *I.*–1881. Presbyterian theologian. Author Discourses of Redemption, etc. *Pub. Apl.*

Robinson, Mrs. Thérèse Albertine [Von Jakob], "Talvi." 1797 *G.*–1870. Wife to E. R. A writer of great learning and ability. Her principal English work is a Historical View of the Language and Literature of the Slavic Nations. She wrote much in German under the pseudonym Talvi. *Pub. Apl.*

Robinson, Wm. S., "Warrington." 1810 *Ms.*–1876. Journalist. Style vigorous and independent. *See Warrington's Pen Portraits with Memoir by Mrs. Robinson. Pub. Le.*

Rockwell, James Otis. 1807 *Ct.*–1831. Poet. Lost at Sea is one of his best poems. *See Griswold's Poets and Poetry of America.*

Roe, Azel Stevens. 1798 *N. Y.*–1886. Novelist. True to the Last, A Long Look Ahead, and Time and Tide are some of his most popular novels. *Pub. Car.*

Roe, Edward Payson. 1838 *N. Y.*–1888. Novelist. Author Barriers Burned Away, Opening a Chestnut Burr, A Face Illumined, His Sombre Rivals, and other religious, semi-sensational, and popular tales. Style pretentious and labored. *Pub. Do.*

Rogers, Wm. Barton. 1805 *Pa.*–1882. Scientist. Author Elements of Mechanical Philosophy, etc.

Rolfe, Wm. James. 1827 *Ms.* ——. Shakespearean scholar. Editor of an annotated edition of Shakespeare in 40 vols., and of Craik's English of Shakespeare; co-author with J. H. Hanson of several classical text-books, and with J. A. Gillet of The Cambridge Physics. *See Lit. World, Oct. 1878. Pub. Har. Os. Pot.*

Rollins, Mrs. Alice Marland [Wellington]. 1847 *Ms.* ——. Poet. Author The Ring of Amethyst. Her verse is all of a high character, the sonnets being particularly fine. *Pub. Put.*

Rollins, Mrs. Ellen Chapman [Hobbs], "E. H. Arr." 1831 *N. H.*–1881. Author New England Bygones, and Old-Time Child-life. *See illustrated edition of the former, with Memoir by Gail Hamilton, 1882. Pub. Lip.*

Root, George Frederick. 1820 *Ms.* ——. Composer. Author of several valuable musical text-books.

Round, Wm. Marshall Fitz. 1845 *R. I.* ——. Novelist and juvenile writer. Author Achsah, Child Marian Abroad, Torn and Mended, Hal and Rosecroft. *Pub. Le. Lo. Wd.*

Rowson, Mrs. Susanna [Haswell]. 1761 *E.*–1824. Novelist. Of her numerous works, the famous Charlotte Temple is best remembered.

Royall, Mrs. Anne. 1769 *Va.*–1854. Novelist and journalist. Author The Black Book, The Tennesseans, etc. Style bitter, vindictive, and personal, and of little merit.

Ruffner, Henry. 1790 *Va.*–1861. Presbyterian religious writer. Author Fathers of the Desert: a Hist. of Monachism, etc.

Rumford, Count. See Thompson, Benj.

Rupp, Isaac Daniel. 1803 *Pa.*–18——. Historian.

Author histories of many Pennsylvania counties,
and An Original Hist. of Religious Denominations
in the United States.

Ruschenberger [roo'shĕn-ber-g̃er], **Wm. S. W.** 1807
N. Y. ——. Surgeon and naturalist. Elements of
Natural Hist., A Voyage Around the World, and
Three Weeks in the Pacific are some of his more
important works. *Pub. Clx.*

Rush, Benjamin. 1745 *Pa.*–1813. Physician. Author Treatise on Diseases of the Mind, and other
valuable medical works. *See Thacher's Medical
Biography.*

Rush, James. 1786 *Pa.*–1869. Son to B. R. Physician. Best known by his standard and exhaustive work The Philosophy of the Human Voice.
The Founder of the Ridgeway Library at Philadelphia. *Pub. Lip.*

Russell, Wm. 1798 *S.*–1873. Elocutionist. Author
Pulpit Elocution, Vocal Culture, etc. *Pub. Den.
Hou.*

Ryan, Abram J., " Father Ryan." 1840 *Va.*–1886.
Poet. Author Poems. Style graceful and fluent.
See edition 1881. Pub. Pi.

Sabine, Lorenzo. 1803 *N. H.*–1877. Historical writer. Author The American Loyalists, etc. *Pub. Lit.*

Sadlier [săd-leer'], **Mrs. Mary Anne [Madden].**
1820 *I.* ——. Novelist and writer of Roman Catholic Sunday-school tales. Author Alice Riordan,
Red Hand of Ulster, etc. *Pub. Sad.*

Samson, George Whitefield. 1819 *Ms.* ——. Author Elements of Art Criticism, Physical Media in
Spiritualism, The Atonement, etc. *Pub. Lip.*

Sanborn, Franklin Benjamin. 1831 *N. H.* ——.
Littérateur. Author Thoreau, in Am. Men of Letters, etc.

Sanderson, John. 1783 *Pa.*-1844. Humorist. Author The American in Paris, and The American in England. Style witty and genial.

Sands, Robert Charles. 1799 *N. Y.*-1832. Poet. Co-author with Eastburn of the once noted poem Yamoyden. *See Life by Verplanck, and Griswold's Poets and Poetry of America.*

Sangster, Mrs. Margaret E. [Munson]. 1838 *N. Y.*
——. Poet and miscellaneous writer. Author Poems of the Household, etc. *Pub. A. T. S. Os.*

Sargent, Epes. 1812 *Ms.*-1880. Poet and littérateur. Author several dramas, and the familiar poem Life on the Ocean Wave. Editor of a popular series of school-books, critical editions of many English poets, and a Cyc. of Poetry. *Pub. Bu. Des. Har. Rob.*

Sargent, John Osborne. 1811 *Ms.* ——. Bro. to E. S. Translator of Grün's Last Knight. *See Harvard Register, June, 1881. Pub. Hou.*

Sargent, Lucius Manlius. 1786 *Ms.*-1867. Temperance writer of note. Author Temperance Tales, Dealings with the Dead, etc.

Sargent, Winthrop. 1825 *Pa.* ——. Historical writer. Author Life of Major André, Hist. Braddock's Expedition, etc. A careful, impartial historian. *Pub. Lip.*

Saunders, Frederick. 1807 *E.* ——. Littérateur. Author Salad for the Solitary, Salad for the Social, New York in a Nut-Shell, etc. *Pub. Car. Ran. Wh.*

Savage, James. 1784 *Ms.*-1873. Genealogist. Author of a Genealogical Dict. of the First Settlers of New England, which has been called the most stupendous work on genealogy ever written.

Savage, Minot Judson. 1841 *Me.* ——. Unitarian theologian. Author Christianity the Science of

Manhood, Beliefs About Man, Belief in God, Life Questions, Poems, etc. An extremely radical thinker. *Pub. El. Le. Loc.*

Saxe, John Godfrey. 1816 *Vt.*-1887. Humorous poet. The Proud Miss McBride, The Money King, and The Rhyme of the Rail are some of his best known poems. Among his graver poems are several sonnets, which are masterpieces of their kind. *Pub. Hou.*

Say, Thomas. 1787 *Pa.*-1834. Naturalist. Author Am. Entomology. *See Le Conte's edition, with Memoir by Ord. Pub. Cass.*

Schaeffer [shä-fer], Charles Wm. 1813 *Md.* ——. Ecclesiologist. Author Early Hist. of the Lutheran Church in the U. S., etc. *Pub. L. P. S.*

Schaff [shäf], Philip. 1819 *Sd.* ——. German Reformed theologian. Author Principles of Protestantism, Hist. of the Christian Church, etc. A prolific writer, whose edition of Lange's Commentary is his greatest work. *See Lit. World, June 20, 1883. Pub. Do. Har. Scr.*

Schem, Alexander Jacob. 1826 *G.*-1881. Statistical and historical writer. *Pub. Le.*

Schliemann, Heinrich. 1822 *P.* ——. Archæologist. Author Troy and its Remains, Mycenæ and Tiryns, Ilios : the City and Country of the Trojans, and Troja. *Pub. Har. Scr.*

Schmucker, Samuel M. 1823 *Va.*-1863. Son to S. S. S. Historian. Author Hist. of the Four Georges, Hist. All Religions, Court and Reign of Catharine II., etc. *Pub. Por. Pott.*

Schmucker, Samuel S. 1799 *Md.*-1873. Lutheran theologian. Author Psychology, etc. *Pub. Har.*

Schoolcraft, Henry Rowe. 1793 *N. Y.*-1864. Ethnologist. The chief of his many valuable works is his Historical Information Concerning the Indian Tribes. *Pub. Clx. Lip.*

Schuyler [sky'lẹr]**, Eugene.** 1840 *N. Y.* ——. Historical writer. Author Peter the Great as Ruler and Reformer, Turkistan, etc. *Pub. Scr.*

Scott, Wm. Anderson. 1813 *Tn.*–188-. Presbyterian theologian. Author The Bible and Politics, Strauss and Renan, The Pacific Expositor, etc. *Pub. P. B.*

Scudder, Horace Elisha. 1838 *Ms.* ——. Littérateur. Author Dream-Children, Stories from my Attic, The Dwellers in Five-Sisters' Court, Stories and Romances, Noah Webster in Am. Men of Letters, the Bodley Books, etc., and editor Am. Poems, Am. Prose, etc. *Pub. Hou.*

Scudder, Samuel Hubbard. 1837 *Ms.* ——. Bro. to H. E. S. Naturalist. Author Butterflies, and numerous scientific monographs. Editor Science. *Pub. Ho.*

Seabury, Samuel. 1801 *Ct.*–1872. High Church theologian. Author Continuity of the Church of England, Mary the Virgin, etc.

Searing, Mrs. Laura C. [Redden], "Howard Glyndon." 1842 *Md.* ——. Poet. Author Sounds from Secret Chambers. *Pub. Hou.*

Sears, Barnas. 1802 *Ms.*–1880. Baptist religious writer. Author Life of Luther, etc.

Sears, Edmund Hamilton. 1810 *Ms.*–1876. Unitarian theologian and poet. Author Regeneration, Foregleams and Foreshadows of Immortality, The Heart of Christ, etc., and the beautiful Christmas hymn " Calm on the listening ear of night." *Pub. Clx. Le. Loc.*

Seccomb, John. 1708 *Ms.*–1792. Humorous rhymer. Author Father Abbey's Will, a once famous piece

of doggerel. *See Tyler's Am. Lit. vol. 2, and Hart's
Am. Lit.*

Sedgwick, Catharine Maria. 1789 *Ms.*–1867. Novelist. Author Hope Leslie, Redwood, etc. Her
juvenile tales, of which Live and Let Live and
Poor Rich Man and Rich Poor Man are good examples, were both excellent and popular. *See Life
and Letters, 1871. Pub. Har. Put.*

Sedgwick, Mrs. Susan [Ridley]. 1789–1867. Wife
to T. S. Writer for the young. Author Walter
Thornley, etc. *Pub. Har.*

Sedgwick, Theodore. 1781 *Ms.*–1839. Bro. to C.
M. S. Jurist. Author Public and Private Economy, Hints to my Countrymen, etc. *See Democratic Rev. Feb. 1840.*

Seelye, Julius Hawtry. 1824 *Ct.* ——. Congregationalist religious writer. Pres. Amherst Coll.
Author Natural Religion, etc. *Pub. Do.*

Seemuller, Mrs. Annie Moncure [Crane]. 1838
Md.–1872. Novelist. Author Emily Chester, Reginald Archer, and Opportunity. Style ingenious,
but somewhat morbid.

Seiss [seess], Joseph Augustus. 1823 *Md.* ——.
Lutheran theologian. The Gospel in the Stars
and The Miracle in Stone are among his chief
works. Style ingenious and imaginative. *Pub.
Lip. Por.*

Sewall, Jonathan Mitchell. 1748 *Ms.*–1808. Poet.
His verse is for the most part forgotten, but his
song War and Washington is yet remembered, and
he was the author of the famous couplet : —

> " No pent-up Utica contracts your powers,
>   But the whole boundless continent is yours."

Sewall, Samuel. 1652 *E.*–1730. Jurist and religious writer. Author The Selling of Joseph, etc.

See Diary of, Tyler's Am. Lit. vol. 2, and Whittier's Prophecy of Samuel Sewall.

Sewall, Thomas. 1787 *Me.*–1849. Physician. Author of a noted work on The Pathology of Drunkenness.

Seward, Wm. Henry. 1801 *N. Y.*–1872. Statesman. Author Diplomatic Hist. of the Civil War, Orations and Speeches, Life J. Q. Adams, etc. *See Autobiography, N. A. Rev. Oct. 1866, and Bartlett's Modern Agitators. Pub. Apl. Por. Complete works, pub. Hou.*

Sharswood, George. 1810 *Pa.*–1883. Jurist of note. Author Law Lectures, Professional Ethics, etc. *Pub. Jo.*

Shaw, Henry W., "Josh Billings." 1818 *Ms.*–1885. Humorist. A writer of much shrewd sense expressed in a pithy, sententious style. *Pub. Car.*

Shaw, Lemuel. 1781 *Ms.*–1861. Jurist of note.

Shea [shā], George. 1827 *I.* ——. Author Alexander Hamilton: a Historical Study, and Nature and Form of the Am. Government. *Pub. Hou.*

Shea, John Augustus. 1802 *I.*–1845. Poet. Author Adolph, Parnassian Wild Flowers, etc.

Shea, John Gilmary. 1824 *N. Y.* ——. Historian. Author The Catholic Church in the U. S., Legendary Hist. of Ireland, Hist. Catholic Indian Missions, etc., translator and editor of Charlevoix's New France, Memoirs and Relations concerning the French Colonies in America, etc. A careful, accurate writer, whose books are of substantial worth. *Pub. Cath. Pi. Sa.*

Shedd, Wm. Greenough Thayer. 1820 *Ms.* —— Presbyterian theologian. Author Hist. of Christian Doctrine, Sermons to the Natural Man, etc. *Pub. Dra. Ran. Scr.*

Shelton, Frederick Wm. 1814 *L. I.*–1881. Humorous and satirical writer. Author The Trollopiad, The Rector of St. Bardolph's, Peeps from the Belfry, etc. *Pub. Wh.*

Shepard, Thomas. 1605 *E.*–1649. Puritan theologian. *See Sermons (3 vols. 1853); also Tyler's Am. Lit. vol. I.*

Sheppard, Furman. 1823 *N. J.* ——. Legal writer. Author Constitutional Text-Book, etc. *Pub. Lo.*

Sherman, Frank Dempster. 1860 *N. Y.* ——. Poet. Author of Madrigals and Catches. *Pub. W.*

Sherman, John. 1772 *Ct.*–1828. Unitarian theologian. Author One God in one Person Only, the first noteworthy defense of Unitarianism in America. *See Sprague's Annals Am. Pulpit.*

Sherwood, John D. 1818 *N. Y.* ——. Littérateur. Author Comic Hist. of the U. S. and numerous magazine articles. *Pub. Hou.*

Shields, Charles Woodruff. 1825 *Ind.* ——. Presb. theologian. Author The Final Philosophy, Religion and Science in their Relations to Philosophy, etc. *Pub. Scr.*

Shillaber, Benjamin P., "Mrs. Partington." 1814 *N. H.* ——. Humorist. Author Life and Sayings of Mrs. Partington, etc. *Pub. Le. Pott.*

Shindler, Mrs. Mary Stanley Bunce [Palmer] [Dana]. 1810 *S. C.* ——. Poet. Best known as the author of The Northern Harp and The Southern Harp.

Sigourney [sĭg′or-nĭ], **Mrs. Lydia Howard [Huntly].** 1791 *Ct.*–1865. Author of some fifty vols. of prose and verse. Of the former, Post Meridian, Letters to My Pupils, and Letters to Young Ladies are the best known examples. Her verse, once so highly praised, has but few readers now. It is graceful and pleasing, but lacks force. *See Griswold's Female Poets of America. Pub. Apl. Bro. Ca. Har. Pott.*

Sikes, Mrs. Olive [Logan]. 1841 *N. Y.* ———. Wife to W. W. S. Dramatist and lecturer. Author of several plays and miscellaneous works. An acute and versatile writer.

Sikes, Wm. Wirt. 1836 *N. Y.*-1883. Miscellaneous writer. Author British Goblins: Welsh Folk-Lore, etc., One Poor Girl, etc. *Pub. Lip. Os.*

Silliman, Benjamin. 1779 *Ct.*-1864. Chemist. Author of numerous scientific works of value and several vols. of travel. *See Life by G. P. Fisher, Am. Journal of Science, May, 1865, and Popular Science Monthly, June, 1883.*

Silliman, Benjamin. 1816 *Ct.*-1885. Son to preceding. Scientist. Author Principles of Physics, etc. *Pub. Iv.*

Simms, Wm. Gilmore. 1806 *S. C.*-1870. Novelist and poet. Of his thirty romances, The Partisan, The Yemassee, and Beauchampe are the best. He was also author of some twelve volumes of poems and of many miscellaneous works. His productions have a recognized value, though his art was not great. *See edition 1882. See Lit. World, Oct. 21, 1882, and Cable's Simms in Am. Men of Letters. Pub. Arm. Har.*

Smith, Mrs. Elizabeth Oakes [Prince]. 1806 *Me.* ———. Wife to Seba S. Poet and miscellaneous writer. The Sinless Child and The Newsboy are among her most popular books.

Smith, Mrs. Frances I. [Burge]. 1826 *R. I.* ———. Author of numerous religious tales. *Pub. Lo. Wh.*

Smith, Henry Boynton. 1815 *Me.*-1877. Presbyterian theologian. Author Faith and Philosophy,

Apologetics, Chronological Hist. of the Church of Christ, Introduction to Christian Theology, etc. A thinker of high rank, with keen, tolerant, and scholarly views. *See Life and Work of, 1881. Pub. Arm. Scr.*

Smith, Captain John. 1579 *E.*–1631. Author True Relation of Virginia, General Hist. of Virginia, etc. Style forcible and picturesque. *See Tyler's Am. Lit. vol. 1, N. A. Rev. Jan. 1867, and Capt. John Smith by C. D. Warner, 1881.*

Smith, John Cotton. 1826 *Ms.*–1882. Episcopal theologian. Author The Church's Law of Development, etc. *Pub. Wh.*

Smith, Richard Penn. 1790 *Pa.*–1854. Dramatist. Fifteen of his plays have been placed on the stage, and were once popular. Caius Marius is one of them.

Smith, Samuel Francis. 1808 *Ms.* ——. Poet. Author of several fine lyrics and hymns, one of which is the familiar " My country 't is of thee." *Pub. Lo.*

Smith, Samuel Stanhope. 1750 *Pa.*–1819. Presbyterian theologian. Pres. Princeton Coll. Author Lectures on the Evidences of the Christian Religion, etc.

Smith, Seba, " Jack Downing." 1792 *Me.*–1868. Humorist. The Letters of Major Jack Downing is his chief work.

Smith, Thomas Buckingham. 1810 *Ga.*–1871. Spanish-American historical writer. Author of many works of value relating to Spanish-American history and literature.

Smith, Wm. 1728 *N. Y.*–1793. Colonial historian. Author Hist. N. Y. from its Discovery to 1732. Style able and clear. *See Tyler's Am. Lit. vol. 2.*

Smith, Wm. 1726 *S.*-1803. Scholar. Author Discourses on Public Occasions, etc. Style graceful and vigorous. *See Tyler's Am. Lit. vol. 2.*

Smyth, Newman. 1843 *Me.* ——. Congregationalist theologian. Author Old Faiths in New Light, The Orthodox Theology of To-Day, The Religious Feeling, etc. *Pub. Scr.*

Smyth, Thomas. 1808 *I.*-1873. Presbyterian theologian. Author Calvin and his Eminence, Ecclesiastical Republicanism, etc.

Sophocles, Evangelinus Apostolides. 1807 *Gr.*-1883. Greek scholar. Author of several Greek text-books and a valuable Greek Dict. of the Roman and Byzantine Periods. *Pub. Lit. Wa.*

Southgate, Horatio. 1812 *Me.* ——. Bp. Constantinople. Religious and miscellaneous writer. Author The Cross Above the Crescent, Parochial Sermons, etc. *Pub. Lip.*

Southworth, Mrs. Emma D. E. [Nevitt]. 1818 *D. C.* ——. Novelist. A prolific author of sensational romances, among the best of which are Ishmael and The Widow's Son. Her plots are skillfully constructed, but the literary merit of her works is slight. *See Hart's Am. Lit. and Lit. World, June 3, 1882. Pub. Pet.*

Spalding, Martin John. 1810 *Ky.*-1872. R. C. Abp. Baltimore. Theological controversialist. Author Review of D'Aubigné's Hist. of the Reformation, Smithsonian Lect. on Modern Civilization, etc. *See Life, by J. L. Spalding. Pub. Pi.*

Sparks, Jared. 1789 *Ct.*-1866. Historian and biographer. Best known by the Am. Biography, which he edited, and of which he was in part the author, and by editions of the works of Franklin and Washington. An accurate, impartial, and discriminating writer. *Pub. Har.*

Spencer, Ichabod Smith. 1798 *Vt.*–1854. Presbyterian religious writer. Author of A Pastor's Sketches, Sermons, etc. *Pub. Do.*

Spencer, Jesse Ames. 1816 *N. Y.* ——. Historian and classical editor. Author Hist. English Reformation, Hist. of the U. S., Sermons, etc. *Pub. Apl. Har. Iv.*

Spofford, Mrs. Harriet Elizabeth [Prescott]. 1835 *Me.* ——. Novelist and poet. Author Azarian, Sir Rohan's Ghost, etc. The Amber Gods is her most characteristic story. Style strongly original, and remarkable for its vividness and luxuriance of description. *See Atlantic Monthly, April, 1882. Pub. Har. Ho. Hou. Rob.*

Spooner, Lysander. 1808 *Ms.*–1887. A prolific writer on religion and politics.

Spooner, Shearjashub. 1809 *Vt.*–1859. Author of a valuable Biographical and Critical Dict. of Painters Engravers Sculptors and Architects, Anecdotes of Painters, etc.

Sprague, Charles. 1791 *Ms.*–1875. Poet. His Ode to Shakespeare is his finest effort, but The Family Meeting and The Winged Worshippers are more generally familiar. *See Griswold's Poets and Poetry of America.*

Sprague, Wm. Buell. 1795 *Ct.*–1875. Annalist and religious writer. His Annals of the Am. Pulpit is the work by which he is best known. It is of great value, and the product of years of careful labor and research. *Pub. Ca. L. P. S. Ran.*

Spring, Gardiner. 1785 *Ms.*–1873. Presbyterian religious writer. Author Power of the Pulpit, The Church in the Wilderness, Sermons, etc. *See Personal Reminiscences of. Pub. Har. Scr.*

Squier [skwīr], Ephraim George. 1821 *N. Y.*–1888.

Archæologist. Author Notes on Central America, Nicaragua, Mexican Hieroglyphics, etc. His works possess much value, but are wanting in vigor and freshness of narration. *Pub. Har.*

Stedman, Edmund Clarence. 1833 *Ct.* ——. Poet and critic. Author Alice of Monmouth, The Blameless Prince, etc. Among his finest poems are Pan in Wall Street and The Lord's-Day Gale. His Victorian Poets is a work of much value, as an example of dispassionate, conscientious, and skillful literary judgment. *See Duyckinck's Cyc. new ed. vol. 2, Scribner's Monthly, Nov. 1873, and Atlantic Monthly, March, 1878. Pub. Hou.*

Steele, J. Dorman. 1836 *N. Y.*–1886. Educational writer. Author of a series of scientific text-books. *Pub. Bar.*

Stella. See Lewis, Mrs.

Stephens, Alexander Hamilton. 1812 *Ga.*–1883. Statesman. Author Hist. of the War between the States, etc. *See Carroll's Twelve Americans, Harper's Mag. Feb. 1876, Life by F. H. Norton, and Life by Johnston and Browne. Pub. Apl. Lip.*

Stephens, Mrs. Ann Sophia [Winterbotham]. 1813 *Ct.*–1886. Novelist. Author of many sensational tales, some of which, like Fashion and Famine, show considerable skill. *See Lit. World, June 3, 1882. Pub. Pet.*

Stephens, John Lloyd. 1805 *N. Y.*–1852. Traveler. Author Central America, Yucatan, Egypt Arabia and the Holy Land, etc. *Pub. Har.*

Stevens, Abel. 1815 *Pa.* ——. Methodist ecclesiologist. Author Hist. M. E. Church in the U. S., Hist. of Methodism, Life of Madame de Staël, etc. *Pub. Har. Phi.*

Stevens, Henry. 1819 *Vt.*-1886. Bibliographer of note.

Stevens, Wm. Bacon. 1815 *Me.*-1887. Bp. Pennsylvania. Author Hist. of Georgia, The Bow in the Cloud, Sermons, etc. *Pub. Clx. Dut. Por. Sto.*

Stiles, Ezra. 1727 *Ct.*-1795. Pres. Yale Coll. Author Hist. of Three of the Judges of Chas. I. Whalley, Goffe, and Dixwell, etc.

Stille [stǐl'le], Alfred. 1813 *Pa.* ——. Physician. Author Elements of General Pathology, The Unity of Medicine, Humboldt's Life and Character, War as an Element of Civilization, etc.

Stillo, Charles Janeway. 1819 *Pa.* ——. Bro. to A. S. Historical writer. Author Historical Development of Am. Civilization, Studies in Mediæval Civilization, etc. *Pub. Lip.*

Stille, Morton. 1822 *Pa.*-1855. Brother to A. S. Physician. Co-author with F. Wharton of a Treatise on Medical Jurisprudence.

Stillman, Wm. James. 1828 *N. Y.* ——. Littérateur and artist. Author Hist. Cretan Insurrection, Poetic Localities of Cambridge, etc. *Pub. Ho. Hou.*

Stith, Wm. 1689 *Va.*-1785. Colonial historian. Author Hist. of Virginia. *See Tyler's Am. Lit. vol. 2.*

Stockton, Francis Richard. 1834 *Pa.* ——. Author Rudder Grange, Tales out of School, etc. *Pub. Scr.*

Stoddard, Charles Warren. 1840 *N. Y.* ——. Littérateur. Author Mashallah : a Flight into Egypt, South Sea Idyls, etc. *Pub. Apl.*

Stoddard, Mrs. Elizabeth D. [Barstow]. 1823 *Ms.* ——. Wife to R. H. S. Novelist and poet. Author The Morgesons, Temple House, etc.

Stoddard, Richard Henry. 1825 *Ms.* ——. Poet

and littérateur. Author Songs of Summer, The King's Bell, The Book of the East, etc., and editor the Bric-à-Brac Series, etc. *See Griswold's Poets and Poetry of America. Pub. Scr.*

Stoddard, Wm. Osborn. 1835 *N. Y.* ——. Novelist. Author Esau Hardery, Dab Kinzer, Saltillo Boys, Wrecked, Verses of Many Days, The Heart of It, etc. *Pub. Put. Scr. W.*

Stone, Edwin Martin. 1805 *Ms.*–1883. Historical writer. Author The Invasion of Canada, Our French Allies in the Revolution, etc.

Stone, James Kent. 1840 *Ms.* ——. Son to J. S. S. Roman Catholic theologian. Author The Invitation Heeded, etc. *Pub. Cath.*

Stone, John Augustus. 1801 *Ms.*–1834. Dramatist. Author Metamora, The Ancient Briton, Fauntleroy, etc.

Stone, John Seely. 1795 *Ms.*–1882. Episcopal theologian. Author The Living Temple, The Christian Sacraments, Sermons, etc. *Pub. Ran.*

Stone, Wm. Leete. 1792 *N. Y.*–1844. Journalist and biographer. Author Lives of Brant, Red Jacket, Letters on Masonry, etc. *See Life, by his son.*

Stone, Wm. Leete, Jr. 1835 *N. Y.* ——. Son to preceding. Historian. Author Hist. of N. Y. City, Life Sir Wm. Johnson, Burgoyne's Campaigns, etc.

Storrs, Richard Salter. 1821 *Ms.* ——. Congregationalist religious writer. Author The Constitution of the Human Soul, Historical Addresses, etc. *Pub. Do. Ran.*

Story, Joseph. 1779 *Ms.*–1845. Jurist of eminence. Author Commentaries on the Constitution of the U. S. (his chief work), on the Conflict of Laws, on Equity and Jurisprudence, etc. A writer of wide research and tolerant spirit. The chief defect in his works is their diffuseness. *See Life, by W. W. Story. Pub. Har. Lit.*

Story, Wm. Wetmore. 1819 *Ms.* ——. Son to J. S. Poet and sculptor. His chief prose works are the life of his father and Roba di Roma. Author He and She : a Poet's Portfolio, The Castle of St. Angelo, etc. A Roman Lawyer in Jerusalem is perhaps his most striking poem. *Pub. Hou. Lip. Lit.*

Stowe, Calvin Ellis. 1802 *Ms.*–1886. Congregationalist theologian. Author Origin and Hist. of the Books of the Bible, Elementary Instruction in Europe, etc.

Stowe, Mrs. Harriet Elizabeth [Beecher]. 1812 *Ct.* ——. Wife to C. E. S. and dau. to Lyman Beecher. Novelist, essayist, and poet. The Minister's Wooing, Old Town Folks, Pearl of Orr's Island, My Wife and I, and Uncle Tom's Cabin are her principal novels. The last is world-famous, and with it her name is inseparably associated. As a piece of literary art, however, The Minister's Wooing must rank as her finest work. Other books of hers are House and Home Papers, The Mayflower, and Religious Poems. *See Atlantic Monthly, July, 1882. Pub. Fo. Hou. Lo. Rob.*

Street, Alfred Billings. 1811 *N. Y.*–1881. Poet. Author of Frontenac, Woods and Waters, Forest Pictures, etc. His verse is meditative and descriptive in tone and excellent in quality. *See Griswold's Poets and Poetry of America.*

Strickland, Wm. Peter. 1809 *Pa.*–1884. Methodist religious writer. Author Hist. Am. Bible Society, The Genius of Methodism, etc. *Pub. Phi.*

Strong, James. 1822 *N. Y.* ——. Methodist theologian. Author English Harmony of the Gospels, Greek Harmony of the Gospels, etc., and co-author with McClintock of a Biblical Encyclopædia. *Pub. Har. Phi.*

Strong, Latham Cornell. 1845 *N. Y.* ——. Poet. Author Castle Windows, Pots of Gold, Poke o' Moonshine, etc. *Pub. Put.*

Strother [strŭth'er], David Hunter, "Porte Crayon." 1816 *Va.*–1888. Humorous writer. His numerous works are illustrated by himself. *See Hart's Am. Lit.*

Stuart, Moses. 1780 *Ct.*–1852. Congregationalist biblical commentator. Of his many works, his valuable Commentaries are the most important. *Pub. Dra.*

Sullivan, James. 1744 *Me.*–1808. Political writer of note. Author Hist. Land Titles of Massachusetts, etc.

Sullivan, Wm. 1774 *Me.*–1839. Political writer. Author Familiar Letters on Public Men of the Revolution, etc.

Summerfield, John. 1798 *E.*–1825. Methodist pulpit orator. *See Sermons, with Memoir by J. Holland. Pub. Har.*

Sumner, Charles. 1811 *Ms.*–1874. Son to C. P. S. Statesman. Author Orations, Speeches, etc. His style is a model of polished and refined yet vigorous English. *See Life, by Pierce, Living Age, March 9, 1878. Pub. Le.*

Sumner, Charles Pinckney. 1766 *Ms.*–1839. Miscellaneous writer. Author Eulogy on Washington, etc.

Sumner, George. 1817 *Ms.*–1863. Son to C. P. S. Writer on international law.

Sumner, Wm. Graham. 1840 *N. J.* ——. Political economist. Author Hist. Am. Currency, What Social Classes Owe to Each Other, Andrew Jackson in Am. Statesmen, Problems in Political Economy, etc. *See Andover Rev. Feb. 1884. Pub. Har. Ho. Hou. Scr.*

Sunderland, La Roy. 1804 *R. I.*-1885. A vigorous writer against Slavery, Spiritualism, and Mormonism.

Sweetser, Moses Foster. 1848 *Ms.* ——. Littérateur. Author The New England Guide-Book, and of a valuable series of art biographies. *Pub. Os.*

Swett, Samuel. 1782 *Ms.*-1866. Author of several valuable historical monographs relating to the Battle of Bunker Hill.

Swing, David. 1830 *O.* ——. Presbyterian theologian. Author Sermons, Club Essays, Truths for To-day, Motives of Life, etc. A leader of liberal thought. *Pub. Jan.*

Swinton, Wm. 1834 *S.* ——. Philologist and military historian. Author Rambles Among Words, Twelve Decisive Battles of the War, Campaigns of the Army of the Potomac, a clear, able narrative, and numerous educational text-books. *Pub. Har. Scr. Un.*

Swisshelm, Mrs. Jane Gray [Cannon]. 1815 *Pa.*-1884. Journalist. Author Half a Century, an autobiography, which see. Style energetic and resolute. *See Hart's Am. Lit. Pub. Jan.*

Symmes, John Cleves. 1788 *N. J.*-1829. Author Symmes' Theory of Concentric Spheres, an attempt to prove that the earth is hollow, open at the poles, and habitable in the interior. *See Harper's Mag. Oct. 1882.*

Talmage [tăl-mǐj or tăm-ǐj], **Thomas De Witt.** 1832 *N. J.* ——. Presbyterian religious writer.

Author Crumbs Swept Up, Sermons, etc. Style inflated and weak. *Pub. Do. Har. Og. Phi.*

Talvi. See Robinson, Mrs. Thérèse.

Tappan, Henry Philip. 1805 *N. Y.*–1881. Philosophical writer. Author Elements of Logic, and several works on the freedom of the will. *Pub. Apl.*

Tappan, Wm. Bingham. 1794 *Ms.*–1849. Poet. Author Poetry of the Heart, Poetry of Life, etc. *See Griswold's Poets and Poetry of America.*

Taylor, Bayard [bi'ard]. 1825 *Pa.*–1878. Poet, novelist, translator, and traveler. Views Afoot, Eldorado, and Byways of Europe are among the best of his works of travel. Hannah Thurston, The Story of Kennet, John Godfrey's Fortune, and Joseph and his Friend are his four novels. Poems of Home and Travel, Poems of the Orient, The Picture of St. John, The Poet's Journal, Lars, The Masque of the Gods, Home Pastorals, and Prince Deukalion comprise his principal volumes of verse. The last is his finest effort in original poetry. The translation of Faust is his greatest work, and the one on which his fame will most securely rest. *See Catholic World, April, 1879, Lippincott's Mag. Aug. 1879, and Life and Letters of Bayard Taylor, by Marie-Hansen Taylor and H. E. Scudder. Pub. Hou. Put.*

Taylor, Benjamin Franklin. 1822 *N. Y.*–1887. Poet. Author Songs of Yesterday, Old Time Pictures, Sheaves of Rhyme, Dulce Domum, etc. Style simple and tender. *Pub. Apl. Arm. Gri.*

Taylor, John. 1750 *Va.*–1824. A political writer, held in much esteem by his contemporaries.

Taylor, Nathaniel Wm. 1786 *Ct.*–1859. Congregationalist theologian. A writer whose views were stated with much ability and persistence.

Taylor, Samuel Harvey. 1807 *N. H.*-1871. Educator. Author Method of Classical Study, etc. Style
accurate and scholarly. *See Memorial compiled by
his last class. Pub. Dra.*

Taylor, Wm. Mackergo. 1829 *S.* ——. Presbyterian religious writer. Author Contrary Winds, The
Limitations of Life, etc. His works are marked by
clear reasoning and devotional feeling. *Pub. Arm.
Har. Ran. Scr.*

Tefft, Benjamin Franklin. 1813 *N. Y.*-1885. Miscellaneous writer. Author The Shoulder-Knot,
Memorials of Prison Life, Methodism Successful,
etc. *Pub. Har. Por.*

Tenney, Mrs. Tabitha [Gilman]. 1762 *N. H.*-1837.
Novelist. Author of the witty, satirical novel Female Quixotism.

Tenney, Sanborn. 1827 *N. H.*-1877. Naturalist.
Author Elements of Zoölogy, etc. *Pub. Bu. Scr.*

Tenney, Wm. Jewett. 1811 *R. I.*-1883. Author
Military and Naval Hist. of the Rebellion, etc.
Pub. Apl.

Terhune, Mrs. Mary Virginia [Hawes], "Marion
Harland." 183-*Va.* ——. Novelist. Author
Alone, Moss-Side, Beechdale, etc., and a widely
known work for housekeepers, entitled Common
Sense in the Household. Alone, her first book,
pub. 1854, has been very popular. *Pub. Car. Scr.*

Thacher, James. 1754 *Ms.*-1844. Physician. Author Am. Medical Biography, Hist. of Plymouth,
Essay on Demonology, etc.

Thatcher, Benjamin Bussey. 1809 *Me.*-1848. Author Indian Biography, Indian Traits, etc. *Pub.
Har.*

Thaxter, Adam Wallace. 1832 *Ms.*-1864. Dramatist.

Thaxter, Mrs. Celia [Laighton]. 1835 *N. H.* ——.
Poet. Author Drift-Weed, Poems, Poems for Children, and a prose volume, Among the Isles of Shoals. Courage, Kittery Church-Yard, The Spaniards' Graves, and The Watch of Boon Island are some of her finest poems. *Pub. Hou.*

Thayer, Alexander Wheelock. 1817 *Ms.* ——. Author Life of Beethoven, The Hebrews and the Red Sea, Brown Papers, etc. *Pub. Dra.*

Thayer, Thomas Baldwin. 1812 *Ms.*–1886. Universalist religious writer. Author Over the River, Christianity vs. Infidelity, Hist. Doctrine of Endless Punishment, etc.

Thayer, Wm. Makepeace. 1820 *Ms.* ——. Author of juvenile works. See The Bobbin Boy, The Pioneer Boy, The Printer Boy, etc.

Thomas, David. 1776 *Pa.*–1859. Pomological and agricultural writer.

Thomas, Edith M. 1854 *O.* ——. Poet and essayist. Author A New Year's Masque. *Pub. Hou.*

Thomas, Frederick Wm. 1811 *R. I.*–1864. Grandneph. to I. T. Novelist. Author Clinton Bradshaw, The Beechen Tree, and Other Poems, etc.

Thomas, Isaiah. 1749 *Ms.*–1831. Printer. Author of a valuable Hist. of Printing, and Founder of the Am. Antiquarian Society at Worcester, Mass.

Thomas, John J. 1810 *N. Y.* ——. Son to D. T. Agricultural writer. Author Rural Affairs, etc.

Thomas, Joseph. 1811 *N. Y.* ——. Son to D. T. Biographical lexicographer. Author of A Pronouncing Gazetteer and Dict. of the World, Gazetteer of the U. S., Medical Dict., Universal Pronouncing Dict. of Biography and Mythology, etc. A writer of tireless energy, and a high authority

11

upon all questions of orthoepy. *See Lit. World,
June 17, 1882. Pub. Lip.*

Thomas, Lewis F. 1815 *Md.* ——. Bro. to F. W.
T. Poet and dramatist. Author of Osceola, etc.

Thompson, Augustus Charles. 1812 *Ct.* ——. Congregationalist religious writer. Author Lyra Cœles-
tis, or Hymns on Heaven, Christian's Consolation,
etc.

Thompson, Benjamin, Count Rumford. 1753 *Ms.*–
1814. Natural philosopher. Author Essays: Political, Economical, and Philosophical, 1798–1806.
*See Cuvier's Éloge de Rumford, Sparks' Am. Bi-
ography, Life by G. E. Ellis, and Atlantic Monthly,
Apr. 1871. Pub. Est.*

Thompson, Daniel Pierce. 1795 *Ms.*–1868. Historical novelist. Author Gaut Gurley, May Martin, Green Mountain Boys, Locke Amsden, etc.
Style breezy and vigorous. *Pub. Hal. Pott.*

Thompson, John R. 1823 *Va.*–1873. Journalist and
poet.

Thompson, Joseph Parrish. 1819 *Pa.*–1879. Religious and miscellaneous writer. Author The Theology of Christ, Man in Genesis and Geology, Lect.
to Young Men, Church and State in the U. S., The
U. S. as a Nation, etc. *Pub. Hou. Ran. Scr. Sh.*

Thompson, Maurice. 1844 *Ind.* ——. Novelist and
poet. Author A Tallahassee Girl, His Second Cam-
paign, Hoosier Mosaics, a volume of sketches, The
Witchery of Archery, and Songs of Fair Weather.
Pub. Os. Scr.

Thompson, Mortimer H., "Q. K. Philander Doesticks." 1830 *N. Y.*–1875. Humorist. Author
Doesticks's Letters, Plu-Ri-Bus-Tah, etc.

Thompson, Wm. Tappan. 1812 *O.*–1882. Humorist. Author Major Jones's Courtship, Major Jones's

Sketches of Travel, and Major Jones's Characters of Pineville. The humor of these books is unmistakable, but it is not refined. *Pub. Apl. Pet.*

Thompson, Zadoc. 1796 *Vt.*–1856. Naturalist. Author Hist. of Vermont, etc.

Thomson, Charles. 1729 *I.*–1824. Author of a noted translation of the Old Testament from the Septuagint.

Thomson, Wm. McClure. 1806 *O.* ——. Missionary. Best known by his excellent work The Land and the Book. *See edition 1883. Pub. Har.*

Thorburn, Grant, "Laurie Todd." 1773 *S.* –1863. Seedsman. The hero of Galt's novel Laurie Todd. Author Todd's Notes on Virginia, Fifty Years' Reminiscences of N. Y., etc. An eccentric and prolific writer. *See Autobiography, 1834, and Fraser's Mag. June, 1833.*

Thoreau [tho-rō], Henry David. 1817 *Ms.*–1862. Naturalist. Author Walden, A Week on the Concord and Merrimac Rivers, Excursions, Maine Woods, Cape Cod, A Yankee in Canada, Early Spring in Massachusetts, etc. An observer of the rarest, closest kind. *See N. A. Rev. Oct. 1865, Fraser's Mag. April, 1866, Memoir by Emerson, Lit. World, March 26, 1881, Harvard Register, April, 1881, Thoreau : his Life and Aims, by Page, Thoreau: the Poet Naturalist, by W. E. Channing, and Thoreau by Sanborn in Am. Men of Letters. Pub. Hou.*

Thornton, John Wingate. 1818 *Me.*–1878. Genealogist and antiquarian. Author Colonial Schemes of Popham and Gorges, The Landing at Cape Anne, First Records of Anglo-American Civilization, The Pulpit of the American Revolution, etc. *Pub. Lo.*

Thornwell, James Henry. 1811 *S. C.*–1862. Presbyterian theologian. Style able and profound.

Thorpe, Mrs. Rosa [Hartwick]. 1850 *Mch.* ——.
Poet. Chiefly known as the author of Curfew Shall
Not Ring To-night. *Pub. Le.*

Thorpe, Thomas Bangs. 1815 *Ms.* ——. Artist and
littérateur. Author The Hive of the Bee Hunter,
etc.

Thwing, Charles Franklin. 1853 *Me.* ——. Littérateur. Author American Colleges, The Reading
of Books, etc. *Pub. Le. Put.*

Ticknor, George. 1791 *Ms.*–1871. Historian. Author Life of W. H. Prescott, and A Hist. of Spanish Literature, a standard work in its department,
but somewhat cold and dry in style. *See London
Quarterly Rev. Oct. 1850, Lippincott's Mag. May,
1876, and Ticknor's Life and Letters. Pub. Har.
Hou. Lip.*

Tilton, Theodore. 1835 *N. Y.* ——. Journalist and
poet. Author The True Church, Swabian Stories,
etc. The Fly is one of his best poems. A ten-
dency to iteration is a noticeable defect in his verse.
Pub. Lip.

Timrod, Henry. 1829 *S. C.*–1867. Poet. His verse
is thoughtful, refined, and exquisitely tender.
Spring in Carolina is one of his best poems. *See
Poems, ed. 1873, with Memoir by Hayne. Pub. Ha.*

Tincker, Mary Agnes. 1833 *Me.* ——. Novelist.
Author Signor Monaldini's Niece, The Jewel in
the Lotus, etc. *Pub. Lip. Rob.*

Titcomb, Timothy. See Holland, J. G.

Todd, John. 1800 *Vt.*–1873. The inventor of the
Index Rerum, and an industrious author of religious works, mainly juvenile in character. *See Life,
and Harper's Mag. Feb. 1876. Pub. Le. Ran.*

Todd, Laurie. See Thorburn, Grant.

Tomes, Robert. 1816 *N. Y.* ——. Littérateur. Author Panama in 1855, Bourbon Prince, My College Days, etc. *Pub. Har.*

Tourgée [toor-zhay'], **Albion Winegar.** 1838 *O.* ——. Political novelist. Editor The Continent. Author A Fool's Errand, Bricks without Straw, Figs and Thistles, Hot Plowshares, etc. *Pub. Fo.*

Towle [tōle], **George Makepeace.** 1840 *D. C.* ——. Littérateur. Author Hist. Henry V., Glimpses of Hist., Modern France, Certain Men of Mark, etc. *Pub. Apl. Har. Le. Rob.*

Townsend, George Alfred, "Gath." 1841 *Del.* ——. Journalist. Author Bohemian Days, Campaigns of a Non-Combatant, The Entailed Hat, Poems, etc. *See Hart's Am. Lit.*

Townsend, Luther Tracy. 1838 *Me.* ——. Theologian. Author God-Man, Credo, The Fate of Republics, Outlines of Christian Theology, etc. *Pub. Apl. Le. Phi.*

Townsend, Virginia Frances. 18— *N. H.* ——. Rel. to L. T. T. Novelist. Author A Woman's Word, One Woman's Two Lovers, Lenox Dare, Protestant Queen of Navarre, etc. *Pub. Le. Lip. Phi.*

Toy, Crawford Howell. 1836 *Va.* ——. Baptist theologian. Author Quotations in the New Testament, Hist. of the Religion of Israel, etc. *Pub. Scr.*

Trafton, Adeline. 1845 *Me.* ——. Novelist. Author Katharine Earle, His Inheritance, and An American Girl Abroad. *Pub. Le.*

Trescot, Wm. Henry. 1823 *S. C.* ——. Political historian. Author Diplomacy of the Revolution, Diplomatic Hist. Washington's Administration, South Carolina in Am. Commonwealths, etc. *Pub. Hou.*

Trowbridge, John Townsend. 1827 *N. Y.* ——.

Novelist and poet. Neighbor Jackwood, Cudjo's Cave, and Lucy Arlyn are his best novels ; Coupon Bonds and The Man Who Stole a Meeting House are among the finest of his inimitable short stories. The Vagabonds is his best known poem, but At Sea and Midsummer are his finest. The last is, in fact, an almost perfect poem. As a writer for young people also Trowbridge has a high rank. *See Hart's Am. Lit. Pub. Har. Hou. Le.*

Trumbull, Henry Clay. 1830 *Ct.* ——. Religious writer. Editor S. S. Times. Author The Knightly Soldier, Kadesh-Barnea, etc. *Pub. Har. Scr.*

Trumbull, John. 1750 *Ct.*–1831. Satirical poet. Author The Progress of Dulness and MacFingal, a Hudibrastic poem once exceedingly popular. *See Stedman's Rise of Poetry in America, and Griswold's Poets and Poetry of America.*

Tucker, George. 1775 *Ba.*–1861. Rel. to St. George T. Jurist. A prolific author, whose Life of Jefferson, Political Hist. of the U. S., and Theory of Money and Banks are his most noted works. *Pub. Lip.*

Tucker, Henry St. George. 1779 *Va.*–1848. Son to St. George T. Jurist. Author Lect. on Natural Law and Government, etc.

Tucker, Luther. 1802 *Vt.* ——. Agricultural writer of note.

Tucker, Nathaniel Beverly. 1784 *Va.*–1851. Son to St. George T. Novelist. The Partisan Leader (pub. 1836), his most noted book, prophesied the secession of the southern states.

Tucker, St. George. 1752 *Ba.*–1827. Jurist. Known to general literature only by the lyric beginning "Days of my youth, ye have glided away." *See Griswold's Poets and Poetry of America.*

Tuckerman, Henry Theodore. 1813 *Ms.*–1871. Critic and essayist. Thoughts on the Poets, Book of the Artists, Biographical Essays, and Artist Life are some of his works. His criticisms are delicate and discriminating, but deficient in force and depth. *Pub. Put. Scr.*

Tudor, Wm. 1779 *Ms.*–1830. Littérateur. Author Gebel Teir, Life James Otis, etc.

Turnbull, Robert James. 1809 *S.*–1877. Baptist theologian. Christ in History is his most important work.

Turner, Samuel Hulbeart. 1790 *Pa.*–1861. Episcopal Biblical commentator. An expositor of high rank, best known by his Commentaries on Hebrews, Romans, Ephesians, and Galatians. Style able, fearless, and accurate. *Pub. Ran.*

Tuthill [tŭt′il], **Mrs. Louisa Caroline [Huggins]**. 1799 *Ct.*–1879. Author of numerous excellent moral tales. I Will be a Gentleman, etc.

Tuttle, Herbert. 1846 *Vt.* ——. Historian. Author Hist. of Prussia, and German Political Leaders. *See Atlantic Monthly, May, 1884. Pub. Hou. Put.*

Twain, Mark. See Clemens.

Tyler, Bennett. 1783 *Ct.*–1858. Congregationalist theologian. Author Hist. New Haven Theology, etc.

Tyler, Moses Colt. 1835 *Ct.* ——. Literary historian. Author The Brawnville Papers, etc., and a Hist. of Am. Literature : vol. 1, 1607–1676 ; vol. 2, 1676–1715. A work of great thoroughness and scholarship. *Pub. Put. Sh.*

Tyler, Royall. 1756 *Ms.*–1826. Humorous writer. Author of The Contrast, a brilliant comedy, The Algerine Captive, etc.

Tyler, Samuel. 1800 *Md.*-1877.   Metaphysician. Author The Progress of Philosophy, Discourse on the Baconian Philosophy, etc.

Tyler, Wm. Seymour. 1810 *Pa.* ——. Classical scholar and theologian. Author Hist. Amherst College, etc. *Pub. Al. Apl. Ran.*

Tyng, Stephen Higginson. 1800 *Ms.*-1885. Low Church theologian. Author The Christian Pastor, Family Commentary on the Gospels, etc. *Pub. Har. Ran. Wh.*

Tyson, Job Roberts. 1804 *Pa.*-1858. Essayist. Author Essay on the Penal Laws of Pennsylvania, and several historical monographs.

Underwood, Francis H. 1825 *Ms.* ——. Littérateur. Author Handbook of English Literature, the novels Lord of Himself and Man Proposes, and biographies of Lowell, Longfellow, and Whittier. *Pub. Le. Os.*

Upham, Charles Wentworth. 1802 *N. B.*-1875. Author Lect. on Witchcraft, Life of Sir Henry Vane, Principles of Congregationalism, etc.

Upham, Thomas Cogswell. 1799 *N. H.*-1872. Metaphysician. Author Elements of Moral Philosophy, Treatise on the Will, Life of Madame Guyon, Principles of the Hidden Life, etc. *Pub. Har.*

Upton, Emory. 1840 *N. Y.*-1881. Tactician. Author Infantry Tactics, The Armies of Asia and Europe, etc. *Pub. Apl.*

Vandenhoff, George. 1820 *E.* ——. Actor and elocutionist. Author Plain System of Elocution, Leaves from an Actor's Note Book, Dramatic Reminiscences, etc. *Pub. Loc.*

Van Lennep, Henry John. 1815 *A. M.*-1889. Traveler. Author Bible Lands, Travels in Asia Minor, etc. *Pub. Har.*

Van Rensselaer [rĕn'sĕl-ạr] **Cortland.** 1808 *N. Y.*– 1860. Presbyterian theologian. Author Essays and Discourses. *Pub. Clx. Lip.*

Van Santvoord, George. 1819 *N. Y.* ——. Jurist. Author Life of Algernon Sidney, Lives of the Chief Justices of the U. S., and several legal works.

Verplanck [vĕr-plănk], **Gulian Crommelin.** 1786 *N. Y.*–1870. Shakespearean scholar. His carefully edited Shakespeare appeared in 1846, and is of much value for its critical notes and comments. Author also of Essays on Revealed Religion, Discourses on American Hist., Art, and Literature. His style is one of great clearness and beauty.

Very, Jones. 1813 *Ms.*–1881. Poet. His verse is mystical in character, but singularly pure and spiritual. *See Poems with Memoir, by W. P. Andrews, 1883, also Atlantic Monthly, July, 1883. Pub. Hou.*

Victor, Mrs. Metta Victoria [Fuller]. 1831 *Pa.* 1885. Novelist and poet. Maum Guinea, Jo Daviess's Client, and The Dead Letter are the best of her numerous stories, Compound Interest one of her best poems.

Vincent, Francis. 1823 *Del.*–1884. Historian. Author Hist. of Delaware, etc.

Vincent, Frank, Jr. 1848 *L. I.* ——. Traveler. Author Land of the White Elephant, Norsk Lapp and Finn, Through and Through the Tropics, etc. *Pub. Har. Put.*

Vincent, John Heyl. 1832 *Al.* ——. Meth. religious and educational writer. *Pub. Phi.*

Vincent, Marvin Richardson. 1834 *N. Y.* ——. Presbyterian writer. Author Faith and Character,

Stranger and Guest, Gates into the Psalm Country, In the Shadow of the Pyrenees, a volume of travels, etc. *Pub. Har. Ran. Scr.*

Vinton, Alexander Hamilton. 1807 *R. I.*–1881. Episcopal religious writer. Author Sermons, etc. *Pub. Dut.*

Wainwright, Jonathan Mayhew. 1792 *E.*–1854. Bp. N. Y. Religious writer. Author The Land of Bondage, Short Family Prayers, etc. *Pub. Apl. Dut.*

Wakefield, Mrs. Nancy Amelia Woodbury [Priest]. 1837 *N. H.*–1870. Poet. Chiefly noted for her poem Over the River.

Walker, Amasa. 1799 *Ct.*–1875. Political economist. Author The Science of Wealth, etc. *Pub. Apl.*

Walker, Francis Amasa. 1840 *Ms.* ——. Son to A. W. Political economist. Author Wages, Money, Money in its Relations to Trade and Industry, Political Economy, etc. *See Lit. World, April, 1878. Pub. Bar. Ho.*

Walker, James. 1794 *Ms.*–1874. Unitarian theologian. Pres. Har. Coll. Author Lect. on Natural Religion, Lect. on the Philosophy of Religion, etc. A thinker of depth and clearness. *Pub. Rob.*

Walker, James Barr. 1805 *Pa.* ——. Presbyterian theologian. His Philosophy of the Plan of Salvation has been widely popular.

Walker, Robert James. 1801 *Pa.*–1869. Political economist of note.

Walker, Sears Cook. 1805 *Ms.*–1853. Astronomer. Author of numerous scientific monographs.

Wallace, Horace Binney. 1817 *Pa.*–1852. Littérateur. Author Literary Criticisms, Art and Scenery in Europe, and several legal works. *Pub. Clx. Lip.*

Wallace, Lewis. 1828 *Ind.* ——. Novelist. Author of The Fair God, an Aztec Story, and Ben Hur, a Tale of the Christ. Style realistic and dramatic. *Pub. Har. Hou.*

Wallace, Wm. Ross. 1819 *Ky.*-1881. Poet. Author The Liberty Bell, etc. *See Griswold's Poets and Poetry of America.*

Wallack, John Lester. 1819 *N. Y.*-1888. Dramatist and actor. Author The Veteran, Rosedale, etc. *See Galaxy Mag. Oct. 1868.*

Wallis, Severn Teackle. 1816 *Md.* ——. Author Glimpses of Spain, Spain: her Institutions Politics and Public Men, etc. *Pub. Har.*

Walsh, Robert. 1784 *Md.*-1858. Political writer. Author An Appeal from the Judgments of Great Britain, Letter on the Genius and Disposition of the French Government, etc. Style strong and dignified. *See Edinburgh Rev. May, 1820, and N. A. Rev. April, 1820.*

Walworth [wŏl'wŭrth], **Mansfield Tracy.** 1836 *N. Y.*-1873. Novelist. His sensational romances are of little value. Beverly and Warwick are perhaps the best. *Pub. Car.*

Ward, Artemus. See Browne, C. F.

Ward, James Warner. 1818 *N. J.* ——. Poet. Author Yorick and Other Poems, and Higher Water, a parody upon Hiawatha.

Ward, Julius Hammond. 1837 *Ms.* ——. Biographer and critic. Author Life of J. G. Percival, The Bible in Modern Thought, etc.

Ward, Nathaniel. 1570 *E.*-1653. Satirist. Author of The Simple Cobbler of Agawam, an able, witty, and vindictive thrust at the existing state of affairs in the writer's day. *See Tyler's Am. Lit. vol. 1.*

Ward, Wm. Hayes. 1835 *Ms.* ——. Editor The Independent. Author religious and Assyriological essays.

Warden, David Baillie. 1788 *I.*-1845. Author of a Statistical Hist. of the U. S., etc.

Ware, Henry. 1764 *Ms.*-1845. Unitarian theologian. Author Letters to Trinitarians and Calvinists, etc.

Ware, Henry, Jr. 1794 *Ms.*-1843. Son to preceding. Unitarian theologian and hymn writer. *See Memoir by John Ware, M. D. Pub. A. U. A.*

Ware, John. 1795 *Ms.*-1864. Son to H. W. Physician. Author several medical works of value.

Ware, John Fothergill Waterhouse. 1818 *Ms.*-1881. Son to H. W., Jr. Unitarian religious writer. Author Wrestling and Waiting, Sermons, War Tracts, etc. *Pub. El. Le.*

Ware, Wm. 1797 *Ms.*-1852. Son to H. W. Historical novelist. Author of Aurelian Julian, Zenobia, Sketches of European Capitals, etc.

Warfield, Mrs. Catherine Anne [Ware]. 1817 *Mi.* ——. Novelist. The Household of Bouverie, her best work, displays fine imaginative powers. *Pub. Pet.*

Waring [wā-rǐng], **George E.** 1833 *N. Y.* ——. Sanitarian. Author The Sanitary Drainage of Houses and Towns, A Farmer's Vacation, The Bride of the Rhine, Tyrol and the Skirt of the Alps, Village Improvements, and Farm Villages, etc. *Pub. Har. Hou. Os. Por.*

Warner, Anna B., "Amy Lothrop." 18— ——. Novelist and religious writer. Dollars and Cents and My Brother's Keeper are her best novels. Co-author with her sister of Say and Seal and other works. *Pub. Ca. Clx. Har. Lip. Ran.*

Warner, Charles Dudley. 1829 *Ms.* ——. Humorist. Author My Summer in a Garden, Back-Log Studies, Baddeck, Saunterings, Being a Boy, Baddeck and that Sort of Thing, Mummies and Moslems, Adirondack Essays, Irving in Am. Men of Letters, Capt. John Smith in Am. Worthies, etc. *Pub. Ho. Hou.*

Warner, Susan, "Elizabeth Wetherell." 1818 *N. Y.* 1885. Sister to A. B. W. Novelist. Author The Wide Wide World, Queechy, The Old Helmet, Stephen: M. D., etc. The first of these has been widely popular in spite of its somewhat strained religious sentimentality. *Pub. Ca. Lip. Put.*

Warren, Mrs. Mercy [Otis]. 1728 *Ms.*-1814. Poet, historian, and dramatist. *See Griswold's Female Poets of America and Mrs. Ellet's Women of the Revolution, vol. 1.*

Washburn, Edward Abiel. 1819 *Ms.*-1881. Broad Church theologian. Author The Social Law of God, Voices from a Busy Life, a volume of poems, etc. Style scholarly and thoughtful. *See Harvard Register, April, 1881. Pub. Wh.*

Washburn, Emory. 1800 *Ms.*-1877. Jurist. Author Sketches of the Judicial Hist. of Massachusetts, and several legal works of value. *Pub. Lit.*

Washington, George. 1732 *Va.*-1799. Pres. U. S. Known to general literature by his Farewell Address. *See Lives by Marshall, Bancroft, Irving, Paulding, Sparks, Weems, Ramsay, etc.*

Wasson, David Atwood. 1823 *Me.*-1887. Theological and philosophical writer of much force.

Waters, Mrs. Clara [Erskine] [Clement]. 1834 *Ms.* ——. Writer on Art. Author Handbook of

Legendary and Mythological Art, Handbook of
Painters, etc., Artists of the 19th Century (with L.
Hutton), Life of Charlotte Cushman, Eleanor Mait-
land, a novel, etc.   *Pub. Hou. Os. W.*

Watson, Elkanah. 1758 *Ms.*-1842. Men and Times
of the Revolution, his best known work, is mainly
autobiographic in character.   *Pub. Apl.*

Watson, Henry C. 1831 *Md.*-1869. Journalist.
Author Camp-fires of the Revolution, Camp-fires
of Napoleon, Romance of History, Lives of the
Presidents, etc.   *Pub. Por.*

Watson, John Fanning. 1780 *N. J.*-1860. Annalist. Chiefly known by his valuable Annals of Philadelphia.   *Pub. Sto.*

Wayland, Francis. 1796 *N. Y.*-1865. Metaphysi-
cian. Pres. Brown Univ. Author Elements of
Moral Science, Intellectual Philosophy, Human
Responsibility, Elements of Political Economy, etc.
A thinker whose conclusions are much valued.
See Memoirs, 1867. Pub. Sh.

Webb, Alexander S. 1835 *N. Y* ——. Son to J.
W. W. Military historian. Author of a valuable
historical work entitled The Peninsula.

Webb, Charles Henry, "John Paul." 1835 *N. Y.*
——. Humorist. Author Liffith Lank, St. 'Twel'mo,
etc. *See Hart's Am. Lit. Pub. Car.*

Webb, James Watson. 1802 *N. Y.*-1884. Journalist. Author Slavery and its Tendencies, etc.

Webber, Charles Wilkins. 1819 *Ky.*-1856. Author the Hunter-Naturalist, Tales of the Western
Border, Old Hicks the Guide, etc. *Pub. Har. Lip.*

Webster, Albert. 1846 *Ms.*-1877. Magazinist.
Among his finest sketches are Little Majesty, An
Operation in Money, and Miss Eunice's Glove.
*See Selected Tales, edited by G. P. Lathrop. Pub
Scr.*

Webster, Daniel. 1782 *N. H.*-1852. Statesman. Known to literature by his legal arguments, state papers, speeches, and orations. A master of English style, whose every line reveals a clear, logical, and brilliant mind. *See Parton's Famous Americans, Am. Cyc., Private Life of, by C. Lanman, Lives by Curtis, Lyman, Smucker, Everett, Fletcher Webster, and Tefft, Atlantic Monthly, Feb. 1882, and Webster, by H. C. Lodge in Am. Statesmen. Pub. Lit. Por.*

Webster, Pelatiah. 1725 *Ct.*-1797. Writer on financial questions.

Webster, Noah. 1758 *Ct.*-1843. Lexicographer. Best known by his famous Spelling Book and his Dict. of the English Language. *See N. A. Rev. April, 1829, and Noah Webster, by H. E. Scudder in Am. Men. of Letters. Pub. Hou. Iv. Me.*

Webster, Richard. 1811 *N. Y.*-1856. Ecclesiologist. Author Hist. of the Presbyterian Church in America.

Weed, Thurlow. 1797 *N. Y.*-1882. Journalist. Style energetic and fearless. *See Autobiography, also Memoir by Thurlow Weed Barnes.*

Weeks, Robert Kelley. 1840 *N. Y.*-1876. Poet. Author Twenty Poems and Episodes and Lyric Pieces. *Pub. Ho.*

Weems, Mason L. 1759 *Va.*-1825. Biographer. Author Lives of Washington, Marion, Penn, Franklin, etc. An entertaining but wholly untrustworthy writer. *Pub. Lip.*

Weiss [wīss], John, 1818 *Ms.*-1879. Radical theologian. Author Lect. on Shakespeare, Am. Religion, Immortal Life, Life of Theodore Parker, etc. *Pub. Apl. Loc. Rob.*

Welby, Mrs. Amelia [Coppuck]. 1821 *Md.*-1852.

Poet. A graceful versifier, whose poems were
once very poj.ular. *See Griswold's Female Poets
of America. See complete works, 1850. Pub.
Apl.*

Weld, Horatio Hastings. 1811 *Ms.*–1888. Essayist
and critic. Author Corrected Proofs, Life of Christ,
Women of the Scriptures, etc.

Wells, David Ames. 1827 *Ms.* ——. Scientist.
Author Familiar Science, etc. *Pub. Har. Iv. Put.*

Welsh, Alfred H. 1850 *O.* ——. Author Develop-
ment of English Literature and Language, English
Literature in the 18th Century, etc. *See Atlantic
Monthly, March, 1883. Pub. Gri.*

Weston, Mrs. Mary C. [North]. 1823 *N. Y.* ——.
Episcopal religious writer. Author Calvary Catechism, Synopsis of the Bible, Jewish Antiquities,
etc. *Pub. Dut.*

Wetherell, Elizabeth. See Warner, Susan.

Wharton, Francis. 1820 *Pa.*–1889. Jurist and Episcopal theologian. Author Criminal Law of the
U. S., Medical Jurisprudence, State Trials of the
U. S., The·Silence of Scripture, Treatise on Theism, etc.

Wheatley, Mrs. Phillis. See Peters, Mrs.

Wheaton, Henry. 1785 *R. I.*–1848. Jurist. Author
Hist. of the Progress of the Law of Nations, Elements of International Law (completed by Lawrence), Hist. of the Northmen, etc. *See Westminster Rev. July, 1847, and Allibone's Dict.*

Whedon, Daniel Denison. 1808 *N. Y.*–1885. Methodist theologian. The Freedom of the Will and a
Commentary on the New Testament are his chief
works. *Pub. Phi.*

Wheeler, Wm. Adolphus. 1833 *Ms.*–1874. Lexicographer. Editor Webster's Dict., and author

Noted Names of Fiction, Familiar Allusions, etc. *See Atlantic Monthly, Aug. 1882. Pub. Hou.*

Whelpley, Samuel. 1766 *Ms.*–1817. Author of a once popular Compend of Hist. and a theological work called The Triangle.

Whipple, Edwin Percy. 1819 *Ms.*–1886. Essayist and critic. Author Character and Characteristic Men, Literature and Life, Essays and Reviews, Success and its Conditions, Literature of the Age of Elizabeth, etc. An eminently trustworthy and discriminating critic. *Pub. Har. Hou.*

Whitcher, Mrs. Frances Miriam [Berry]. 1812 *N. Y.*–1852. Humorist. Author of the famous Widow Bedott Papers. *Pub. Arm.*

White, Andrew Dickson. 1832 *N. Y.* ——. Historical writer. Pres. Cornell Univ. Author The Warfare of Science, Lect. on Modern Hist., etc. *See Hart's Am. Lit. Pub. Apl.*

White, Richard Grant. 1822 *N. Y.*–1885. Shakespearean scholar and littérateur. Author of Words and Their Uses, Every-Day English, England Without and Within, etc. His critical edition of Shakespeare in 12 vols. appeared in 1865, and the Riverside edition in 1883. A writer of strong individuality with an entertaining, incisive, and sometimes dogmatic style. *See Atlantic Monthly, Sep. 1880 and Feb. 1882. Pub. Hou.*

White, Wm. 1748 *Pa.*–1836. Bp. Penn. Low Church theologian. Author Memoir of the P. E. Church, etc. *See Life by Bird Wilson, 1839. Pub. Dut.*

Whitehead, Wm. Adee. 1810 *N. J.*–1884. Historical writer. Author of several valuable historical works relating to New Jersey.

Whiting, Wm. 1813 *Ms.*–1873. Jurist. His chief

work, The War Powers of the President and the
Legislative Powers of Congress, has been widely
circulated. *See Duyckinck's Cyc. Am. Lit.*

Whitman, Mrs. Sarah Helen [Power]. 1803 *R. I.-*
1878. Poet. Author Hours of Life, and Other
Poems, Edgar Poe and his Critics, etc. A Still
Day in Autumn is her finest poem, and one of rare
beauty. *See Easy Chair of Harper's Mag. Sept.
1878. - Pub. Hou.*

Whitman, Walt. 1819 *N. Y.* ——. Poet. Author
Leaves of Grass, Drum Taps, etc. His style is
rhapsodical and his expressions frequently coarse
and repellant, while his descriptions often sink to
the level of a catalogue. O Captain, My Captain,
a fine poem, and perhaps his best, is one of the
few rhymed poems he has written. *See Scribner's
Mag. Nov. 1880, Lit. World, Nov. 19, 1881, and
Walt Whitman, by R. M. Bucke. Pub. Os. Rob.
Wor.*

Whitmore, Wm. Henry. 1836 *Ms.* ——. Genealogist of note. Author Am. Genealogy, etc.

Whitney, Mrs. Adeline D. [Train]. 1824 *Ms.* ——.
Novelist and poet. Author of Faith Gartney, The
Gayworthys, Hitherto, We Girls, The Other Girls,
Real Folks, Sights and Insights, Odd or Even, etc.;
and Mother Goose for Grown Folks, and Pansies,
two vols. of verse. Style picturesque and forcible,
but marred by too frequent moralizing. A writer
of the purest aims and of far-reaching influence.
Pub. Hou.

Whitney, Anne. c. 1820 *Ms.* ——. Poet and
sculptor. Bertha is her best poem, and one of
great merit.

Whitney, Joseph Dwight. 1819 *Ms.* ——. Miner-
alogist. Author The Mineral Wealth of the U. S.,
etc. *Pub. Lip.*

Whitney, Wm. Dwight. 1827 *Ms.* ——. Bro. to J. D. W. Philologist of eminence. Language and the Study of Language is his most popular book. His rank is among the very first linguists. His work is accurate and profound, but the style is somewhat involved. *Pub. Apl. Gi. Ho. Scr.*

Whittemore, Thomas. 1800 *Ms.*-1861. Ecclesiologist. Author Hist. of Modern Universalism, etc.

Whittier, John Greenleaf. 1807 *Ms.* ——. Poet. Snow Bound, Miriam, Among the Hills, and The Tent on the Beach are the best of his longer poems ; My Soul and I, The Eternal Goodness, In School Days, The Last Walk in Autumn, The Playmates, and My Psalm, the finest of his shorter poems. As a prose writer he is known by Old Portraits and Modern Sketches, Leaves from Margaret Smith's Journal, etc. *See Scribner's Mag. Aug. 1879, Harper's Mag. Feb. 1883, Century Mag. Dec. 1883, Hazeltine's Chats About Books, and Biography of, by Underwood. Pub. Hou. Os.*

Whittingham, Wm. Rollinson. 1805 *N. Y.*-1879. Bp. Md. High Church theologian and scholar of eminence. *See Life, by Wm. F. Brand. Pub. Apl.*

Wigglesworth, Michael. 1631 *E.*-1705. Religious poet. His two long poems, The Day of Doom and Meat out of the Eater, were once extraordinarily popular, but more by reason of their lurid theology than for their poetical merit. *See Tyler's Am. Lit. vol. 2.*

Wilcox, Carlos. 1794 *N. H.*-1827. Poet. Author The Age of Benevolence. *See Duyckinck's Cyc. Am. Lit., and Griswold's Poets and Poetry of America.*

Wilde, Richard Henry. 1789 *I.*-1847. Poet.

Known chiefly as the author of the graceful lyric
My Life is like the Summer Rose. *See Griswold's
Poets and Poetry of America.*

Wiley, Calvin Henderson. 1819 *N. C.* ——. Novelist and educational writer. Author Alamance,
Roanoke, etc. *See Hart's Am. Lit. Pub. Bar.*

Wilkinson, Wm. Cleaver. 1833 *Vt.* ——. Poet
and littérateur. Author Poems, A Free Lance in
the Field of Life and Letters, etc. His Webster
ode is his most noted poem. *Pub. Scr.*

Willard, Mrs. Emma [Hart]. 1787 *Ct.*–1870. Educational writer. *See Life, by John Lord, and Hart's
Am. Lit. Pub. Bar.*

Willard, Samuel. 1640 *Ms.*–1707. Puritan theologian. Of his many works A Complete Body of
Divinity is the best known.

Williams, John. 1664 *Ms.*–1729. Author of The
Redeemed Captive, a graphic picture of heroism
and suffering, the narrative being an account of
personal adventures among the Indians.

Williams, John. 1817 *Ms.* ——. Bp. Ct. Theologian. Author Studies on the English Reformation,
Sermons, etc. *Pub. Dut.*

Williams, Roger. 1606 *W.*–1683. Theologian and
controversialist. The first upholder of the doctrine
of liberty of conscience in its entirety. A strong,
forceful, and liberal thinker. *See Bancroft's Hist.
U. S., Tyler's Am. Lit. vol. 1, and Mudge's Footprints of Roger Williams.*

Williams, Samuel Wells. 1812 *N. Y.* 1884. Missionary. His valuable book on China, The Middle
Kingdom, is his principal work. *Pub. Scr.*

Williams, Wm. R. 1804 *N. Y.*–1885. Baptist religious writer. Author Religious Progress, God's
Rescues, or Discourses on Luke, etc.

Willis, Nathaniel Parker. 1806 *Me.*-1867. Poet and littérateur. Author of Scripture Poems, Melanie, Hurrygraphs, People I have Met, Pencillings by the Way, etc. Style polished and refined, but marred occasionally by affectations. A talented writer, who deliberately chose to win a transient popularity instead of a permanent fame by the performance of lasting work. *Pub. Clx. Scr.*

Willson, Byron Forceythe. 1837 *N. Y.*-1867. Author of The Old Sergeant, and Other Poems. *See Atlantic Monthly, March, 1875. Pub. Hou.*

Wilson, Alexander. 1766 *S.*-1813. Ornithologist. The founder of Am. ornithology. Author Am. Ornithology. A keen, close observer, possessing a lively, imaginative style. *See Life, by G. F. Ord. Pub. Por.*

Wilson, Mrs. Augusta J. [Evans]. 1835 *Ga.* ——. Novelist. Author of Beulah, Macaria, Vashti, St. Elmo, etc. A popular writer whose works, while displaying considerable power, are faulty in construction, and overweighted with psychological details and general information. *Pub. Car.*

Wilson, Henry. 1812 *N. H.*-1875. Statesman. Author Hist. of Anti-Slavery Measures, Rise and Fall of the Slave Power in America, etc. An exhaustive, impartial writer. *See Life and Public Service of, by G. E. Nason. Pub. Hou.*

Wilson, James Grant. 1832 *S.* ——. Littérateur. Poets and Poetry of Scotland, Mr. Secretary Pepys and his Diary, Love in Letters, etc. *Pub. Har. Put.*

Wilson, John. 1802 *S.*-1868. His best known work is an exhaustive Treatise on English Punctuation. *Pub. Pot.*

Wilson, Wm. Dexter. 1816 *N. H.* ——. Episcopal

theologian. Author Hist. of the Reformation in England, The Church Identified, Psychology, The Foundations of Religious Belief, etc. An able and learned thinker. *Pub. And. Apl. Dut.*

Winchell, Alexander. 1824 *N. Y.* ——. Geologist. Author Sketches of Creation, Pre-Adamites, Doctrine of Evolution, World Life, etc. Style able and scholarly. *Pub. Gri. Har.*

Wines, Enoch Cobb. 1806 *N. J.*-1879. Author of several works on education and prison discipline.

Wingate, Charles Frederick. 1847 *N. Y.* ——. Sanitarian. Author Views and Interviews on Journalism, Plumbing and House Drainage, etc.

Winslow, Edward. 1595 *E.*-1655. Historical and controversial writer. Author Good News from New England, Hypocrisy Unmasked, New England's Salamander, etc. *See Tyler's Am. Lit. vol. 1.*

Winsor, Justin. 1831 *Ms.* —— Librarian Harvard University. Editor Memorial Hist. of Boston, etc.

Winter, Wm. 1836 *Ms.* ——. Poet and critic. Author Poems, The Trip to England, The Jeffersons, English Rambles, and editor works of Geo. Arnold, John Brougham, and Fitz-James O'Brien. Azrael, My Witness, and Fidele are among his finest poems. *Pub. Os.*

Winthrop, John. 1588 *E.*-1649. Colonial historian. Author Hist. New England from 1630 to 1649. *See Tyler's Am. Lit., and Atlantic Monthly, Jan. 1864.*

Winthrop, Robert Charles. 1809 *Ms.* ——. Descendant of preceding. Author of Addresses and Speeches, and a Life of Gov. John Winthrop. *Pub. Lit.*

Winthrop, Theodore. 1828 *Ct.*-1861. Descendant of J. W. Novelist. Author John Brent, Cecil Dreeme, Edwin Brothertoft, Canoe and Saddle,

Love on Skates, etc. Style fresh, versatile, and brilliant. *See Atlantic Monthly, Aug. 1861, and Aug. 1863, and Life and Poems of.* Pub. Ho.

Wirt, Wm. 1772 *Md.*-1834. Statesman. Author Life of Patrick Henry, Letters of the British Spy, etc. *See Memoir, by J. P. Kennedy.* Pub. Clx. Har. Por.

Wise, Daniel, "Francis Forrester." 1813 *E.* ———. Methodist religious writer. Author of numerous popular moral and religious works. *Pub. Le. Phi.*

Wise, Henry Augustus. 1819 *N. Y.*-1869. Writer of sea tales and works of adventure. Author The Story of the Gray African Parrot, Captain Brand, etc. *Pub. Har.*

Wister, Mrs. Annis Lee [Furness]. 1830 *Pa.* ———. Dau. to Wm. H. Furness. A noted and skillful translator of many German novels. *Pub. Lip.*

Wister, Mrs. Owen. See Wister, Mrs. Sarah.

Wister, Mrs. Sarah [Butler]. 1835 *Pa.* ———. Dau. to Frances Kemble. Littérateur. Author the poem A Boat of Glass, translations from Alfred de Musset, etc.

Witherspoon. John. 1722 *S.*-1794. Political and religious writer. Pres. Princeton Coll. Author Ecclesiastical Characteristics, Thoughts on Am. Liberty, etc. W. possessed a vigorous, witty, and often sarcastic style.

Wood, Wm. 15— *E.*-1639. Author New England's Prospect, a descriptive work partly in verse. *See Tyler's Am. Lit. vol. 1.*

Woodberry, George Edward. 1855 *Ms.* ———. Littérateur. Author A Hist. of Wood Engraving, The North Shore Watch: a Threnody, Poe in Am. Men of Letters, etc. *See Atlantic Monthly, May, 1883.* Pub. Har. Hou.

Woods, Leonard. 1774 *Ms.*-1854. Congregationalist theologian. Author Letters to Unitarians, etc. *See Parks' Life and Character of.*

Woodward, A. Aubertine, " Auber Forestier." 1841 *Pa.* ——. Translator of note from the German and Norse, co-translator with Anderson of Björnson's novels, and author of Echoes from Mist-Land, and many literary sketches and monographs. *Pub. Gri.*

Woodworth, Francis C. 1812 *Ct.*-1859. Neph. to S. W. Author of many excellent books for young people. *Pub. Clx.*

Woodworth, Samuel. 1785 *Ms.*- 1842. Poet. Principally remembered for his famous lyric The Old Oaken Bucket.

Woolman John. 1720 *N. J.*-1772. Quaker moralist. Author of Essays and Epistles, and a noted Journal, which last has been edited by the poet Whittier. *Pub. Hou.*

Woolsey, Sarah Channing, " Susan Coolidge." 18— *O.* ——. Poet and writer for children. Niece to T. D. W. Her verse is tender in expression, careful in conception, and musical in form. *Pub. Rob.*

Woolsey, Theodore Dwight. 1801 *N. Y.* ——. Philosophical writer. Pres. Yale Coll. Author Political Science, Communism and Socialism, Introduction to the Study of International Law, Essay on Divorce and Divorce Legislation, etc. *See Lit. World, May, 1878. Pub. Bro. Scr.*

Woolson, Mrs. Abba [Goold]. 1837 *Me.* ——. Lecturer on English Literature. Author Woman in American Society, Dress Reform, Browsings Among Books. *Pub. Rob.*

Woolson, Constance Fenimore. 18— *N. H.* ——.

Novelist. Author Castle Nowhere, Lake County Sketches, Two Women : a poem, Rodman the Keeper : Southern Sketches, and the novels Anne and For the Major. *See London Academy, July 21, 1883. Pub. Apl. Har. Os.*

Worcester, Joseph Emerson. 1784 *N. H.*-1865. Lexicographer. His greatest work is his Universal and Critical Dict. of the English Language. *Pub. Lip.*

Worcester, Noah. 1758 *N. H.*-1837. Congregationalist controversialist. Author of A Respectful Address to the Unitarian Clergy, etc.

Worcester, Samuel. 1770 *N. H.*-1821. Bro. to N. W. Congregationalist controversialist. Author Letters to Dr. Channing on the Unitarian controversy, etc.

Worcester, Samuel Melanchthon. 1801 *Ms.*-1866. Son to S. W. Author Essays on Slavery, etc.

Work, Henry Clay. 1832 *Ct.*-1884. Song writer of note. Author Marching Through Georgia, Grandfather's Clock, and many other popular songs.

Wright, Chauncey. 1830 *Ms.*-1875. Philosopher. Author Philosophical Discussions. A thinker of rare powers. *See Biographical Sketch, by Chas. Eliot Norton, and Fiske's Darwinism and other Essays. Pub. Ho.*

Wright, Fanny. See D'Arusmont in Addenda.

Wright, Mrs. Julia [McNair]. 1840 *N. Y.* ——. A prolific writer of religious tales, mainly anti-Romanist in character. Author Almost a Nun, Priest and Nun, etc. *Pub. P. B. Por.*

Wright, Robert Wm. 1816 *Vt.*-1885. Satirical poet. Author The Church Knaviad, Vision of Judgment, The Pious Chi-Neh, etc. Style sharp and incisive.

Wyman, Jeffries. 1814 *Ms.*–1874. Scientist of note, and author of many scientific monographs of much value. *See Atlantic Monthly, Nov. 1874.*

Xariffa. See Townsend, Mrs.

Yeomans, Edward Dorr. 1829 *Ms.*–1868. A noted translator of German theological works.

Youmans [yoo′manz], **Eliza Ann.** 1827 *N. Y.* ——. Author scientific text-books. *Pub. Apl.*

Youmans, Edward Livingston. 1821 *N. Y.*–1887. Bro to E. A. Y. Chemist. Author Handbook of Physical Science, The Culture Demanded by Modern Life, etc. Editor The Popular Science Monthly. *Pub. Apl.*

Youmans, Wm. Jay. 1818 *N. Y.* ——. Bro. to E. A. Y. Co-author with Huxley of Elements of Physiology and Hygiene. *Pub. Apl.*

Young, Alexander. 1800 *Ms.*–1854. Author Chronicles of the Pilgrim Fathers, a valuable work of reference, Library of Old English Prose Writers, etc.

Young, Charles Augustus. 1834 *N. H.* ——. Astronomer. Author The Sun, A General Astronomy, etc. *Pub. Gi.*

ADDENDA.

Adams, Brooks. 1848 *Ms.* ——. Son to Chas. Francis Adams. Author Massachusetts in Am. Commonwealths. *Pub. Hou.*

Adams, Charles Follen. 1842 *Ms.* ——. ˙Humorous poet. Author Leedle Yawcob Strauss, and Other Poems, etc. *Pub. Le.*

Adams, Henry. 1838 *Ms.* ——. Bro. to B. A. Author John Randolph in Am. Statesmen, and Life of Albert Gallatin. *See Atlantic Monthly, Jan.* 1883. *Pub. Hou. Lip.*

Adams, Henry Carter. 1852 *Ia.* ——. Political economist. Author monographs on the History of Taxation in the U. S., etc. *Pub. J. H. U.*

Adams, John Glover. 1807 *N. Y.*–1884. Physician and medical biographer.

Aimwell, Walter. *See Simonds.*

Allen, Alexander Viets Griswold. 1841 *Ms.* ——. Episcopal theologian. Author Continuity of Christian Thought. *Pub. Hou.*

Allmond, Marcus Blakey. 1851 *Va.* ——. Poet. Author Estelle.

Angell, Joseph K. 1794 *R. I.*–1857. Author of a noted Treatise on the Common Law of Watercourses, The Law of Tide Waters, The Limitation of Actions, etc.

Annan, Annie Rankin. 1847 *N. Y.* ——. Poet.

Arnold, Samuel Greene. 1821 *R. I.* ——. Historian. Author History of the State of Rhode Island and Providence Plantations, Life of Patrick Henry, etc. *Pub. Apl.*

Atkinson, Edward. 1827 *Ms.* ——. Political economist. Author The Distribution of Products.

Atkinson, Wm. Parsons. 1820 *Ms.* ——. Bro. to E. A. Author The Right Use of Books, History and the Study of History, etc. *Pub. Rob.*

Bacon, Henry. 1839 *Ms.* ——. Artist. Author A Parisian Year, Parisian Art and Artists. *Pub. Os. Rob.*

Bailey, James Montgomery. 1841 *N. Y.* ——. Author Life in Danbury, England from a Back Window, The Danbury Boom, etc. *Pub. Le.*

Baldwin, Mrs. Lydia Wood. 1836 *Ms.* ——. Author Rubina, and A Yankee School-Teacher in Virginia. *Pub. Fu.*

Barr, Mrs. Amelia Edith [Huddleston]. 1833 *E.* ——. Novelist. Author Jan Vedder's Wife, etc. *Pub. Apl. Do.*

Bates, Katharine Lee. 1859 *Ms.* ——. Poet.

Beard, George Miller. 1859 *Ct.*–1883. Physician. Author treatises on Stimulants and Narcotics, Eating and Drinking, etc. *Pub. Wo.*

Beers, Mrs. Ethelinda [Elliott]. 1827 *N. Y.*–1879. Poet. Author All Quiet Along the Potomac, and Other Poems.

Beers, Henry Augustin. 1847 *N. Y.* ——. Author A Century of Am. Literature, Odds and Ends: a volume of verse, Willis in Am. Men of Letters, etc. *Pub. Ho. Hou.*

Bellamy, Charles Joseph. 1852 *Ms.* ——. Author The Breton Mills : a novel, Everybody's Lawyer, and The Way Out: Suggestions for Social Reform. *Pub. Put.*

Bellamy, Edward. 1850 *Ms.* ——. Bro. to C. J. B. Novelist. Author Dr. Heidenhoff's Process, and Miss Ludington's Sister. *Pub. Apl. Os.*

Bellamy, Mrs. Elizabeth Whitfield [Croom], "Kamba Thorpe." 1838 *Fl.* ——. Novelist. Author Four Oaks, and Little Joanna. *Pub. Apl. Car.*

Benedict, David. 1779 *Ct.*-1874. Baptist historian. Author Hist. of the Baptists, Hist. of All Religions, Fifty Years Among the Baptists, Compendium of Church Hist., Hist. of the Donatists, etc.

Bianciardi, Mrs. Elizabeth Dickinson [Rice]. 18— *Ms.*-1885. Author At Home in Italy, and two volumes of poems. *Pub. Hou. Ran.*

Billings, John Shaw. 1839 *Ind.* ——. Hygienic writer of note.

Blaikie, Wm. 1843 *N. Y.* ——. Author How to Get Strong, Sound Bodies, etc. *Pub. Har.*

Blaine, James Gillespie. 1830 *Pa.* ——. Author Twenty Years of Congress, etc.

Blake, Mrs. Lillie [Devereux] [Umstead]. 1835 *N. C.* ——. Lecturer and writer on social reforms. Author Fettered for Life, etc.

Bloede, Gertrude, "Stuart Sterne." 1845 *Sxy.* ——. Poet. Author Angelo, Giorgio and Other Poems, etc. *Pub. Hou.*

Bolles, Albert Sidney. 1845 *Ct.* ——. Author Chapters in Political Economy, The Conflict Between Labor and Capital, Industrial Hist. of the U. S., Financial Hist. of the U. S. 1774-1860, etc. *Pub. Apl.*

Booth, Mary Louise. 1831 *L. I.*-1889. Ed. Harper's Bazar. Author Hist. of City of New York, and translator of note.

Bostwick, Mrs. Helen Louise [Barron]. 1826 *N. H.* ——. Poet. Author Buds : Blossoms : and Berries.

Branch, Mary Bolles. 1841 *L. I.* ——. Author the well-known poem The Petrified Fern.

Brewer, Thomas Mayo. 1821 *Ms.*–1880. Ornithologist. Author Hist. N. A. Birds, Oölogy of N. A., etc.

Brooks, Wm. Keith. 1849 *O.* ——. Biologist. Author Development of Lingula, Development of the Am. Oyster, Handbook of Invertebrate Zoölogy, The Law of Heredity, etc. *Pub. Cass. Mur.*

Brotherton, Mrs. Alice [Williams]. 18— *O.* ——. Poet and littérateur. Author Sailing of King Olaf.

Brown, Samuel Gilman. 1813 *Me.*–1885. Pres. Hamilton College. Author Biography of Self-Taught Men, Life of Rufus Choate, etc. *Pub. Lit.*

Bunce, Oliver Bell. 1828 *N. Y.* ——. Littérateur. Author Life Before Him, Bensly, The Adventures of Timias Terrystone, Bachelor Bluff, My House : an Ideal, Don't, a popular little work on deportment, and the dramas Marco Bozzaris and Love in '76. *Pub. Apl. Scr.*

Butterworth, Hezekiah. 1839 *R. I.* ——. Poet. Editor Youth's Companion. Author Zig-Zag Journeys, and other juvenile works, etc. *Pub. Est. Lo.*

Butts, Mrs. Mary Frances [Barber]. 1836 *R. I.* ——. Poet and writer for young people. Author Three Girls, Lottie, Nellie's New Home, Lizzie and her Friends, The Frolic Series, etc. *Pub. A. T. S., C. P. S.*

Cheney, Mrs. Ednah Dow [Littlehale]. 1824 *Ms.* ——. Author Gleanings in the Field of Art, etc. *Pub. Le.*

Cheney, John Vance. 1848 *N. Y.* ——. Poet and littérateur. Author The Old Doctor. *Pub. Apl.*

Collier, Thomas Stephens. 1842 *N. Y.* ——. Poet.

Conant, Samuel Stillman. 1831 *Me.*-1885. Littérateur.

Cone, Helen Gray. 1859 *N. Y.* ——. Poet. Author Oberon and Puck.

Congdon, Charles Tabor. 1821 *Ms.* ——. Journalist.

Coolbrith, Ina Donna. 18— *Il.* ——. Poet. Author The Perfect Day.

Cornwell, Henry Sylvester. 1831 *N. H.*-1886. Poet and physician. *See Poems pub. 1879.*

Craddock, Charles Egbert. *See Murfree.*

Croly, Mrs. Jennie [Cunningham], "Jennie June." 1831 *E.* ——. Journalist. Originator of duplicate correspondence. Author Talks on Women's Topics, For Better or Worse, etc. *Pub. Le.*

Cullum, George Washington. 1812 *N. Y.* ——. Writer on military science.

Curtis, Benjamin Robbins, Jr. 1855 *Ms.* ——. Son to B. R. C. Author Dottings Round the Circle, and editor Life and Writings of B. R. Curtis, and Jurisdiction of the Courts of the U. S. *Pub. Hou. Lit.*

Curtis, Mrs. Caroline Gardiner [Cary], "Carroll Winchester." 1827 *N. Y.* ——. Novelist. Author From Madge to Margaret, and The Love of a Lifetime. *Pub. Cu. Le.*

Cutler, Elbridge Jefferson. 1831 *Ms.*-1870. Poet. Author War Lyrics.

Dangé, Henri. *See Hammond, Mrs.*

D'Arusmont, Frances [Wright]. 1795 *S.*-1852. Social reformer. Author Altorf: a tragedy, Views of Society and Manners in America, A Few Days in Athens, etc. *See Gilbert's The Pioneer Woman.*

Davidson, Thomas. 1841 *S.* ——. Writer on art and philosophy.

Dole, Nathan Haskell. 1852 *Ms.* ——. Co-author with Rambaud of Young Folks' Hist. of Russia. Author Hist. Turko-Russian War of 1877–78. Literary editor Philadelphia Press.

Drisler, Henry. 1818 *N. Y.* ——. Classical scholar. Author A Greek-and-English Lexicon, etc. *Pub. Har.*

Ely, Richard Theodore. 1854 *N. Y.* ——. Political economist. Author French and German Socialism in Modern Times, The Past and Present of Political Economy, etc. *Pub. Har. J. H. U.*

Field, David Dudley. 1806 *Ms.* ——. Bro. to H. M. F. Jurist. *See Speeches, Arguments, and Miscellaneous Papers edited by A. P. Sprague.* *Pub. Apl.*

Foote, Mrs. Mary [Hallock]. 1847 *N. Y.* ——. Novelist and artist. Author The Led Horse Claim, etc. *Pub. Os.*

French, Alice, "Octave Thanet." 1850 *Ms.* ——. Author Knitters in the Sun. *Pub. Hou.*

Gardner, Eugene C. 1836 *Ms.* ——. Architect. Author Homes and All About Them, The House that Jill Built, etc. *Pub. Fo. Os.*

Genung [je-nŭng'], John Franklin. 1850 *N. Y.* ——. Author A Study of In Memoriam. *Pub. Hou.*

Gilder, Wm. Henry. 1835 *Pa.* —— Bro. to R. W. G. Author Schwatka's Search, and Ice Pack and Tundra. *Pub. Scr.*

Gildersleeve, Basil Laneau. 1831 ——. Greek scholar of note. *Pub. Har. Un.*

Goodwin, Wm. Watson. 1831 *Ms.* ——. Greek scholar of note. Author A Greek Grammar, etc. *Pub. Gi.*

Griswold, Mrs. Frances Irene [Burge] [Smith]. *See Smith, Mrs. Frances.*

Guiney [gī-nī], Louise Imogen. 1861 *Ms.* ——. Poet and essayist. Author Songs at the Start, and Goose-Quill Papers. *Pub. Cu. Rob.*

Gustafson, Axel, " Carl Bremer." 18— *Sn.* ——. Author The Foundation of Death : a Study of The Drink Question. *Pub. Gi.*

Gustafson, Mrs. Zadel [Barnes]. 1841 *Ct.* ——. Wife to A. G. Poet and littérateur. Author Meg : a Pastoral, Can the Old Love, etc. *Pub. Le. Os.*

Hagen, Hermann August. 1817 *P.* ——. Entomologist of note.

Hallowell, Richard Price. 1835 *Pa.* ——. Author The Quaker Invasion of Massachusetts. *Pub. Hou.*

Hammond, Mrs. Henrietta [Hardy], " Henri Dangé." 1854 *Va.*–1883. Novelist. Author The Georgians and A Fair Philosopher. *Pub. Os.*

Hanaford, Mrs. Phebe Ann [Coffin]. 1829 *Ms.* —— Author Life of Abraham Lincoln, Life of Geo. Peabody, etc.

Hayne, Wm. Hamilton. 1856 *S. C.* ——. Son to P. H. Poet.

Hayward, Edward Farwell. 1851 *Ms.* ——. Poet. Author Willoughby, Patrice, and Ecce Spiritus. *Pub. Cu.*

Hazeltine, Mayo Williamson. 18— *Me.* ——. Author Chats About Books, British and American Education, etc.

Headley, Phineas Camp. 1819 *N. Y.* ——. Bro. to J. T. H. Author Women of the Bible, The Island of Fire, Young Folks' Heroes of the Rebellion, Lives of Josephine, Lafayette, etc. *Pub. Le.*

Hennequin [en'-căn], Alfred. 1846 *F.* ——. Dramatist and author of educational essays and Anglo-French text-books. *Pub. Apl. Iv.*

Higginson, Stephen. 1743 *Ms.*-1828. Author Essays by Laco, reprinted as Ten Chapters in the Life of John Hancock, and Defence of Jay's Treaty.

Holden, George Henry. 1848 *Ms.* ——. Author Canaries and Cage Birds, etc. *Pub. Fo.*

Holmes, Oliver Wendell, Jr. 1841 *Ms.* ——. Son to O. W. H. Jurist. Author The Common Law, etc. Editor Kent's Commentaries. *Pub. Lit.*

Hopkins, Mrs. Louisa Parsons [Stone]. 1834 *Ms.* ——. Poet and educational writer. Author Motherhood, Breath of the Field and Shore, Cosmic Geography, Handbook of the Earth, etc. *Pub. Le.*

Hoppin, Augustus. 1828 *R. I.* ——. Artist and littérateur. Author Recollections of Auton House, A Fashionable Sufferer, Two Compton Boys, etc. *Pub. Hou.*

Hoppin, James Mason. 1820 *R. I.* ——. Cousin to A. H. Author Notes of a Theological Student, Old England, Life of Admiral Foote, Memoirs of Henry Armitt Brown, Homiletics, and Pastoral Theology. *Pub. Apl. Do. Fu. Har. Hou. Lip.*

Howe, Edgar Watson. 1854 *Ind.* ——. Novelist. Author The Story of a Country Town, and The Mystery of The Locks. *Pub. Os.*

Howe, Maud. 1853 *Ms.* ——. Dau. to S. G. H. Novelist. Author A Newport Aquarelle, and The San Rosario Ranch. *Pub. Rob.*

Howison, George Holmes. 1834 *Md.* ——. Mathematician. Author Treatise on Analytic Geometry, etc.

Hutchinson, Ellen Mackay. 18— ——. Poet.
Author Songs and Lyrics. *Pub. Os.*

Hutton, Laurence. 1843 *N. Y.* ——. Littérateur.
Author Literary Landmarks of London, etc. *Pub.
Os.*

Jacobi, Mrs. Mary [Putnam]. 1842 *E.* ——. Physician. Author The Martyr to Science, etc.

Janson, Kristofer. 1841 *N.* ——. Novelist and
poet. Author From the Parishes, The Spellbound
Fiddler, etc. *Pub. Gri.*

Jenkins, John Stilwell. 1818 *N. Y.*-1852. Biographer. Author The Heroines of History, Lives
of the Governors of N. Y., Political Hist. N. Y.,
Hist. Mexican War, etc.

Johnston, Alexander. 1849 *L. I.* ——. Political
historian. Author Connecticut in Am. Commonwealths, Handbook of American Politics, etc. *Pub.
Hou.*

Jones, Charles Colcock. 1804 *Ga.*-1863. Presbyterian theologian. Author The Church of God,
etc.

Jones, Charles Colcock, Jr. 1831 *Ga.* ——. Archæologist. Author Ancient Tumuli in Georgia,
Antiquities of the Southern Indians, The History
of Georgia, etc. *Pub. Hou.*

Jones, Leonard Augustus. 1832 *Ms.* ——. Editor
Am. Law Register. Author Law of Mortgages of
Personal Property, Treatises on the Law of Mortgages of Real Property, on the Law of Pledges, on
the Law of Pledges and Collateral Securities, on
the Law of Railroad and other Corporate Securities, etc. *Pub. Hou.*

June, Jennie. *See Croly.*

Kaler, James Otis. 1846 *Me.* ——. Writer for young people. Author Toby Tyler, Left Behind, Mr. Stubbs's Brother, Tom and Tip, Raising the Pearl, etc. *Pub. Har.*

Kennedy, Wm. Sloane. 1850 *O.* ——. Author Lives of Longfellow and O. W. Holmes, Wonders and Curiosities of the Railway, etc. *Pub. Cass. Gr.*

Kenyon, James Benjamin. 1858 *N. Y.* ——. Poet. Author Out of the Shadows, The Fallen and Other Poems, and Songs in All Seasons. *Pub. Cu. Lip.*

Kimball, Harriet McEwen. 1834 *N. H.* ——. Poet. Author Swallow Flights of Song. *Pub. Dut.*

Kouns [coons], Nathan Chapman. 1833 *Mo.* ——. Novelist. Author Arius the Libyan, and Dorcas the Daughter of Faustina. *Pub. Apl.*

Knox, Thomas Wallace. 1835 *N. H.* ——. Journalist and traveler. Author Overland Through Asia, Camp-fire and Cotton-field, Backsheesh, Underground, The Boy Travelers in the Far East, How to Travel, Pocket Guide Around the World, The Voyage of the Vivian, Hunting Adventures on Land and Sea, etc. *Pub. Har.*

Leonowens, Mrs. Anna Harriette [Crawford]. 1834 *W.* ——. Author The English Governess at the Siamese Court, The Romance of the Harem, and Life and Travels in India. *Pub. Por.*

Litchfield, Grace Denio [dē-nī'-o]. 1849 *N. Y.* ——. Novelist. Author Only an Incident, The Knight of the Black Forest, etc. *Pub. Put.*

Lothrop, Mrs. Harriet M., "Margaret Sidney." 1844 *Ct.* ——. Author Five Little Peppers and How They Grew, The Pettibone Name, So as by Fire, Half Year at Brockton, What the Seven Did, etc. *Pub. Lo.*

Lowe, Mrs. Martha A. [Perry]. 1829 *N. H.* ——.
Poet. Author The Olive and the Pine, Love in
Spain and Other Poems, The Story of Chief Jo-
seph, etc. *Pub. Cu.*

Mabie, Hamilton Wright. 1846 ——. Editor
Christian Union. Author Norse Stories Retold
from the Eddas. *Pub. Rob.*

Mason, Mrs. Caroline Atherton [Briggs]. 1823
Ms. ——. Poet. Do they Miss me at Home is
her most noted poem.

Millet, Francis Davis. 1846 *Ms.* ——. Artist and
littérateur.

Mitchell, Mrs. Lucy Myers [Wright]. 1845 *Per.*
-1888. Author History of Ancient Sculpture. *Pub.
Do.*

Mitchell, Samuel Augustus. 1792-1868. Geographer of note.

Montgomery, George Edgar. 1855 *N. Y.* ——.
Poet and littérateur. Author Songs of Real Life.

Moore, Charles Leonard. 1854 *Pa.* ——. Poet.
Author Poems Antique and Modern. *Pub. Pott.*

Morgan, Appleton. 1849 *Me.* ——. Littérateur.
Author Laws of Literature, The Shakespearean
Myth, A History of the Shakespeare Text, etc.
Pub. Clke.

Morgan, Henry. 1823 *Ms.*-1884. Author Boston
Inside Out, etc.

Morgan, Lewis Henry. 1819-1881. Ethnologist.
Author League of the Iroquois, Systems of Con-
sanguinity and Affinity of the Human Family, The
American Beaver and his Works, Ancient Society,
etc. *Pub. Ho.*

Murfree, Mary Noailles, "Charles Egbert Craddock." 185- *Tn.* ——. Novelist. Author In the

Tennessee Mountains, Where the Battle was Fought, The Prophet of the Great Smoky Mountains, Down the Ravine, etc. *Pub. Hou. Os.*

Murray, Wm. Henry Harrison. 1840 *Ct.* ——. Author Adventures in the Wilderness, Adirondack Tales, Deacons, Music Hall Sermons, The Perfect Horse, etc. *Pub. Le.*

Nadal, Ephraim Syme. 18—— ——. Essayist. Author Essays at Home and Elsewhere, Impressions of London Social Life, etc. *Pub. Mac. Scr.*

Nason, Elias. 1811 *Ms.*–1887. Author Gazetteer of Massachusetts, Life John A. Andrew, etc.

Nichols, James Robinson. 1819 *Ms.*–1888. Scientist. Author What: When: and Where, Fireside Science, Chemistry of the Farm, The New Agriculture, etc. *Pub. Cu.*

Nye, Bill. *See Nye, Edgar.*

Nye, Edgar Wilson. 1850 *Me.* ——. Humorist. Author Bill Nye and Boomerang, Forty Liars and Other Lies, Baled Hay, Bill Nye's Blossom Rock, etc.

Ober, Frederick Albion. 1849 *Ms.* ——. Naturalist and traveler. Author Camps in the Caribbees, Young Folks' Hist. Mexico, The Silver City, Travels in Mexico, Mexican Resources and Guide to Mexico. *Pub. Le.*

Oberholtzer, Mrs. Sara Louisa [Vickers]. 1841 *Pa.* ——. Poet and littérateur. Author Violet Lee and Other Poems, Come for Arbutus, Hope's Heart Bells: a novel, etc. *Pub. Lip.*

O'Connor, Wm. Douglas. 1833 *Ms.* ——. Littérateur. Author Harrington, The Good Gray Poet, etc.

Oliver, Mrs. Grace Atkinson [Little] [Ellis]. 1844 *Ms.* ——. Littérateur. Author Lives of Mrs. Barbauld, Maria Edgeworth, Theodore Parker, and Dean Stanley, and editor Tales of Maria Edgeworth, Essays of Mrs. Barbauld, Tales and Poems of Ann and Jane Taylor, etc. *Pub. Cu. Os. Rob.*

Oswald, Felix Leopold. 1845 *Bm.* ——. Naturalist. Author Physical Education, Summerland Sketches, Zoölogical Sketches, etc. *Pub. Apl. Lip.*

Otis, James. *See Kaler.*

Penn, Arthur. *See Matthews, J. B.*

Preble, George Henry. 1816 *Me.*–1885. Author History of the American Flag, etc. *Pub. Os. Put.*

Putnam, George Palmer. 1814 *Me.*–1872. Publisher. Author The Tourist in Europe, American Facts, The World's Progress, etc. *Pub. Put.*

Pyle, Howard. 1853 *Del.* ——. Artist and littérateur. Author The Merrie Adventures of Robin Hood, and Within the Capes : a novel. *Pub. Scr.*

Rexford, Eben Eugene. 1848 *N. Y.* ——. Poet and novelist. Silver Threads Among the Gold is his best known poem.

Rich, Hiram. 1832 *Ms.* ——. Poet.

Rogers, Horatio. 1836 *R. I.* ——. Editor Hadden's Journal and Orderly Books.

Roosevelt, Robert Barnwell. 1829 *N. Y.* ——. Author The Game Fish of N. A., Game Birds of the Northern States, etc.

Roosevelt, Theodore. 1858 *N. Y.* ——. Neph. to R. B. R. Author The Naval War of 1812, Hunting Adventures of a Ranchman, etc. *Pub. Put.*

Ropes, John Codman. 1836 *Ra.* ——. Military

historian.   Author The Army under Pope, etc.
Pub. Scr.

Royce, Josiah. 1855 *Cal.* ——. Author The Religious Aspect of Philosophy, California in Am.
Commonwealths, etc. *Pub. Hou.*

Ruggles, Samuel Bulkley. 1800 *Ct.*-1881. Publi-
cist.

Sadlier, Anna Teresa. 1856 *Q.* ——. Dau. to Mrs.
Sadlier. Novelist. Author Seven Years and Mair,
The King's Page, Ethel Hamilton, Names that
Live: a volume of biographies, and many trans-
lations from the French, Italian, and German.
Pub. Har. Sad.

Saltus, Edgar Evertson. 185- *N. Y.* ——. Author
Balzac: a Study, and The Philosophy of Disen-
chantment. *Pub. Hou.*

Scharf, John Thomas. 1843 *Md.* ——. Historian.
Author Chronicles of Baltimore, Hist. Maryland,
Hist. Baltimore, Hist. Western Maryland, Hist.
City of St. Louis, Hist. Philadelphia, etc. *Pub.
Lip. Pi.*

Schurz [shurts], Carl. 1829 *P.* ——. Orator of
eminence. Author Henry Clay in Am. Statesmen,
etc. *Pub. Hou.*

Scollard, Clinton. 1860 *N. Y.* ——. Poet. Author Pictures in Song, a collection of graceful and
artistic verse. *Pub. Put.*

Shaler, Nathaniel Southgate. 1841 *Ky.* ——. Geologist. Author Kentucky in Am. Commonwealths, General Geology, etc. *Pub. Clke. Gi. Hou.*

Shaw, Albert. 1857 *O.* ——. Author Icaria: a
chapter in the History of Communism. *Pub. Put.*

Shinn, Charles Howard. 1852 *Ts.* ——. Author
Mining Camps. *Pub. Scr.*

Shurtleff, Ernest Warburton. 1862 *Ms.*——. Poet. Author Poems, Easter Gleams. *Pub. Cu.*

Sidney, Margaret. *See Lothrop, Mrs.*

Sill, Edward Rowland. 1841 *Ct.*–1887. Poet.

Simonds, Wm., "Walter Aimwell." 1822 *Ms.*– 1859. Writer for the young. Author The Aimwell Stories, The Boys' Own Guide, etc.

Simpson, Matthew. 1811 *O.*–1884. Methodist pulpit orator of eminence. Author Lectures on Preaching, A Hundred Years of Methodism, etc. *Pub. Har. Phi.*

Smith, Mrs. Mary Prudence [Wells], "P. Thorne." 1840 *N. Y.*——. Author The Browns, Child Life on a Farm, Jolly Good Times at School, and other juvenile tales. *Pub. Rob.*

Smith, Mrs. May Louise [Riley]. 1842 *N. Y.*——. Poet. Sometime is her best known poem.

Snider, Denton Jaques. 1841 *O.*——. Author System of Shakespeare's Dramas, A Walk in Hellas, Delphic Days, Agamemnon's Daughter, etc. *Pub. Jon. Os.*

Spalding, John Lancaster. 1840 *Ky.*——. Neph. to M. T. S. R. C. Bp. of Peoria. Author Life of Most Rev. M. J. Spalding, Essays and Reviews, Religious Mission of the Irish People and Catholic Colonization, Lectures and Discourses, etc. A thinker of much force and clearness.

Spalding, Solomon. 1761 *Ct.*–1816. Author The Manuscript Found, the basis of the Mormon bible. Pub. 1812.

Spofford, Ainsworth Rand. 1825 *N. H.*——. Librarian of Congress, Compiler Am. Almanac and Treasury of Facts.

Sprague, Mary Aplin. 18— *O.*——. Novelist. Author An Earnest Trifler. *Pub. Hou.*

Stauffer, Francis Henry. 1832 *Pa.* ——. Novelist and journalist.

Steiger, Ernst. 1832 *Sxy.* ——. Bibliographer and publisher.

Sterne, Stuart. *See Bloede.*

Stimson, Frederick Jesup, " J. S. of Dale." 1855 *Ms.* ——. Author Guerndale, The Crime of Henry Vane, and co-author with J. T. Wheelwright of Rollo's Journey to Cambridge. *Pub. Scr.*

Sturgis, Russell. 1836 *Md.* —— Art critic.

Taylor, Alfred. 1831 *Pa.* ——. Author Peeps at Our Sunday Schools, etc. *Pub. Phi.*

Thanet, Octave. *See French.*

Thayer, Joseph Henry. 1828 *Ms.* ——. Congregationalist biblical scholar.

Thompson, Robert Ellis. 1844 *I.* ——. Political economist. Editor Penn Monthly. Author Elements of Political Economy. *Pub. Por.*

Thorne, P. *See Smith, Mrs. Mary.*

Thorpe, Kamba. *See Bellamy, Mrs.*

Todd, Charles Burr. 1849 *Ct.* ——. Journalist and magazinist. Author Life and Letters of Joel Barlow. *Pub. Put.*

Torrey, Bradford. 1843 *Ms.* ——. Essayist. Author Birds in the Bush. *Pub. Hou.*

Townsend, Mrs. Mary Ashley, "Xariffa." 18— ——. Poet. Author Xariffa's Poems, Down the Bayou, etc. *Pub. Os.*

Trumbull, James Hammond. 1821 *Ct.* ——. Editor Colonial Records of Ct., Roger Williams's Key to the Languages of North America, etc. The highest authority upon Indian languages.

Van Brunt, Henry. 1832 *Ms.* ——. Writer on architecture.

Van Buren, Martin. 1782 *N. Y.*-1862. Pres. U. S. Author An Inquiry into the Origin and Causes of Political Parties in the U. S. *See Van Buren in Am. Statesmen. Pub. Hou.*

Vannah, Letitia Catharine. 1857 *Me.* ——. Poet and littérateur. Author Verses. *Pub. Lip.*

Van Rensselaer, Mrs. Mariana [Griswold]. 1851 *N. Y.* ——. Art critic.

Venable, Wm. Henry. 1836 *O.* ——. Poet. Author June on the Miami and Other Poems, The Teacher's Dream, Melodies of the Heart, etc. *Pub. Clke. Put. Va.*

Ward, Lester Frank. 1841 *Il.* ——. Author Dynamic Sociology, etc. *Pub. Apl.*

Ward, Samuel. 1814 *N. Y.*-1884. Author Lyrical Recreations. *Pub. Hou.*

Warren, Wm. Fairfield. 1833 *Ms.* ——. Pres. Boston University. Author Paradise Found : the Cradle of the Human Race at the North Pole. *Pub. Hou.*

Watson, Paul Barron. 1861 *N. J.* ——. Author Marcus Aurelius Antoninus. *Pub. Har.*

Watterson, Henry. 1840 *D. C.* ——. Journalist. Editor Louisville Courier-Journal.

Wendell, Barrett. 1856 *N. Y.* ——. Novelist. Author The Duchess Emilia. *Pub. Os.*

Wilder, Burt Green. 1841 *Ms.* ——. Writer on anatomy and physiology. *Pub. Put.*

Wiley, Isaac William. 1825 *Pa.*-1884. Methodist writer. Author The Fallen Missionaries, The Religion of the Family, China and Japan, etc.

Wilstach, John Augustine. 1824 *D. C.* ——. Author of a Translation into English Verse of the complete works of Virgil. *Pub. Hou.*

Wilstach, Joseph Walter. 1857 *Ina.* ——. Son to J. A. W. Author Horatian Odes, and Montalembert: a Character Study. *Pub. Cath.*

Winchester, Carroll. *See Curtis, Mrs.*

Wright, Elizur. 1804 *Ct.*–1885. Reformer. Author of A Curiosity of Law and a translation of La Fontaine's Fables.

Anagnos, Mrs. Julia Romana [Howe]. 1844–1886. Poet.

Blake, Mrs. Mary Elizabeth [McGrath]. 1840 *I.* ——. Poet and littérateur. Author Poems, The Merry Months All, Youth in Twelve Centuries, On the Wing. *Pub. Hou. Le. Lo.*

Conway, Katharine Eleanor. 1853 *N. Y.* ——. Poet. Author On the Sunrise Slope and co-author with Mrs. Waters of Christian Symbols. *Pub. Cath.*

Fullerton, William Morton. 1865 *Ct.* ——. Journalist and littérateur. Literary editor Boston Advertiser.

Peck, Samuel Minturn. 1854 *Al.* ——. Poet. Author Cap and Bells. *Pub. W.*

Roche, James Jeffrey. 1847 *I.*–1889. Poet. Author Songs and Satires.

Savage, John. 1828 *I.*–1888. Poet and Littérateur. Author Lays of the Folkstead, Modern Revolutionary History of Ireland, Our Living Representative Men, Life of Andrew Johnson, Fenian Heroes and Martyrs, and several plays.

Stallo, John Bernard. 1823 *G.* —— Scientist, Author General Principles of the Philosophy of Nature, The Concepts and Theories of Modern Physics. *Pub. Ap.*

Starr, Eliza Allen. 1824 *Ms.* ——. Art writer. Author Patron Saints, Pilgrims and Shrines, Songs of a Lifetime.

Thayer, William Roscoe. " Paul Hermes." 1859. *Ms.* ——. Poet. Author The Confessions of Hermes, Hesper : a drama.

American Statesmen.

A Series of Biographies of Men conspicuous in the Political History of the United States.

EDITED BY

JOHN T. MORSE, Jr.

———•———

The object of this series is not merely to give a number of unconnected narratives of men in American political life, but to produce books which shall, when taken together, indicate the lines of political thought and development in American history. The volumes now ready are as follows. —

John Quincy Adams. By JOHN T. MORSE, JR.
Alexander Hamilton. By HENRY CABOT LODGE
John C. Calhoun. By DR. H. VON HOLST.
Andrew Jackson. By PROF. W. G. SUMNER.
John Randolph. By HENRY ADAMS.
James Monroe. By PRES. DANIEL C. GILMAN.
Thomas Jefferson. By JOHN T. MORSE, JR.
Daniel Webster. By HENRY CABOT LODGE.
Albert Gallatin. By JOHN AUSTIN STEVENS.
James Madison. By SYDNEY HOWARD GAY.
John Adams. By JOHN T. MORSE, JR.
John Marshall. By A. B. MAGRUDER.
Samuel Adams. By JAMES K. HOSMER.
Thomas H. Benton. By THEODORE ROOSEVELT
Henry Clay. By Hon. CARL SCHURZ. 2 vols.
Patrick Henry. By MOSES COIT TYLER
Gouverneur Morris. By THEODORE ROOSEVELT
Martin Van Buren. By EDWARD M. SHEPARD.
George Washington By HENRY CABOT LODGE.
2 vols.

IN PREPARATION.

Benjamin Franklin. By JOHN T. MORSE, JR.
Others to be announced hereafter. Each volume, 16mo, gilt top, $1.25; half morocco, $2.50.

ESTIMATES OF THE PRESS.

"JOHN QUINCY ADAMS."

That Mr. Morse's conclusions will in the main be those of posterity we have very little doubt, and he has set an admirable example to his coadjutors in respect of interesting narrative, just proportion, and judicial candor. — *New York Evening Post.*

Mr. Morse has written closely, compactly, intelligently, fearlessly, honestly. — *New York Times.*

"ALEXANDER HAMILTON."

The biography of Mr. Lodge is calm and dignified throughout. He has the virtue — rare indeed among biographers — of impartiality. He has done his work with conscientious care, and the biography of Hamilton is a book which cannot have too many readers. It is more than a biography; it is a study in the science of government. — *St. Paul Pioneer-Press.*

"JOHN C. CALHOUN."

Nothing can exceed the skill with which the political career of the great South Carolinian is portrayed in these pages. The work is superior to any other number of the series thus far, and we do not think it can be surpassed by any of those that are to come. The whole discussion in relation to Calhoun's position is eminently philosophical and just. — *The Dial* (Chicago).

"ANDREW JACKSON."

Prof. Sumner has, . . . all in all, made the justest long estimate of Jackson that has had itself put between the covers of a book. — *New York Times.*

One of the most masterly monographs that we have ever had the pleasure of reading. It is calm and clear. — *Providence Journal.*

"JOHN RANDOLPH."

The book has been to me intensely interesting. . . . It is rich in new facts and side lights, and is worthy of its place in the already brilliant series of monographs on American Statesmen. — Prof. MOSES COIT TYLER.

Remarkably interesting. . . . The biography has all the elements of popularity, and cannot fail to be widely read. — *Hartford Courant.*

———

"JAMES MONROE."

In clearness of style, and in all points of literary workmanship, from cover to cover, the volume is well-nigh perfect. There is also a calmness of judgment, a correctness of taste, and an absence of partisanship which are too frequently wanting in biographies, and especially in political biographies. — *American Literary Churchman* (Baltimore).

The most readable of all the lives that have ever been written of the great jurist — *San Francisco Bulletin.*

———

"THOMAS JEFFERSON."

The book is exceedingly interesting and readable. The attention of the reader is strongly seized at once, and he is carried along in spite of himself, sometimes protesting, sometimes doubting, yet unable to lay the book down. — *Chicago Standard.*

The requirements of political biography have rarely been met so satisfactorily as in this memoir of Jefferson. — *Boston Journal.*

———

"DANIEL WEBSTER."

It will be read by students of history; it will be invaluable as a work of reference; it will be an authority as regards matters of fact and criticism; it hits the key-note of Webster's durable and ever-growing fame; it is adequate, calm, impartial; it is admirable. — *Philadelphia Press.*

The task has been achieved ably, admirably, and faithfully. — *Boston Transcript.*

"ALBERT GALLATIN."

It is one of the most carefully prepared of these very valuable volumes, . . . abounding in information not so readily accessible as is that pertaining to men more often treated by the biographer. . . . The whole work covers a ground which the political student cannot afford to neglect. — *Boston Correspondent Hartford Courant.*

Frank, simple, and straightforward. — *New York Tribune.*

"JOHN ADAMS."

A good piece of literary work. . . . It covers the ground thoroughly, and gives just the sort of simple and succinct account that is wanted. — *Evening Post* (New York).

"SAMUEL ADAMS."

Thoroughly appreciative and sympathetic, yet fair and critical. . . . This biography is a piece of good work — a clear and simple presentation of a noble man and pure patriot; it is written in a spirit of candor and humanity. — *Worcester Spy.*

A brilliant and enthusiastic book, which it will do every American much good to read. — *The Beacon* (Boston).

"HENRY CLAY."

We have in this life of Henry Clay a biography of one of the most distinguished of American statesmen, and a political history of the United States for the first half of the nineteenth century. In each of these important and difficult undertakings, Mr. Schurz has been eminently successful. Indeed, it is not too much to say that, for the period covered, we have no other book which equals or begins to equal this life of Henry Clay as an introduction to the study of American politics. — *Political Science Quarterly.*

"PATRICK HENRY."

Professor Tyler has not only made one of the best and most readable of American biographies; he may fairly be said to have reconstructed the life of Patrick Henry, and to have vindicated the memory of that great man from the unappreciative and injurious estimate which has been placed upon it. — *New York Evening Post.*

*** *For sale by all booksellers. Sent, post-paid, on receipt of price by the Publishers,*

HOUGHTON, MIFFLIN AND COMPANY,

BOSTON AND NEW YORK.

American Men of Letters.

EDITED BY

CHARLES DUDLEY WARNER.

———•———

A series of biographies of distinguished American authors, having all the special interest of biography, and the larger interest and value of illustrating the different phases of American literature, the social, political, and moral influences which have moulded these authors and the generations to which they belonged.

———

Washington Irving. By CHARLES DUDLEY WARNER.
Noah Webster. By HORACE E. SCUDDER.
Henry D. Thoreau. By FRANK B. SANBORN.
George Ripley. By OCTAVIUS BROOKS FROTHINGHAM.
J. Fenimore Cooper. By THOMAS R. LOUNSBURY.
Margaret Fuller Ossoli. By T. W. HIGGINSON.
Ralph Waldo Emerson. By OLIVER WENDELL HOLMES.
Edgar Allan Poe. By GEORGE E. WOODBERRY.
Nathaniel Parker Willis. By HENRY A. BEERS.
Benjamin Franklin. By JOHN BACH MCMASTER.

IN PREPARATION.

Nathaniel Hawthorne. By JAMES RUSSELL LOWELL.
William Cullen Bryant. By JOHN BIGELOW.

Others to be announced hereafter.

Each volume, with Portrait, 16mo, gilt top, $1.25 ; cloth, uncut edges, paper label, $1.50 ; half morocco, $2.50.

"WASHINGTON IRVING."

Mr. Warner has not only written with sympathy, minute knowledge of his subject, fine literary taste, and that easy, fascinating style which always puts him on such good terms with his readers, but he has shown a tact, critical sagacity, and sense of proportion full of promise for the rest of the series which is to pass under his supervision. — *New York Tribune.*

It is a very charming piece of literary work, and presents the reader with an excellent picture of Irving as a man and of his methods as an author, together with an accurate and discriminating characterization of his works. — *Boston Journal.*

It would hardly be possible to produce a fairer or more candid book of its kind. — *Literary World* (London).

"NOAH WEBSTER."

Mr. Scudder's biography of Webster is alike honorable to himself and its subject. Finely discriminating in all that relates to personal and intellectual character, scholarly and just in its literary criticisms, analyses, and estimates, it is besides so kindly and manly in its tone, its narrative is so spirited and enthralling, its descriptions are so quaintly graphic, so varied and cheerful in their coloring, and its pictures so teem with the bustle, the movement, and the activities of the real life of a by-gone but most interesting age, that the attention of the reader is never tempted to wander, and he lays down the book with a sigh of regret for its brevity. — *Harper's Monthly Magazine.*

It fills completely its place in the purpose of this series of volumes. — *The Critic* (New York).

"HENRY D. THOREAU."

Mr. Sanborn's book is thoroughly American and truly fascinating. Its literary skill is exceptionally good, and there is a racy flavor in its pages and an amount of exact knowledge of interesting people that one seldom meets with in current literature. Mr. Sanborn has done Thoreau's genius an imperishable service. — *American Church Review* (New York).

Mr. Sanborn has written a careful book about a curious man, whom he has studied as impartially as possible; whom he admires warmly but with discretion; and the story of whose life he has told with commendable frankness and simplicity. — *New York Mail and Express.*

It is undoubtedly the best life of Thoreau extant. — *Christian Advocate* (New York).

"GEORGE RIPLEY."

Mr. Frothingham's memoir is a calm and thoughtful and tender tribute. It is marked by rare discrimination, and good taste and simplicity. The biographer keeps himself in the background, and lets his subject speak. And the result is one of the best examples of personal portraiture that we have met with in a long time. — *The Churchman* (New York).

He has fulfilled his responsible task with admirable fidelity, frank earnestness, justice, fine feeling, balanced moderation, delicate taste, and finished literary skill. It is a beautiful tribute to the high-bred scholar and gener-ous-hearted man, whose friend he has so worthily por-trayed. — *Rev. William H. Channing* (London).

"JAMES FENIMORE COOPER."

We have here a model biography. The book is charm-ingly written, with a felicity and vigor of diction that are notable, and with a humor sparkling, racy, and never obtrusive. The story of the life will have something of the fascination of one of the author's own romances. — *New York Tribune.*

Prof. Lounsbury's book is an admirable specimen of literary biography. . . . We can recall no recent addition to American biography in any department which is supe-rior to it. It gives the reader not merely a full account of Cooper's literary career, but there is mingled with this a sufficient account of the man himself apart from his books, and of the period in which he lived, to keep alive the interest from the first word to the last. — *New York Evening Post.*

"MARGARET FULLER OSSOLI."

Here at last we have a biography of one of the noblest and the most intellectual of American women, which does full justice to its subject. The author has had ample material for his work, — all the material now available, perhaps, — and has shown the skill of a master in his use of it. . . . It is a fresh view of the subject, and adds important information to that already given to the public. — REV. DR. F. H. HEDGE, in *Boston Advertiser.*

He has filled a gap in our literary history with excel-lent taste, with sound judgment, and with that literary skill which is preëminently his own. — *Christian Union* (New York).

Mr. Higginson writes with both enthusiasm and sym-pathy, and makes a volume of surpassing interest. — *Commercial Advertiser* (New York).

"RALPH WALDO EMERSON."

Dr. Holmes has written one of the most delightful biographies that has ever appeared. Every page sparkles with genius. His criticisms are trenchant, his analysis clear, his sense of proportion delicate, and his sympathies broad and deep. — *Philadelphia Press.*

A biography of Emerson by Holmes is a real event in American Literature. — *Standard* (Chicago).

"EDGAR ALLAN POE."

Mr. Woodberry has contrived with vast labor to construct what must hereafter be called the authoritative biography of Poe, a biography which corrects all others, supplements all others, and supersedes all others. — *The Critic* (New York).

The best life of Poe that has yet been written, and no better one is likely to be written hereafter. This is high praise, but it is deserved. Mr. Woodberry has spared no pains in exploring sources of information; he has shown rare judgment and discretion in the interpretation of what he has found. — *Commercial Advertiser* (New York).

"NATHANIEL PARKER WILLIS."

Prof. Beers has done his work sympathetically yet candidly and fairly and in a philosophic manner, indicating the status occupied by Willis in the republic of letters, and sketching graphically his literary environment and the main springs of his success. It is one of the best books of an excellent series. — *Buffalo Times.*

"BENJAMIN FRANKLIN."

One of the most interesting and instructive volumes of the series, overflowing with instructive matter concerning the Bostonian whose name is so closely identified with the history of Philadelphia, and, indeed, with that of the whole country as it existed in his day. The pictures which are given of the momentous period in which he lived are full of vigor, and betray an astonishing amount of research in many directions. The simplicity of style and the critical ability so abundantly displayed make the work very fascinating reading throughout. The estimate of Franklin's character, ability, and attainments is a very just one. — *Boston Gazette.*

** *For sale by all Booksellers. Sent, post-paid, on receipt of price by the Publishers,*

HOUGHTON, MIFFLIN AND COMPANY,
BOSTON AND NEW YORK.